Hidden Treasures

Hidden Treasures

Mapping Europe's sources of competitive advantage in doing business

Donald Kalff and **Andrea Renda**

With contributions from:
Willem Pieter De Groen
Karel Lannoo
Felice Simonelli
Nadina Iacob
Jacques Pelkmans

Centre for European Policy Studies (CEPS)
Brussels

CEPS is an independent policy research institute in Brussels. Its mission is to produce sound policy research leading to constructive solutions to the challenges facing Europe. The views expressed in this book are entirely those of the authors and should not be attributed to CEPS or any other institution with which they are associated or to the European Union.

Cover illustration: Kiselev Andrey Valerevich (Shutterstock)

ISBN 978-94-6138-746-2
© Copyright 2019, CEPS

All rights reserved. No part of this publication may be reproduced, stored in a retrieval system or transmitted in any form or by any means – electronic, mechanical, photocopying, recording or otherwise – without the prior permission of the Centre for European Policy Studies.

Centre for European Policy Studies
Place du Congrès 1, B-1000 Brussels
+32 (0)2 229.39.11
info@ceps.eu – www.ceps.eu

Contents

Executive Summary	i
Hidden Treasures: Mapping Europe's sources of competitive advantage in doing business	vii
1. The Legal System: Uncovering EU advantages	11
2. The Financing of Investments and Working capital of Companies: Europe's unique recipe	27
3. Corporate Governance: in Search of the European Enterprise	45
4. Innovation: Europe's most hidden treasure?	69
5. Patents: a not-so-hidden treasure, now at risk	99
6. Competition Policy: Should Europe beg to differ?	111
7. Taxes: can Europe outperform the rest of the world?	125
8. A Commitment to Eradicate Corruption	137
9. Trade and the Single Market: Exploiting Synergies Further	149
10. Leading the World in Technology Rules and Standards	171
11. Epilogue: Fairness, Quality, Sustainability and Trust as the Common Features of Europe's Hidden Treasures	195
References	203
Description of the research team	235
Notes	239

List of Figures and Tables

Figure 1. Time needed to resolve litigious civil and commercial cases (2016)	17
Figure 2. Perceived independence of courts and judges (2016-2018)	19
Figure 3. Major obstacles to exporting for SMEs in the five largest EU member states	25
Figure 4. Share of bank and non-bank financing in total non-financial corporation debt financing in the euro area and the United States (outstanding amounts; percentages)	28
Figure 5. Enterprises by size of business (2016)	30
Figure 6. Employment by size of business (2016)	31

Figure 7. Number of bank relationships by size of business (October 2017-March 2018)..32
Figure 8. Use of internal and external financing by euro area enterprises across by size of business (October 2017-March 2018) 33
Figure 9. Bank branches and stakeholder value banks (2017).....................35
Figure 10. Distribution of banks across ownership structures and countries (% of assets in EU member states)................................35
Figure 11. Distribution of foreign-born residents with low versus high level of education, by OECD destination country, 2015-2016, in%..75
Figure 12. Excluding FAANG stocks, index returns would have been negative in 1H2018..78
Figure 13. SME funding: the first year of Horizon 2020 versus FP7...........81
Figure 14. Evolution of existing Joint Undertakings 84
Figure 15. Article 185 Partnerships launched to date...................................85
Figure 16. The new landscape of Partnerships in Horizon Europe compared to Horizon 2020..87
Figure 17. The European Battery Alliance 88
Figure 18. The IPCEI on Microelectronics...91
Figure 19. Total Patent Applications in the top 5 Patent Offices, 1883-2016...103
Figure 20. Google trends chart for "Unitary Patent", 1/1/2010 - 24/08/2019 106
Figure 21. Countries with rules on abuse of economic dependence, 2011..114
Figure 22. Trade Liberalisation and economic growth...............................150
Figure 23. Patents on quantum computing technology 175

Table 1. Example of common and civil law countries..................................12
Table 2. Key differences between the Shareholder, Stakeholder and European Models...62
Table 3. Global Innovation Index 2018 rankings...70
Table 4. Cities of the world, various indicators...72
Table 5. Main EU instruments to fight against corruption 139
Table 6. Overview of corruption indicator scores across the EU and the G20 countries 142
Table 7. Overview of EU's FTAs in four categories....................................162

EXECUTIVE SUMMARY

Europe is often presented as a declining global power, in which red tape, incumbency interests and governance flaws hamper economic performance, innovation and productivity. Part of this can be traced back to the inherent challenge and ambition of the European integration project; but also to external factors, including the rise of the United States as a global superpower during the 20th century, and the worldwide diffusion of ideas, especially in politics and economics, that had seldom originated in Europe, or that were tailored to its particular legal, economic and social traditions. Until recently, Europe has sought to carve out its model and role in global governance by mimicking many US policy approaches: shareholder capitalism, deregulation and unconstrained movement of capital. As the global community increasingly sees the rise of protectionist stances, and a growing inability to face emerging challenges such as sustainable development and the breath-taking rise of disruptive digital technologies, Europe should seek to burnish its best qualities to reclaim its position in the global order, to the benefit of all. The prospect of Brexit, while certainly not favourable for the Union, paradoxically opens up new opportunities to face emerging challenges with a greater degree of cohesion.

This book, a joint effort between Donald Kalff and Andrea Renda and benefiting from the contribution of CEPS researchers and a number of very helpful discussants, aims at identifying and exploring Europe's 'hidden treasures', competitive advantages often covered by dust that could, if adequately nurtured, bring the 'Old Continent' back to the forefront of the global order. In our approach, a hidden treasure must meet specific characteristics: in particular, it should be a feature of the economy, legal system or legal tradition of the EU or a subset of its member states, which was (or is) receiving insufficient attention in public policy, and which has the potential to increase Europe's competitiveness and overall positioning in the global context. Uncovering and promoting hidden treasures is a timely and much-needed exercise, as the EU approaches its post-elections transition and the global governance context appears to be changing rapidly, shaping a new playing field in which Europe has no obvious allies, and is increasingly challenged by superpowers with different, if not diverging, priorities.

Our findings show that Europe's unique balance between freedom, justice and fairness provides a solid basis for identifying hidden treasures. For example, we consider that the conspicuous advantages offered by continental European contract law, starting with the good faith requirement in in contract formation, have not been sufficiently capitalised on, which may have contributed to the overall belief that the EU legal system is inherently less efficient than the US one. The main obstacles that can be identified are the inefficiency of the judiciary in many countries, the cost of access to justice for smaller firms and citizens, and the lack of a robust set of rules protecting the interests of smaller contractors in relational contracts. This is why we believe that the EU should consider taking action to promote the use of civil law, improve the effectiveness and efficiency of legal institutions, and remove the remaining obstacles to trade in the single market.

Moreover, as is widely known in the EU financial institutions, banks form the most important source of external financing for companies, whereas in the US the capital markets contribute more to the financing of corporations and the broader economy. As we explore in Chapter 2, most European banks adhere to the 'relationship model', in sharp contrast to the 'transaction model' that dominates in the US. This lets them gain deep insights into the history and prospects of their clients as well as their markets and competitors, and to play an important role in helping clients upgrade their investment programmes by backing or rejecting investment proposals. The contribution of relationship banking to the economy as a whole is real and should be more strongly emphasised at the EU level, and highlighted as an opportunity and a source of competitiveness for Europe, rather than as a cumbersome legacy of the past.

Furthermore, researchers have started to uncover the existence of a fundamental trade-off between mainstream corporate governance and the ability of a firm to innovate and successfully address societal challenges. This has resulted in mounting criticism of the 'Shareholder Model' typical of US capitalism, mostly coming from inside the US and the UK. What emerges is that both shareholder and stakeholder capitalism feature problems, as exemplified by American and German corporate disasters. And indeed, in Europe, the most advanced companies have moved beyond these standard models, a fact that deserves to be brought into the limelight. These developments are helping to delineate a distinct 'European Enterprise Model', which puts the creation of economic value, rather than the generation of profit, at centre stage. Such an organisational form features dispersed leadership combined with a heavy emphasis on the quality of decision making. It can only be managed based on principles, not rules. Its culture is characterised by fairness, both internally and when dealing with suppliers, customers and partners. And all this is enshrined in articles of association that become the corporate constitution.

Much in the same vein, the EU has a real chance to build a new approach to innovation and competition, more inclusive and oriented towards sustainable development and well-being. This will take political courage and coordinated action with member states, some of which score very highly in global innovation rankings. One opportunity to uncover this innovation potential is provided by the upcoming transition to "mission-oriented innovation policy" in the future Horizon Europe, the EU's €100 billion research and innovation programme: within that context, Europe should help small and large companies, universities and government research organisations to forge tailor-made coalitions, powered by trust as a basis for cooperation.

Within this context, European patents may be used as a true 'quality seal': obtaining a European patent should become a way to escape from the 'noise' generated by bad quality patents around the world. This can improve patent justice and certainty, particularly for small and medium-sized companies, and restore the patent system in Europe as a catalyst for innovation efforts and investment. In the neighbouring area of competition law, there is a growing divergence between US and EU rules. During her mandate, Commissioner Vestager seems to have spotted a hidden treasure: an extremely rich set of national experiences that extends the reach of competition-related rules way beyond the remit of Article 102 TFEU. Rather than being an obstacle, this now appears as an opportunity, to be reaped especially in key sectors such as retail commerce, agri-food, and the platform economy, and to be expanded to other sectors such as biotech, new materials and nanotechnology.

We also see potential treasures in the way the EU deals with taxation and corruption. In Europe, minimum standards have been achieved on the quality of tax codes and tax rulings, and the handling of tax filings is more efficient in comparison with the US. Europe's tax treasure, however, remains hidden due to the great heterogeneity of tax regimes and, most importantly, the overall lack of cooperation between member states, which leaves numerous loopholes. The move towards a common consolidated corporate tax base, coupled with the deployment of RegTech for regulatory monitoring and compliance purposes, could help Europe exploit the quality of its tax system to the benefit of all. More generally, Europe is better placed than most when it comes to effective policymaking as well as doing business: however, while the legal instruments and institutions to prevent and fight corruption are available in all member states, enforcement in many of them is insufficient. The direct cost of corruption in the EU of up to a trillion euros per year needs to be brought down without delay.

Europe also has a chance to lead the global community thanks to its primacy in trade policy, and its emerging leadership in the regulation of emerging digital technologies. EU trade policy is already a sparkling gem, but additional policy coherence would make the EU a potential leader in 'responsible globalisation'. And on digital technologies such as artificial intelligence, blockchain, the internet of things and 5G, Europe can claim to possess three advantages: a solid, comprehensive legal framework; the size of its single market; and a potential for leadership in the global quest for fundamental rights and sustainable development, at a time when the US is backtracking and China does not yet appear ready to lead. Establishing a comprehensive policy framework to enable the contribution of digital technologies to the Sustainable Development Goals would be optimal in placing the EU as global leader both in the SDG arena, as well as in the technological one.

These are our main findings. But we believe that the list could be much longer, and the treasure trove much richer. Most importantly, we believe that Europe's unique balance between freedom ('of', not 'from'), justice and fairness can make it the perfect place for the next generation of capitalism. Fairness, reasonableness, good faith, pre- and post-contractual obligations are time-tested principles and part of the heritage of continental Europe. These principles are enshrined in many laws and regulations. They give guidance to individuals, small, medium-sized and large companies in their different roles as customer, supplier and partner. They also provide the basis for most of the hidden treasures: in contract formation, in dealings between tax officials and taxpayers, in financing small enterprises, in the 'European Enterprise Model', in joint efforts to innovate, in granting patents, in competition law and enforcement and in the EU trade agreements. The fight against corruption can be seen as crucial to protecting these principles, just as the export of European standards is essential so as to spread them around the world.

This book also shows that these principles are vital in meeting the economic challenges of our time: insufficient investment, lack of socially relevant innovation, and slowing productivity growth. The book shows that the 'Shareholder Model' of capitalism fails conspicuously on all three fronts. The EU-27 offers an ideal environment for alternative enterprise models that can make a positive difference. Pursuit of the creation of economic value, rather than short-term profit, unshackles investments. And the counter-argument that well-designed financial markets would incorporate long-term economic value in their fundamentals is not convincing: financial markets are far from perfect, and incorporate imperfect signals, biases and herd behaviour to an extent that their ability to provide correct information signals is questionable at best.

Our book also leads to two additional, essential findings related to technology and sustainability. On the one hand, Europe can harness the potential of digital technology 'for good', by setting ethical and policy standards through the sheer size of its single market, as well as through procurement, certification and trade policy. Europe's 'secret sauce' on digital technology can fill an existing gap in global governance, and help the Old Continent find room for its approach to economic policy at the global level. This is crucially related to Europe's ability to treat technology as a means, not an end: in this respect, the upcoming ethical guidelines on artificial intelligence and the observed effectiveness of legislation such as the General Data Protection Regulation and on platform-to-business trading practices will be essential to gauging Europe's ability to play a decisive role in this expanding arena.

This also leads to a more general consideration regarding the broader, long-term picture. Looking at current trends such as the resurgence of nationalism in politics, deterioration in the rule of law (also in some European countries), new protectionist stances and tariff wars in trade, short-termism in social policy and recurring denials of climate change, the SDG agreement reached in September 2015 by 193 countries seems to belong to a distant era. In the absence of any strong political will, the pursuit of the SDGs looks more dependent on technological breakthroughs and global private initiatives than on the alignment of governmental agendas in the leading blocs. Recent reports have confirmed that, with the exception of Scandinavian countries, all high-income countries are far from a trajectory that would lead them to achieve the 17 goals, and they struggle in particular with the four objectives related to sustainable consumption and production patterns, climate action, aquatic life and life on land.

To date, the EU has not shown sufficient ability to step up its efforts. In a recent stocktaking exercise of the past five years, Eurostat found slow progress in certain areas of sustainable development and a worrying rise in inequality. It is now time to shift gear: the financial crisis is over, the Silicon Valley model is plateauing, and the world is witnessing the rise of less democratic, less open forces in both developed and developing countries, as well as in the private sector. The Old Continent can push back against these worrying trends.

We believe Europe's hidden treasures offer an essential, compelling starting point to rethink Europe by retrieving its lost identity and strengthening its self-confidence.

HIDDEN TREASURES:
MAPPING EUROPE'S SOURCES OF COMPETITIVE ADVANTAGE IN DOING BUSINESS

Policymakers and businessmen often present Europe very negatively when it comes to entrepreneurship and innovation: a land of red tape, a deadly mix of precaution and bureaucracy where doing business is difficult, if not impossible. This is reflected in various slogans and declarations, aimed at highlighting Europe's embedded risk-aversion and strong suspicion of innovation;[1] the deep entrenchment of incumbent interests (Guinea and Erixon, 2019); and the under-development of non-banking sources of finance such as venture capital. Commentators often point at the United States as the land of innovation and 'ease of doing business', in which companies can grow faster and become more profitable on the basis of a wider spectrum of possibilities for early and mature stage funding. Silicon Valley has taken on mythical proportions as echoed in countless speeches and presentations, while the innovation-friendliness of regulatory agencies, Congress and even the Supreme Court are highlighted as sources of superior competitiveness on the other side of the Atlantic (Epstein, Landes and Posner, 2017). The almost uncontested supremacy of US tech giants such as Apple, Google, Microsoft, Facebook, Amazon has generated significant envy in Europe, leading politicians to ask themselves why Europe was not able to spawn such dynamic new firms.[2]

One of the corollaries of this theorem is that Europe should simplify its laws and align them with the more agile and dynamic US legal framework. Indeed, the past decades have witnessed attempts to achieve stronger regulatory convergence between the

US and Europe, based on the underlying belief that the two blocs were similar enough, and complementary enough, to warrant an even closer relationship (Hamilton and Pelkmans, 2015). The negotiations on the Transatlantic Trade and Investment Partnership (between 2013 and 2016) have, however, revealed significant differences both in horizontal, cross-cutting policies, as well as in sectoral legislation and in the overall enforcement of legal rules: a divergence that, especially on the US side, was interpreted as a sign of the superiority of the US legal and regulatory system vis-à-vis the older, less competitive EU one. This prejudice is equally present in Europe and the United States, and has spread throughout the global business community, where the US legal system is very influential, if not predominant. The intimate relation between the origins of contract law in UK common law and the *lex mercatoria* (merchant law) and the strong influence of the Anglo-Saxon tradition in the development of international law and policy (through the 'Washington Consensus') have left traces on the perception of common law as a superior framework for doing business. Since the mid-1960s, some US scholars also started to highlight the alleged superior tendency of common law towards economic efficiency (Posner, 1972). Based on this view, in a nutshell, Europe should take the US as a model, and its regulatory framework as an agenda.

At the same time, the ongoing disruption in international politics and global governance is signalling a time of unrest and unease in the United States as well. President Trump's "Make America Great" agenda came with the stated desire to deconstruct the administrative state, and pull the US out of important global and regional accords such as NAFTA, the TPP and COP21. Fears that China may, and ultimately will overtake the US as the world's largest economy are tangible and palpable in the US, and this is producing more protectionism and a resurgence of old-style industrial policy through market bans (recently, with Chinese tech giant Huawei) and trade tariffs.

In such a fast-changing environment, the United States seem to be discovering the limits of their own highly-praised economic and regulatory model. In a widely read NBER paper, Gutierrez Gallardo and Philippon (2017) observe that while until the 1990s US markets were more competitive than European markets, today European markets display lower concentration, lower excess profits, and lower regulatory barriers to entry. In an earlier contribution, Vogel (2012) explained how Europe came to become a leader in risk regulation and governance, and Wiener et al. (2011; but see also IRGC, 2017) ended up largely dismantling the myth that Europe is allergic to risk and innovation. Recent regulatory innovations such as the General Data Protection Regulation (GDPR) and the Ethics Guidelines for Trustworthy Artificial Intelligence show signs of a renewed EU ambition to become a 'norm leader' at the global level. From an entrepreneurial perspective, it is indeed remarkable that many European businesses managed to remain competitive on world markets, despite the wide range of competitive advantages enjoyed by American companies: a large homogeneous home market, a largely integrated legal and fiscal system, a common language and low energy costs.[3]

Against this background, the jury is out as to whether Europe is experiencing a time of renaissance, or a phase of inevitable, even irreversible decadence. The patchy and complex process of economic and social integration and the difficulty in responding to mounting global competition have led Europe to gradually lose sight of a number of precious legacy and prospective advantages over its global competitors: such advantages mostly refer to the robustness of Europe's set of values and its institutional setup. Some of them appear in vibrant relief, whereas many are only visible in a few member states; and others are simply covered by dust, waiting for someone to rediscover them. This is what this book seeks to achieve, by shedding light on ten "treasures" that Europe can rediscover and rely upon to restore a more sustainable growth. Such treasures encompass a wide spectrum of topics such as the overall quality of the legal system (Chapter 1), the patterns and traditions of corporate finance and governance (Chapters 2-3); the dynamics of innovation and more specifically the untapped potential of EU patents (Chapters 4-5); the quality and direction of competition rules (Chapter 6); the framework for taxation and the relative lack of widespread corruption (Chapters 7-8); Europe's possible future enhanced role as a trade superpower (Chapter 9) and, last but not least, its ability to become a norm leader in emerging high-tech markets (Chapter 10).

In developing our thoughts on Europe's hidden treasures, we were supported by colleagues and friends who ended up sharing, if not all the details, at least the spirit and direction of our research. In particular, we wish to acknowledge the collaboration of several CEPS researchers, including Karel Lannoo (Chapters 3 and 7); Willem Pieter de Groen (Chapter 2); Jacques Pelkmans (Chapter 9); Felice Simonelli and Nadina Iacob (Chapter 8). We also thank a number of friends and colleagues from EU institutions, who offered comments on selected hidden treasures at various moments since we decided, in July 2018, to embark into this adventure. They include Arnaldo Abruzzini, Nicholas Ashford, Annemieke van der Beek, Helena Braun, Filomena Chirico, Frank Heemskerk, Paul Nemitz, Stephan Raes, Joachim Schwerin, Luc Soete, Pawel Swieboda, Lucio Vinhas de Souza, John Zysman and all the participants at the session on Hidden Treasures we organised during the CEPS Ideas Lab in February 2019.

1. THE LEGAL SYSTEM: UNCOVERING EU ADVANTAGES

The quality of the legal system is a globally recognised driver of growth. The efficiency and effectiveness of the civil justice system, the quality of legal institutions and the independence of the judiciary are included among the most important preconditions for growth. For example, in 1990, Mancur Olson observed that "a society cannot have much borrowing and lending or obtain many of the other gains from mutually advantageous trade unless individuals and firms have the right to make contracts with one another that will be impartially enforced". And in the same year, Douglass North argued that "the inability of societies to develop effective, low cost enforcement is the most important source of both historical and contemporary under-development in the Third World". Similarly, indicators such as the World Bank's Worldwide Governance Indicators have sharpened our understanding of how the quality of institutions and the certainty generated by a strong rule of law can have a positive impact on economic development. Recent studies such as Han et al. (2014) showed that good governance, including regulatory and institutional quality and the control of corruption, is associated with both a higher level of per capita GDP as well as higher rates of GDP growth over time (Han, Khan and Zhuang, 2014).

Against this background, Europe still presents a heterogeneous landscape when it comes to the quality of the legal framework, as testified by the World Bank's Doing Business reports, as well as the EU Justice Scoreboard.[4] Among the most evident challenges Europe faces, the most widely acknowledged are the difficulty in achieving coordination and suitable rules in the EU's complex multi-level governance; the mix of legal cultures featured by member states; the lack of a fully fledged single market when it comes to basic aspects of transactions such as redress and even parcel delivery; the lack of reliable and speedy judicial remedies in some member states; the presence of corruption in a subset of EU countries; and, obviously, the language barriers faced by citizens and businesses. Under these layers of dust, however, our first treasure is hidden: the inherent quality of the EU legal system can become, with adequate support, a driver of future growth and investment.

1.1 Common law versus civil law: an endless querelle

Is the legal system in the EU designed in a way that tends, over time, towards the selection of more efficient, business-friendly rules? In academia, a dispute has emerged since the 1960s on whether common law jurisdictions, such as the US and the UK, are more conducive towards efficiency than civil law jurisdictions. This debate can shed some light on the possible future efficiency orientation of the EU legal system, especially if Brexit leads the EU to strengthen its civil law dimension. At risk of oversimplification,[5] in this chapter we assume that the EU legal system post-Brexit could move towards a civil law system.[6]

Table 1. Example of common and civil law countries

Common Law	French Civil Law	German Civil Law	Scandinavian Civil Law
England and Wales	France	Germany	Sweden
USA	Italy	Austria	Norway
Canada	Spain	Switzerland	Denmark
Australia	Portugal	Japan	Iceland
New Zealand	Belgium	South Korea	Finland
India	Netherlands	Taiwan	
Nigeria	Romania	Slovenia	
Malaysia	Brazil		
Singapore	Argentina		
Ireland	Mexico		
Burma	Chile		
Jamaica	Angola		
Barbados	Egypt		
Zimbabwe	Lebanon		
Pakistan	Turkey		

Source: Garoupa et al. (2014).

There is a lot of literature on the comparison between civil law and common law from the standpoint of efficiency, fuelled by the writings of Richard Posner and others in the 1960s in the United States, mostly as part of the rise of the so-called law and economics movement (Posner, 1972; Parisi, 2004; Renda, 2011; Calabresi, 2017). Posner's argument mostly rested on the idea that judges, lacking other criteria to solve disputes, would rely on Paretian efficiency tests (such as Kaldor-Hicks efficiency); whereas the more rigidly codified rules in civil law would not allow for such an exercise (Rubin, 1977; Deffains, 2011). Posner pushed his argument so far that he advocated the transformation of the United States into a "cost-benefit state", in which every interaction between the public sector and private market forces would be triggered by (potential) Pareto efficiency considerations. Posner's views, as well as those of other influential Chicago School economists such as Milton Friedman, were very influential, and permeated the global debate on the nature and shape of international private law, which still incorporates key dimensions of common law systems (Picker, 2008).

These views were also later echoed by other authors in the corporate governance and finance domains, as will be explained in more detail below, in Chapter 2. This sectoral debate was initiated by work authored by La Porta, Lopez-de-Silanes, Shleifer and Vishny (1997), which found that the legal system to which a country belongs, the content of laws, and the quality of law enforcement affected not only the degree of protection afforded to creditors' rights, but also the performance of capital markets. In the views of La Porta et al., common law countries provide stronger investor protection than civil law ones. Levine (2003) later extended the analysis to the banking system, finding that countries with more stringent enforcement of contracts and closer creditor protection also had a more developed banking system and higher economic growth rates. These authors converged with Posner's hypothesis, comforting the idea that civil law is less efficient than common law because it neglects economic effects on the behaviour of economic actors.

Recent contributions, however, have gone in a different direction, with authors arguing that civil law can in principle provide more legal certainty and a smoother corporate and economic development over time compared to common law. Back in 1988, Gordon Tullock (1988; 1997) suggested that, because of its nature, and its distinction between narrow holdings and *dicta*, common law can only develop very tight, narrow rules, whereas rules that are produced for civil codes, conversely, are broad and general in application. Tullock argued that it is much harder to manipulate lawmakers at the general level than it is to manipulate them at the narrow level through special interest pressures: since code provisions are very general, they can resist special interest pressures better than the narrow rules of the common law system.[7] In 2000, Aristides Hatzis observed that "an indication of the superiority of civil law, especially in the field of contracts, is that over the last two centuries, common law has consistently copied the institutions of civil law"; and added that "the particularistic and pragmatic approach of the Roman and civil law has proven to be more efficient than that of the rigid, theoretical approach of common law". Moreover, Garoupa et al. (2016) observe that the 'legal origins' theory, alongside its 'policy version' (the Doing Business reports of the World Bank) incorrectly selects a particular bundle of legal doctrines in order to measure the efficiency of a particular legal system, thereby erring in favour of the common law efficiency hypothesis. In their opinion, a different set of legal doctrines produces a different conclusion, and as a result the "identification of the efficiency of the common law is much more intricate and multifaceted than anticipated by the literature" (Garoupa et al., 2016).

The current debate shows that deciding which legal system is more efficient is at once a time-consuming and a tentative exercise, and that the supposed superiority of common law has never been fully demonstrated in practice, but still greatly inspired the work of international organisations and the development of international private law. Looking at specific fields of law, however, may lead to totally opposite conclusions, which may be very important for the future of the EU legal system, currently trapped in an often self-declared inferiority position. Among the key elements that affect the overall efficiency of the EU legal system, it is worth recalling the role of default rules, and in particular good faith obligations, in contract law; and the different patterns and cultures of litigation in the US and the EU. We explore them below.

1.2 The hidden treasure of the efficiency of EU contract law

A sound and reliable legal framework is of increasing importance in international business and innovation. This is due to the fact that more and more innovative enterprises operate on a project basis in the context of open innovation projects, which require a variety of expertise and resources for the development of new products and services, from their inception to roll out. Open innovation, in particular, leads to the need to build tailor-made coalitions of institutions and enterprises (Chesbrough, 2003). In this context, both bilateral and relational contractual schemes (Williamson, 1979) are essential to the working of innovation projects, and the availability of a well-shaped legal framework can significantly reduce transaction costs, facilitating partners by offering efficient default options and helping partners avoid detailed, complex negotiations, in which typically the strongest parties have more resources and superior bargaining power (see below, Chapter 6).

In the EU-27, and particularly in the civil law tradition, a generic good faith obligation applies to contract negotiation (*inter alia*, leading to pre-contractual liability), agreement and execution.[8] This implies that, regardless of the specific mentioning of good faith in the contractual document, parties are expected to behave in good faith throughout the whole contractual process and can be held liable if they fail to comply with the *bona fide* standard. If properly implemented, this can sharply reduce the risk of investing in the building of such coalitions, as the freedom to step out, once promising negotiations are under way, is limited.[9] Fairness and reasonableness are closely associated with the good faith obligation: the latter makes behaviour more predictable, which in turn helps to build trust among the parties.

Ejan Mackaay (2013) and other law and economics scholars have studied the differences between the two systems in depth, and Philippe (2018) explores "best effort clauses" on the two sides of the Atlantic. Key differentiating factors include the existence of general obligations to behave in good faith in the pre-contractual, contractual and post-contractual phases of contracts. Notable cases in which the European system has shown the potential benefits of *bona fide* requirements include *Phillips Petroleum Cu Ltd. UK v Enron*

Europe Ltd. (EWCA, 1996). In particular, the issue of pre-contractual liability has been subject to a completely diverging treatment in civil law and common law systems.[10] Although courts in common law juridical systems recognise the existence of a duty of good faith while contracts are in force, they hesitate to consider it during the period of contractual negotiations. The resistance and the reservations towards the good faith doctrine are based on the fear that its acceptance might threaten the fundamental principles of private autonomy and freedom to contract.[11] A good example is *Walford v Miles*, in which the House of Lords ruled that pre-contractual duties, derived from good faith, are contrary to the prosecution of self-interest and to contractual freedom, which encompass the possibility of ending negotiations at any time (Cumberbatch, 1992). Contrary to what happens in common law, the Roman-Germanic legal tradition orders long ago accepted the notion of *culpa in contrahendo*, developed by von Jhering in the 19th century (von Jhering, 1861; Kessler and Fine, 1964).

The lack of trust-oriented obligations has led to significant differences in contracting in the US and the EU. It is well known that commercial contracts are far more extensive and exhaustive than contracts in civil law legal orders (Cordero-Moss, 2007; 2014). As observed by Freire (2016), in common law countries "transaction costs are higher as a larger amount of time is expended in negotiations and direct costs, such as lawyers and legal advisers' fees, are also more significant"; whereas in civil law countries, "contracts have fewer stipulations because contracting parties seem to trust that the existing legal and jurisdictional mechanisms are able to fill in the gaps or revise the contract when unforeseen circumstances occur. Ultimately, they trust that judicial decisions will have the ability to understand the immediate aims expressed by the parties but, above all, the substantive goals underlying the contract. Thus, a general principle of good faith, established by law, enables parties to delegate in the judicial system the interpretation and revision of contracts according to their best interests. Confidence is strengthened by the existence of a general rule of honesty and loyalty that functions as a conduct criterion and as the legal basis for courts to interpret the will that led to the agreement and to fulfil the gaps in contracts" (Freire, 2016). Hence, unlike what occurs in the US and the UK, contracts in the EU-27 do not have to specify all the undesirable behaviour and steps of all the partners. In many cases framework agreements suffice, as all partners are bound by the principles of reasonableness and fairness.[12]

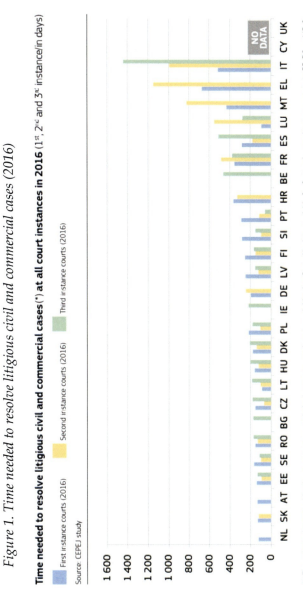

Figure 1. Time needed to resolve litigious civil and commercial cases (2016)

These features of corporate life increase the likelihood that attempts to build coalitions will succeed, considerable costs will be saved, value will be created sooner rather than later and, most importantly, the coalition will be far more agile in adapting to changing circumstances. The obligation to meet post-contractual obligations provides a stimulus to build a solid reputation as a partner. A soft asset that over time will increase in value. If and when a conflict arises, the courts will go back to the original intentions of the partners and in fact fill in the apparent holes in the contract.

1.3 The dust of obstacles to the efficiency of legal systems in the EU

Our first treasure is hidden under layers of dust, which may have contributed to the overall belief that the EU legal system is inherently less efficient than the US one. The main obstacles that can be identified are the limited capacity and significant inefficiency of the judiciary in many countries, the cost of access to justice for smaller firms and citizens, and the lack of a robust set of rules protecting the interests of smaller contractors in relational contracts.[13]

For what concerns the inefficiency of the judiciary, it suffices to look at the current statistics on the time needed to resolve cases in the member states, from the EU 2018 Justice Scoreboard. In two member states, more than 1,000 days are needed on average just to obtain an appeals decision (2nd instance).

In specific areas of EU law, the Justice Scoreboard confirms the heterogeneity of findings. For competition cases, more than one third of member states report first instance cases lasting more than three years. In only a quarter of member states does the consumer protection authority take a decision in a case covered by EU consumer law in less than three months on average. And in the field of money laundering, while in about half of member states the first instance court proceedings take up to a year on average, these proceedings take around two years on average in several member states that are facing challenges.

Figure 2. Perceived independence of courts and judges (2016-2018)

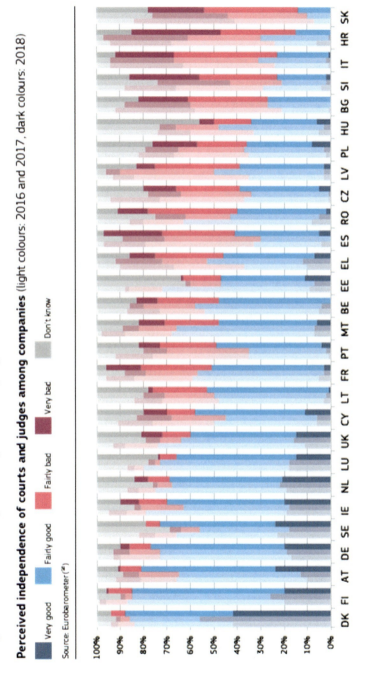

The Justice Scoreboard also indicates important concerns related to the perceived lack of independence of the judiciary in many EU member states. This, too, can be a deadly blow to the superiority of EU contract law, as the latter's efficiency chiefly depends on the timely and independent action of the judge in interpreting the parties' will in a given contract.

Even more significant differences between the EU and the US, and among EU countries are found in the domain of litigation and enforcement. Gordon Tullock (1988) famously critiqued the system of dispute resolution in the United States, arguing that the adversarial system of adjudication exacerbates rent dissipation in litigation.[14]

Overall evidence reveals that litigation is more frequent, and settlements are more common in the US compared to the EU. This is due to several factors: for example, on fee-shifting rules, Carbonara, Parisi and Von Wangenheim (2015) identify a hidden virtue of the English rule over the American rule, showing that an increase in fee-shifting may reduce total litigation costs and lead to desirable outcomes in socially valuable litigation. All in all, however, the US seems to feature a comprehensive set of plaintiff-friendly procedural rules, which help injured parties in filing a lawsuit (and then most often in settling it). Suffice it to recall that, in the field of antitrust rules, more than 95% of EU antitrust cases are public enforcement cases, possibly ending in administrative sanctions; whereas in the US, more than 90% of cases are private enforcement cases, ending with damage awards if successful; and 99% of these cases are settled before trial (Renda et al., 2008). The key challenge for the European Commission in its past attempts to stimulate private antitrust enforcement in Europe was to avoid creating the US "litigation culture" while at the same time strengthening the EU's "compensation culture".[15]

All in all, it is important to realise that the use of the legal system, and the disciplining effect it exerts on the parties in contractual relationships, are a function of the effectiveness of the system itself. The advantages offered by EU contract law cannot be fully exploited if the parties cannot fully rely on the legal system: the flexibility granted by the obligation to behave in good faith and by the contextual interpretation of contracts gets lost if the parties cannot go to court easily and rely on an independent and competent judge. This is of utmost importance, especially if one considers that the diffusion of open innovation schemes and the platform economy determine the rise of various forms of contracting as prominent forms of organisation in the modern economy (Bénézech, 2012). More specifically, with increasingly modular products and complex value chains, large companies have the option of outsourcing entire phases of their value chains to smaller companies by establishing relational contracting schemes, whereas large platforms essentially rely on the market (and thus, individual contracting) as an alternative to more complex hierarchical structures (Coase, 1937, 1960; Renda, 2019). A hybrid governance scheme between in- and outsourcing is represented by 'relational contracting', which configures long-term contractual relationships, often based on trust and a relatively sophisticated governance (Williamson, 1979; 1985).

Against this background, the requirement of good faith in contracting can be a boost for smoother and more efficient commercial relationships between large and smaller firms: at the same time, if not coupled with adequate arrangements in terms of specific SME-friendly policies, appropriate provisions for access to justice and conflict resolution, such requirements could become a curse for SMEs and for society at large, as larger companies would have the temptation to rely too much on open innovation schemes and relational contracting, knowing that they will be able to abuse their superior bargaining position over time (Brunswicker, 2012). In other words, if our first 'hidden treasure' is not adequately coupled with side measures, it may end up promoting inefficient governance decisions and an over-reliance on B2B contracting as opposed to pure market transactions or the in-sourcing of production. This, in turn, leads to what will become a dominant theme in this book: the lack of a dedicated set of EU policies that support SMEs in approaching commercial relationships and dispute resolution when dealing with larger businesses: a situation that is hardly covered by existing policies such as EU competition rules on abuse of dominance (Articles 102 TFEU), or the Small Business Act.

1.4   Policy implications

Our analysis of the advantages offered by civil law especially for B2B cooperation in complex value chains and open innovation projects has far-reaching consequences for the EU agenda in the years to come. We recommend four main actions: the promotion of civil law over common law, especially in contract formation; the strengthening of the civil court system to speed up procedures and to improve the quality of the business environment at the national level; the removal of barriers for SMEs to access the civil court system; and the introduction of specialised civil courts on issues related to Information and Communication Technology, Biotech and Energy. Below, we provide more details on each of these recommendations.

1.4.1   Promote civil law over common law in contract formation

The Commission and the member states should consider actively promoting the use of civil law over the use of common law in contract formation, especially when contracts involve Anglo-Saxon and EU-27 companies. Initiatives to raise awareness of the merits of civil law among entrepreneurs are highly advisable, and long overdue (Hadjemmanuil, 2018; Escobar Ribas, 2017). The use of civil law can be promoted and endorsed in various ways, mostly by leveraging the financial and commercial power of the single market. For example, EU institutions such as the European Commission and the European Investment Bank provide financial support to small and large firms in many shapes and forms to projects and programmes. The use of civil law could be both incorporated in the terms of reference, and also used as a 'conditionality', i.e. a mandatory condition for the eligibility to receive funding.

Escobar Ribas (2018) observes that Brexit will have significant implications for particular aspects of business contracts, in particular for what concerns interpretation, applicable law and on Brexit as grounds for termination. But recent research also demystifies the view that the popularity of English law is due to its quality or substantive merits (Vogenauer, 2013). Empirical evidence shows that the choice of law is usually "determined by familiarity and the dominant position of English law firms"; and that in cross-border transactions, parties do not engage in 'contract law shopping', but rather leave this activity to large law firms. The latter often use English law as part of a 'package', alongside insurance and arbitration in London. Whether Brexit can break this habit and bring back civil law as a default option, together with arbitration on the continent, for both large and small firms, remains to be seen.

1.4.2   Invest in improving the court system

The EU and its member states should invest in the court system, to make the use of civil law attractive to all comers. At the very minimum, the cost-cutting that has taken place over the past decade needs to be rolled back: investment in the quality of institutions and in particular courts, should regularly feature in the types of reforms that member states are asked to implement and monitor under the European Semester: available statistics show that the quality of the legal system is positively correlated with sustainable growth. The trend towards specialised courts for specific, highly technical subjects (corporate governance, patents, information technology, competition) should be subject to more in-depth analysis, and endorsed where beneficial (Ginsburg and Wright, 2013). Including reforms of the court system in the Semester would also be consistent with a commitment, within the Agenda 2030, to mainstream SDGs into every aspect of EU policy: as a matter of fact, goal 16 aims *inter alia* at strengthening institutions for sustainable development, and courts are important institutions in this respect.

Another promising avenue for the single market is the recent trend towards the introduction of English as an optional language in civil courts, which can facilitate non-nationals in settling controversies by using civil or even common law as appropriate (Kern, 2012). This transition is going to become even more urgent after Brexit, since many commercial and financial contracts rely on UK common law and would therefore become bereft of a forum for settling controversies in continental Europe. Apart from international arbitration cases, the availability of courts to settle international disputes in English in countries like France, Germany and the Netherlands is increasingly a reality, which will lead to further hybridisation between civil (procedural) law and common law, and even growing interpretation of the law by courts in common law cases.[16] The inherent risk is that this trend towards English-speaking courts leads to increased use of common law: we argue that the EU should avoid facilitating this tendency and should proactively seek to promote civil law.

For example, the Netherlands set up a new international Commercial Court, which opened its doors in Amsterdam on 1 January 2019. The major 'selling point' of the Court is that the entire proceedings can be conducted in English, including any written statements, communication with the Court and hearings. Furthermore, the procedural rules of the Netherlands Commercial Court also provide the flexibility for proceedings to be conducted in the civil law tradition or in a manner similar to proceedings in international arbitration or common law jurisdictions. By providing this flexibility, the Netherlands Commercial Court aims to make proceedings recognisable for international parties. The Netherlands Commercial Court will hear international civil or commercial disputes, provided that the parties have expressly agreed to confer jurisdiction on the Netherlands Commercial Court.

1.4.3 Remove barriers to access to justice for SMEs

Improving the legal system is also, and especially, important for weaker parties lacking the financial resources to sustain litigation for a long period. In particular, SMEs' access to the courts should be greatly improved, especially in a cross-border setting (see Figure 3). This would encourage enterprises to be scrupulous in meeting their contractual obligations and could very well reduce the number of court cases. In addition, there is a large unmet need for innovative, cheap and fast methods to resolve conflicts. Experiments are underway in different member states, many of which are geared to forms of triage to ensure that only cases with merit reach the legal system.

In 2017, with specific reference to the need for SMEs to ensure adequate protection of Intellectual Property Rights (IPRs), a manifesto published by an umbrella organisation (IP Europe) advocated fairer access to justice for European SMEs, by specifically mentioning stronger IPR protection in all jurisdictions, the promotion of a fair, fit-for-purpose legal system so that SMEs can protect their inventions and cost-effectively challenge those, notably large companies, who infringe their patents and profit from their inventions without taking out a licence; ensuring that the guarantees and bonds required from SMEs seeking injunctions against large companies are not prohibitive, and that all courts in Europe have the discretion to set bonds that do not deprive SMEs of their access to justice; the adoption of pro-SME measures, including easier access to Courts and reduced fees in all jurisdictions to ensure that any litigation and costs supported by SMEs in protecting their R&D investments are not beyond their financial reach. The Manifesto also included an urgent call on the Commission to implement the non-legislative supporting measures mentioned in the Communication "Putting intellectual property at the service of SMEs to foster innovation and growth".[17]

Figure 3. Major obstacles to exporting for SMEs in the five largest EU member states

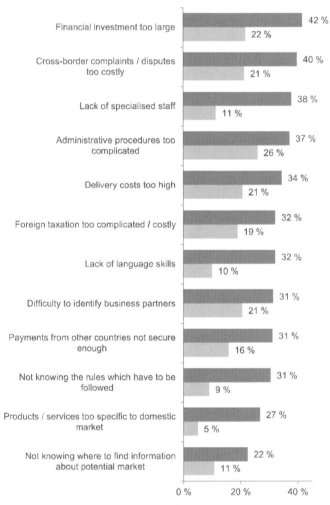

■ SMEs without exporting experience in the five largest EU member countries

▪ SMEs with exporting experience in the five largest EU member countries

Source: Abel-Koch ed., 2018.

1.4.4 Create specialised civil courts for ICT, Biotech and Energy

The creation of specialised courts, in charge of solving disputes related to specific sectors that are thought to be particularly technical (e.g. intellectual property, competition) or atypical, worthy of specific resource allocation (family law), is a consolidated practice in a number of member states. The EU institutions could decide to set up specific courts for sectors that are considered to be particularly strategic for the EU agenda, as well as likely to feature heavy litigation to the detriment of small, innovative companies. But also large companies could profit from the availabilities of a network of courts throughout the territory of the EU, with specialised knowledge in highly technical sectors. The key benefit of competent courts being available would need to be weighed against the perils of repeated interaction between the courts and the litigants. This is why good governance, strong independence of the judiciary and a high level of transparency are needed in this domain.

1.4.5 Create EU-level dispute resolution mechanisms for SMEs

In addition to creating specialised courts at the national level, the EU could take the initiative to create mechanisms for dispute resolution at the EU level, designed in a way that would favour the collection of confidential complaints, and also avoid smaller firms refraining from accessing the justice system for fear of retaliation by their larger counterparts. In fact, as will be observed below in Chapter 6, competition rules barely protect smaller businesses in Europe, if not in the rather uncommon cases in which antitrust law can be invoked. Creating ad hoc rules to protect SMEs in cases of abuse of superior bargaining power, strategic behaviour and abuse of economic dependency, and coupling these rules with centralised enforcement mechanisms to ensure easier access to justice for SMEs would boost the business environment for European SMEs, and in turn promote the competitiveness of the whole continent. This would also be very much in line with the creation of a more 'decentralised' single market, with a more fragmented and local market structure, as will be evoked below in Chapter 10. And it could be made available in particular if small businesses had access to a dedicated European enterprise statute, tailored to their needs, which will be described in the next chapter.

2. THE FINANCING OF INVESTMENTS AND WORKING CAPITAL OF COMPANIES: EUROPE'S UNIQUE RECIPE

A competitive economy must provide adequate sources of financing to innovative enterprises, whatever their size. At the same time, the economics literature never converged on an unambiguous conceptualisation of the relationship between financial markets development and economic growth. A recent literature review by Paun et al. (2019) largely confirms this view. For example, in an analysis focused on Latin America, Blanco (2009) finds that "while economic growth causes financial development, financial development does not cause economic growth"; Naceur et al. (2017) observe that "financial development does not appear to be a magic bullet for economic growth", and that they could not find an "unambiguously positive relationship between financial development, investment, and productivity"; studies on Africa … show that "financial liberalization failed to increase economic growth" for the overwhelming majority of surveyed countries; whereas Gries, Kraft and Meierrieks (2009) analyse 16 sub-Saharan African countries, concluding that "finance, growth and openness do not share significant long-run relationships".

The financial crisis that hit the global economy in 2007 shed more light on the nature of the relationship between finance and growth, leading economists to identify cases of excessive financialisation of the economy (Mazzucato, 2018). Prochniak and Wasiak (2017) focus on EU and OECD economies in the period 1993–2013, concluding that "an excessively large size of the financial system … may negatively impact GDP dynamics". And Haiss, Juvan and Mahlberg (2016) study 26 European countries in the period 1990-2009, concluding that under current conditions, "the financial sector is not capable of dampening unsustainable levels of indebtedness, risk-taking and leverage or to avoid euphoria in the markets".

At the same time, economics literature is almost unanimous in finding a positive impact of well-developed, sophisticated capital markets on economic growth. This spurred a heated debate at the EU level, where the private equity market is under-developed compared to the United States (EIB, 2018). In fact, over the 2007–15 period, the average venture capital-backed US company received five times more than its EU counterpart, i.e. €6.3 million compared with €1.3 million (AFME, 2017); the gap between the US and Europe is especially wide at the scale-up stage (EIB, 2018), whereas at the start-up stage, there is relatively little difference in the amount of funding.

Figure 4. Share of bank and non-bank financing in total non-financial corporation debt financing in the euro area and the United States (outstanding amounts; percentages)

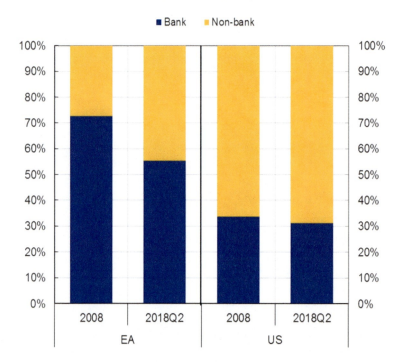

Source: ECB, Federal Reserve System. Latest observation: Q2 2018.

As a result, there are significant differences in the way businesses are financed in the US and the EU: while the size of the financial system is broadly comparable, the EU banking sector is about twice the size of the US banking sector. This is partially due to a difference in accounting standards and (with Fannie Mae and Freddie Mac) a different way of financing mortgage loans; but even when these two factors are accounted for, the banking sector remains substantially more important as a financing source in the EU than in the US. This difference will become even larger post-Brexit.

Although the relatively larger role of banks might provide EU corporates with fewer options for funding of investments and business activities, this might fit better the demands of the (on average) smaller companies operating in the EU. Moreover, the EU banking system is more stakeholder-focused, especially when it takes the form of cooperative and savings banks, which permits a longer-term perspective and requires lower rates of return than listed commercial banks.

With the launch of the Capital Markets Union project in 2015, the European Commission aimed to develop the EU's capital markets, which is characterised as "under-developed and fragmented" in its action plan.[18] Looking at financing for companies, the European Commission sees opportunities for venture capital markets and securitisation in particular. This, however, raises the question whether capital markets are indeed the solution for all businesses, or only for a limited number of large corporations. Banks, historically the main funding source for the large majority of EU corporations, are currently confronted with a transformation. A combination of new legislative and supervisory requirements in the aftermath of the 2007-9 global financial crisis and digitalisation is challenging their existing business models and market practices. Although the transformation is contributing to more efficient and safer financial markets, they might potentially also have some negative unintended consequences for the financing of corporations and in particular SMEs. The transformation, for instance, challenges relationship banking and stakeholder banking models, which are traditionally important in the financing of EU SMEs. This suggests that actions should be taken to preserve these historic strongholds in EU corporate finance.

2.1 Tailoring the financial system to the EU's traditional and market features

Financing demand and supply differs substantially across business sizes, primarily due to different levels of information asymmetry. In general, there is substantially more accessible information available about publicly listed and large companies than about SMEs and private companies. SMEs, with the exception of some high-growth potential companies, are also subject to less scrutiny from analysts than large companies (Petersen and Rajan, 2002).

Figure 5. Enterprises by size of business (2016)

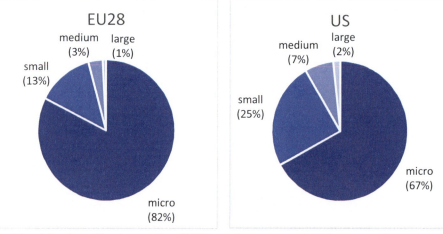

Note: Number of businesses for all EU member states excl. Lithuania and Luxembourg. For Sweden, UK and US, the data are for 2015.
Source: OECD Data Portal (2018). https://data.oecd.org/entrepreneur/enterprises-by-business-size.htm#indicator-chart

Small and micro-enterprises are relatively more important for the EU than the US economy. Looking at the sizes of the companies, there are substantial differences between the EU and the US. In both, micro companies (0 to 9 employees) form the majority of companies, but in the US the relative weight of small (10 to 49 employees), medium-sized (50 to 249 employees) and large companies (more than 250 employees) is almost twice that in the EU (see Figure 5).

Figure 6. Employment by size of business (2016)

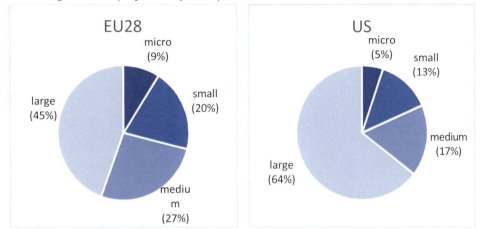

Note: Employees by business size for all EU member states excl. Lithuania and Luxembourg. For Sweden, UK and US, the data are for 2015.
Source: OECD Data portal (2018). https://data.oecd.org/entrepreneur/employees-by-business-size.htm#indicator-chart

In terms of activity, SMEs are also substantially more important for the EU economy (see Figure 6). Large companies form less than 2% of the businesses in the EU and the US, but are responsible for the majority of the employment in the US (64%). In turn, the micro, small and medium-sized enterprises in the EU are jointly responsible for more than half of employment (56%).

Large and publicly listed companies are required to disclose much more information about their financial performance and activities. Moreover, this information for larger and publicly listed companies is also subject to more intense scrutiny from accountants and auditors, than that for SMEs. In addition, lenders to both smaller and larger companies collect additional private information about the creditworthiness of companies during the lending relationship (e.g. receivables and payments). This information is, however, only available to a limited number of lenders that are not keen on sharing it, given the competitive advantage it offers. In fact, the smaller the company size, the lower the average number of its bank relationships, and thus the smaller the number of banks that possess the information required to assess its creditworthiness (see Figure 7).

Figure 7. Number of bank relationships by size of business (October 2017-March 2018)

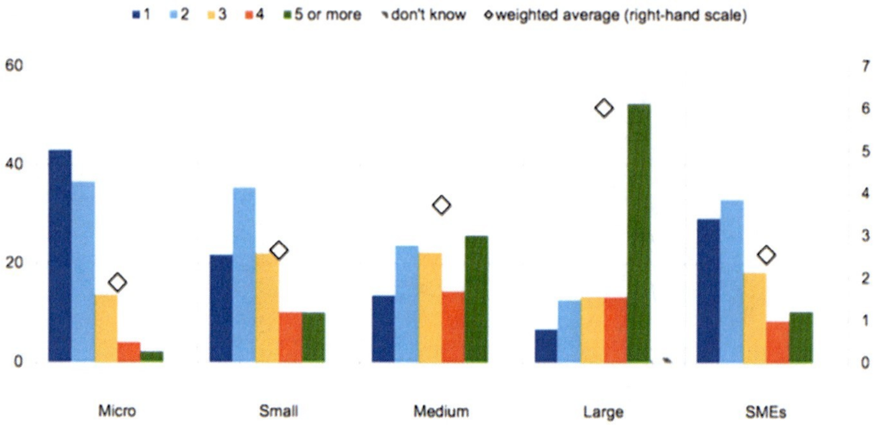
1
2
3
4
5 or more
don't know
weighted average (right-hand scale)
60
40
20
0
7
6
5
4
3
2
1
0
Micro
Small
Medium
Large
SMEs

Source: ECB (2018).

Traditionally, information collection to determine the creditworthiness of SMEs is very labour intensive. With limited hard information available, soft information is more important for SMEs. This information is collected over time due to relationships between lenders and borrowers (Berger and Udell, 2000). The soft information is not stored in databases, but in the minds of the loan officers of banks. In addition to the labour-intensive information collection, the smaller amounts involved also contribute to the higher costs of lending to SMEs.

It is not coincidental that banks are currently the main financers of SMEs. Banks have a comparative advantage over other lenders in providing financing to SMEs. First, most banks operate larger bank branch networks that, besides loans to SMEs, also provide financial and non-financial services (e.g. cash handling, insurance, real estate brokerage) to households and other customers. This allows banks to distribute the relatively high cost of operating a bank branch among its various services. Second, European banks offer highly efficient payment systems and arrange savings and investment accounts. Banks are also well positioned to cover both private and business demand for services, which is crucially important for micro and small companies. Their comprehensive insight into the skills and attitudes of the entrepreneur, their private finances and business is extremely valuable to avoid both false positives (e.g. granting loans that should have been rejected) and false negatives (e.g. denying loans to creditworthy entrepreneurs and ventures).

Figure 8. Use of internal and external financing by euro area enterprises across by size of business (October 2017-March 2018)

Source: ECB (2018).

Banks also constitute the most important source of finance for large companies, which on average require higher amounts and more varied types of financing than SMEs, including also capital markets financing (equity and debt securities). In turn, on average SMEs use fewer sources of financing than large companies, mainly internal funds and bank financing. Besides loans, credit lines, trade credit, factoring and leasing can also be provided by banks. However, in some cases these are provided by alternative financers. Some of these forms of financing such as factoring and leasing are fully collateral-based and therefore require less information on the company and are also more often provided by alternative financers. Capital markets are a relatively insignificant source of financing for SMEs, with only a very small share of primarily high-growth potential SMEs obtaining equity and to a lesser extent debt financing through exchanges and other (unregulated) capital markets.

The EU banking sector has evolved to address the financing needs of SMEs. In particular, many stakeholder-owned banks such as savings and cooperative banks still have relatively large branch networks through which they primarily serve SMEs and households (see Figure 9). These stakeholder value banks are mostly owned by their customers, foundations or governments. The stakeholder-owned banks are distinguished from commercial banks with profit maximisation as their main target by having other objectives such as serving their owners (i.e. local households and companies) or contributing to local socio-economic development. Stakeholder-owned banks are dominant in Austria, Belgium, Cyprus, Finland, France, Germany, Greece, Italy, Ireland, The Netherlands, Slovenia, Poland and Portugal (see Figure 10). In the US, credit unions could be considered as stakeholder value banks, but they are relatively small in size.

Stakeholder value banks in the EU have numerous different business models and governance structures. According to empirical evidence, their performance and efficiency are fairly similar to those of commercial banks. However, there are potential economic, systemic and welfare benefits that can be derived from having a diverse banking sector in general and more cooperative banks in particular. Indeed, a more diverse banking sector increases competitiveness, financial stability and economic growth (Ayadi et al., 2010).

Figure 9. Bank branches and stakeholder value banks (2017)

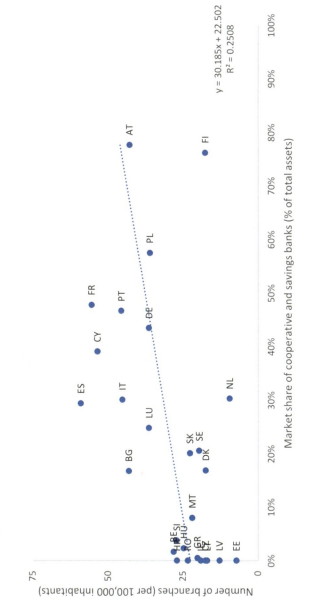

Source: ECB (2018).

36 | THE FINANCING OF INVESTMENTS AND WORKING CAPITAL OF COMPANIES

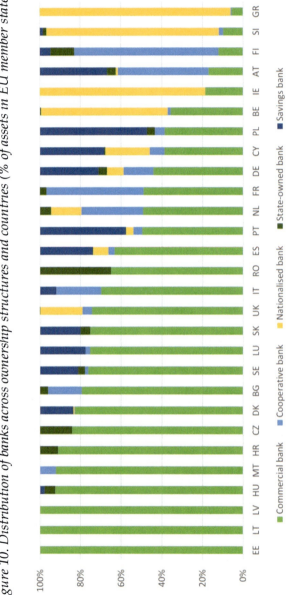

Figure 10. Distribution of banks across ownership structures and countries (% of assets in EU member states)

Source: Ayadi et al. (2016).

2.2 Europe's diverse banking system is a hidden treasure

Legislation introduced after the 2007-9 global financial crisis and the digital transformation challenges the existing business models of many banks and in particular stakeholder-owned banks as the regulation and supervision of banks in the EU and especially in the euro area has been strengthened and extended. First, capital requirements have been reinforced and complemented with leverage ratio and liquidity ratios. This required all banks to raise their capital levels, which is more challenging for most stakeholder-owned banks as they cannot issue equity. Second, with the introduction of the resolution mechanism, the orderly unwinding of distressed systemic banks or a way of ensuring their continuity needs to be arranged. This scheme, however, only considers commercial (private bail-in) and public solutions (recapitalisation via resolution fund). This means that in cases where a stakeholder-owned bank is resolved, it is likely to become a commercial bank. Third, the supervision in the euro area has been consolidated at the ECB. ECB supervision is more data-heavy, which is problematic for stakeholder-owned banks and others whose lending is traditionally based more on soft information. Fourth, the newly adopted, more stringent regulation is also accompanied by higher compliance costs. This is challenging, in particular for the stakeholder-owned banks that often manage many banking licences, obliging some of them to consolidate their organisation or networks over the past few years.

Digitalisation makes it easier for banks and other financial institutions to collect more frequent hard information at a distance and potentially reduces the need for the collection and storage of soft information, which requires a denser branch network and closer proximity to companies. However, it can only overcome the difficulties to a limited extent, as soft information is by definition hard to express quantitatively (Stein, 2002; Uzzi, 2000). In addition, the digital transformation potentially challenges the business model of stakeholder-owned and other banks that operate many branches, and might also reduce lending to small, new and high-growth potential companies. For these companies, for which less hard information is available and soft information is more important in assessing their creditworthiness, credit is likely to become more costly and/or scarce (Begenau et al., 2018). In addition, fintech and big-data-driven alternative lenders are more likely to lend to borrowers with high creditworthiness (Buchak et al., 2017). In this latter respect, perhaps the biggest threat to relationship banking is the possibility for big tech companies to gain access to information held by banks: the recent provisions on open banking introduced by the second EU Payment Services Directive (PSD2) risk creating a situation in which extremely precious customer information is taken from banks and delivered into the hands of technology giants.

2.3 Does Europe really need more venture capital?

The previous chapters have helped us identify a key issue related to the financing needs of European companies. While economists agree that more sophisticated capital markets often accompany growth, the extent to which this is a case of correlation, or one of causation, is still far from settled. Moreover, the quest for more venture capital seems a bad fit for the needs of European SMEs: more generally, such a stance should not overshadow the need for quality capital, rather than growth at all costs. In fact, venture-backed start-ups often face huge pressure to perform: either succeed rapidly, or fail fast (and if possible, gracefully). And the literature exploring the links between the financialisation of the economy, venture capital, the rise of inequality and the gradually growing instability of the economy is becoming richer every week.

A decade has passed since newly elected European Commission President Barroso invoked venture capital as one of the four reforms that would bring Europe back to sustained growth after the financial crisis wave (together with energy liberalisation, the reduction of red tape and the services directive). Those ideas and hopes, today, appear preposterous at best. Scholars like Mariana Mazzucato (2018), Kate Raworth (2016), Lynn Stout (2012) and George Stiglitz (2017; 2018) have since vehemently criticised 'shareholder capitalism' as too narrow and ultimately unfit for the age of sustainable development. And economists and market analysts start to realise that 'patient capital' and a more balanced model of capitalism can offer more stable growth opportunities to SME-dominated economies like those in the EU.[19] Venture capital is of course welcome, but it comes in many different guises and is in many cases far too expensive in terms of the cost of dividends and/or of serving the loans taken out by the owners as well as in terms of lost entrepreneurship. Funds work very much under a short-term perspective, aimed at securing a successful exit, and exploiting the fiscal advantage of debt over equity. Mixing the personal interests of the fund managers and the fund is not necessarily a driver of successful scale-up and the best way to leverage European entrepreneurship. On the other hand, commercial banks are also struggling to provide small loans, as costs have risen and staff has been reduced. All this produces the very well documented 'valley of death', where promising prototypes become stranded and perish.

And yet, boosting venture capital still seems to be the master plan in the EU, in particular through the complex and ambitious array of initiatives that fall under the umbrella name of the Capital Markets Union. However, the EU business structure in which SMEs have a more prominent position still requires, at least for the time being, a bank-dominated system, and possibly the co-existence of a variety of business models, together with legislation that does not undermine the stability and overall incentives of stakeholder-owned banks. Soft information is likely to play a more important role for the financing of especially small, new and high-growth potential companies. This means that policies in this domain should allow banks to collect and use soft information to assess the creditworthiness of SMEs.

An important strand within the literature seeks to understand the models, mechanisms, and the general nature of bank financing for SMEs. The consensus in most of the literature is that small and domestic banks provide more financing to SMEs (Berger & Udell, 1998, 2006; Hassan et al., 2017; Hernandez-Canovas & Martinez-Solano, 2010), since "small and domestic banks have more capacity to engage in relationship lending, the use of soft information and continuous personalized contacts to lend to SMEs" (Beck, Demirguc-Kunt, & Peria, 2011; Hassan et al., 2017; Hakenes et al., 2014). The argument is that relationship lending reduces the information asymmetry between SMEs and banks (Esho and Verhoef, 2018). Beck et al. (2017) find, on the basis of interviews with bank CEOs in 397 banks across 21 countries, that relationship lending is particular useful during times of economic downturn; this is due, *inter alia,* to the fact that, since relationship lenders acquire valuable information during the lending relationship, they can also more easily adapt their lending conditions to changing circumstances (Agarwal and Hauswald, 2010; Bolton, Freixas, Gambacorta, and Mistrulli, 2016).

European enterprises can and should take advantage of the diversity of the EU banking system with commercial banks, cooperative banks and savings banks. Most European banks adhere to the 'relationship model' in sharp contrast to the 'transaction model'. They have deep insights into the history and prospects of their clients as well as their markets and competitors. They know the main players, their strengths and weaknesses. Relationship banking remains the superior route to banks' risk management: *Svenska Handelsbanken* is a shining example in this respect. Relationship banks play an important role in helping their clients to upgrade their investment programme by backing and by rejecting investment proposals. The contribution of relationship banks to the economy as a whole is real and should be more strongly emphasised at the EU level.[20]

2.4 Policy implications

Our discussion of corporate finance in Europe is intimately related to the analysis of the particularity of the EU legal system, as well as the dynamics and features of continental EU corporate governance and innovation. Brexit, when it occurs, will leave Europe bereft of a vibrant capital market, as well as of the most financialised large economy compared to other large member states. This may offer an opportunity to revisit the overall approach to SME financing, focusing on the acquisition of quality information regarding the prospects of existing ventures, as well as countless possibilities for mentoring and nurturing talent without falling prey to short-termism and the urge to deliver on investment. This approach may lead to important consequences for EU policymakers in the next legislature. Below, we explore a few steps that may bring value to the future EU: the preservation and promotion of relationship lending (including in emerging fintech intermediaries), the creation or expansion of house funds by institutional investors, and the provision of various forms of mentoring and support to promising SMEs, possibly through a blending of instruments, rather than a siloed approach to financing (see more detail on this latter point in Chapter 4).

2.4.1 Preserve and promote the diversity of banking models in Europe

The EU legislative and policy framework should allow for a diverse banking sector, including, in particular, stakeholder-owned banks that focus on SMEs. This implies that the policy framework does not amplify scale advantages, and that diverse ownership of banks is preserved. The resolution and supervisory framework should allow for cooperative and savings banks to continue operating as such after resolution. Moreover, supervisors should take the ownership structure into account: stakeholder-owned banks have limited possibilities to attract external capital, which means that they sometimes require longer transition periods to meet higher capital requirements or recover. This also means that provisions on capital requirements may have to differentiate between listed and non-listed banks, as the combination of the pursuit of shareholder return on investment (ROI) and the use of IFRS makes the former more vulnerable.[21]

2.4.2 Explore in-depth how banks decide on loans to SMEs

In the banking domain, the European Commission should support a study into the way banks handle loan applications and the decision criteria that are applied. At present, these decisions appear to be mostly based on readily available information, such as corporate accounts and tax returns, which have very little predictive value. This is in line with the predominant arms' length approach to banking. On the contrary, evaluation on the basis of productivity, investment record and the intellectual property on 'a virtual balance sheet' and other factors could help avoid two types of mistakes: approving loans that should have been rejected ('false positives') and rejecting loans that should have been approved ('false negatives'). DG GROW undertook a study in 2013, which explored credit assessment tools used by banks and provided useful recommendations (CSES and Panteia, 2014). At the time, however, it was quite difficult to assess the way banks handle loan applications and the decision criteria that they apply, due to the vast spectrum of rating models used by banks (either standardised or internal). Existing practices and new forms of interaction and feedback should be further explored in the coming years.

2.4.3 Leverage fintech solutions based on the relationship model

The digital transformation of banking is leading to a proliferation of business models, some of which may offer opportunities to consolidate our "hidden treasure". As a matter of fact, besides Internet giants, part of the fintech universe is actually based on relationship models: this includes crowdfunding, peer-to-peer lending, and ICOs/tokens that in general emerge bottom-up at a small scale. This part of fintech is, in a way, the digital twin of the old savings and cooperative banks, building on trust and close connectivity, only without those traditional banks as such (although hybrid models exist) but based on digital entities and cryptocurrencies. If Europe succeeds in helping such initiatives to scale up and spread best practices, the new generation of financial services and intermediation will incorporate the benefits of the relationship model with the agility of fintech. This may require specific approaches to competition policy (see Chapter 6), aimed at preserving the possibility for smaller players to compete on an equal footing with large tech giants.

2.4.4 Incentivise institutional investors to set up equity funds for SMEs

Institutional investors, generally with long-term obligations, should be incentivised to invest in in-house funds for SMEs, run by quality staff. Banks could start equity funds as long as these are organisationally separate from the main bank and separately financed. Ideally, these funds should be accompanied by a portfolio of services, including equity, loans, lease products and export financing. This would enable SMEs to avoid private equity and its associated cost and, more importantly, to design their own procedures and criteria for granting loans.

The EIB is the prime example of an independent, highly entrepreneurial and safe bank and EU institutions are right to gradually expand its role. Member states are exploring the foundation of development banks, and some of them already rely on extremely strong institutions (e.g. France, Germany, Italy). The European Commission is also setting up a dedicated body in charge of promoting the scale-up of promising firms, the so-called European Innovation Council, and is mobilising funding for innovative projects through both InvestEU and Horizon Europe. Altogether, if coupled with adequate policy reforms aimed at creating a level playing field and a rich, diverse banking environment, these initiatives could lay the foundations of a new, different model, rooted in Europe's legal and economic approach to innovation, competition and corporate governance (see the next three chapters).

3. Corporate Governance: In Search of the European Enterprise

The way in which the internal supervision, management, and decision-making of large companies is structured has a strong influence on their incentives and behaviour. Traditionally, the literature on comparative corporate governance has focused on transatlantic differences between the 'Shareholder Model' adopted in the US, which leads companies to primarily pursue the interests of shareholders, directors and management; and the 'Stakeholder Capitalism' model adopted by many European corporations, which tends to address a broader group of stakeholders. This debate is echoed in other parts of academic scholarship, such as the business ethics literature, which has debated extensively on whether managers should prioritise primarily or exclusively the interests of shareholders (*à la* Milton Friedman), or whether they should consider or balance the interests of a wider group of stakeholders (Agle & Mitchell, 2008; Campbell, 2007; Freeman, 1994; Phillips, 1997).

Similarly to what occurred in the case of common and civil law systems, here too the academic literature has traditionally looked at common law as a more growth-friendly system: the emergence of the 'law and finance' debate (La Porta et al., 1997) led to an initial conclusion, that the common law system generally provides "a more favourable basis for financial development and economic growth, and on the other hand, the French branch of the civil law tradition is the least favourable in this respect" (Graff, 2008). These economists mostly looked at the relationship between law (in the form of investor protection) and financial development, using as a variable the legal family or legal origin (i.e. French civil law, German civil law, Scandinavian civil law and common law). The underlying hypothesis is that England, France and Germany developed different legal styles of controlling business due to their unique histories. Today, within continental Europe distinctions are made between the French tradition, where the dominant stockholder is usually a family or a company, the German tradition, characterised by a "universal bank" that holds a considerable share, and the Nordic countries, where families play an important role (Cools, 2005).

In fact, there are differences in the way corporations are organised in different parts of the world, and the literature has broadly confirmed the influence of the legal tradition in affecting corporate structure and governance. As recalled by Sofie Cools (2008), the "Berle and Means corporation", with many dispersed shareholders and control in the hands of management, is not a worldwide phenomenon. In other parts of the world, different corporate ownership structures exist (Musacchio and Turner, 2013). The index developed by La Porta et al. (1997) is still being relied upon extensively as a quantitative measure of investor protection. On that basis, scholars have found that investor protection correlates with broad and deep capital markets, higher dividend pay-outs, higher corporate valuation, better access to external finance, more efficient capital allocation, and the extent of exchange rate depreciation and stock market collapse during a crisis. They have uncovered correlations with a country's cultural profile, the value of control benefits, and many other factors, or used the index as a control variable. This stream of literature dominated the scene in academia for more than two decades and led its pioneers to rank among the most often quoted authors in the history of social sciences.

However, the views of La Porta and his colleagues have been criticised even before the financial crisis of the late 2000s by a number of scholars, in particular as regards the so-called "anti-director" index used in the Law and Finance paper (Vagts, 2002). Some scholars have highlighted biases in the selection of legal variables, as well as a lack of rigour in the coding of laws and other statistical fallacies (e.g. Milhaupt and Pistor, 2008; Spamann, 2010); other scholars have argued that La Porta and his colleagues gave too much importance to the law, neglecting the influence of history and politics on corporate governance and finance (Coffee, 2000; Cheffins, 2001; Roe and Siegel, 2009); in a recent paper, Gerhard Schnyder, Mathias Siems and Ruth Augilera (2018) argue that the Law and Finance paper did not take law seriously enough. Aguilera and Williams (2010) espouse a similar view by calling it "inaccurate, incomplete, and important". The diffusion of this stream of literature has indeed determined the emergence of a real inferiority complex in Europe, where scholars have started to overtly advocate for adherence to the Anglo-Saxon model of corporate governance. In fact, as observed, among others, by Heremans and Bosquet (2011), the findings of the 'law and finance' literature have been influential in policy making, including corporate governance codes and even EU legislation to converge toward the Anglo-Saxon corporate governance model. Governments have taken action to change corporate law, and push their corporations towards more dispersed ownership, or increased influence of institutional investors in management.

On a parallel, completely separate front, the academic literature on business ethics reacted disapprovingly to this view of corporate governance, starting long before La Porta and his colleagues. In particular, a *querelle* emerged already in the past decades between the focus on shareholder interests of the "Shareholder Theory" of Milton Friedman (1962), who took a laissez-faire approach to the social responsibility of business (described as limited to using resources and engaging in activities designed to increase profits); and Freeman's (1984) seminal formulation of "Stakeholder Theory", which, while not denying that profitability should be a goal of corporations, sees the primary purpose of the corporation as being a vehicle to manage stakeholder interests. The latter theory, which echoes a social function of private initiative and property that is typical of many European legal systems, has become one of the most prominent theories both within business ethics (Phillips, 2003) and the wider field of management, as well as a dominant paradigm for corporate social responsibility (McWilliams & Siegel, 2001). Most importantly, as recalled by Rönnegard and Smith (2018), the 'shareholder primacy norm' based on the initial contributions of Milton Friedman has been considered as a key obstacle to corporate social responsibility, since it "hinder managers from considering the interests of other corporate stakeholders besides shareholders" (Campbell, 2007; Evan and Freeman, 1983; Phillips, Freeman & Wicks, 2003).

Should Europe reconsider its approach to corporate governance to enable a stronger link between corporate strategy and Agenda 2030? Are European legal traditions (e.g. the French, the German, the Scandinavian) a hidden treasure, which puts Europe in a privileged position to seek sustainability and prosperity in the mid- to long-term? After twenty years of research and lively debate fuelled, *inter alia*, by the Law and Finance approach, it is time to bury the hatchet, and develop a more balanced view of corporate governance structures, and most importantly a functional one, which looks at Europe's mid-term goals. Below, we explore the differences between the Shareholder and Stakeholder theories of the corporation in greater depth, and propose a 'third way', the European Enterprise Model, which fits the needs and particularities of Europe's unique legal, economic and social environment and puts the focus on economic value creation by means of growth and improved productivity.

3.1 What if we got it all wrong?

Piercing the veil of corporate governance structures, it appears that the polarisation of the debate along the dichotomy between the Anglo-Saxon and other legal traditions has sacrificed more important and granular issues, such as: the limited time supervisory board members allot to their complicated tasks; the combination of advice and supervision and the unhealthily close relationship between the Chairman of the Supervisory Board and the Chief Executive, cutting out other members of the Board and the Management team at critical moments. Likewise, the attention devoted to the issues of diversity on the board and executive remuneration overshadows more fundamental problems: for example, the restriction of corporate governance to the arrangements between the shareholder, the board and the management of the company, ignoring the works councils and other forms of employee participation. More generally, corporate governance depends on the positioning of the company in its socio-economic context and on the source of its legitimacy. In this respect, rather than focusing only on the 'shareholder primacy norm', alternative forms such as cooperatives pursue the interests of their members; foundations, a much-underestimated vehicle for economic activity, pursue their interests as laid down in their articles of association; and in millions of family businesses it is considered self-evident that the interests of the company and its contributions to society at large should take centre stage.

An example of the focus adopted by mainstream corporate governance theory is the trade-off between the 'insider' and 'outsider' models of share ownership. The insider model arises in companies with share registers dominated by a controlling shareholder or a small group of shareholders (Edmans, 2014); whereas in the outsider model, individual shareholders are 'outsiders' who may lack the incentive to actively engage in governance issues. The insider model is common in privately-held companies, but also among listed companies in continental Europe and in most other non-English speaking countries around the world; the outsider model of company ownership is common in many large UK- and US-listed corporations, and often arises because institutional investors and their asset managers – which dominate the share registers of Anglo-American listed companies – prefer to diversify their investments across large portfolios of equities and other asset classes.

The starting point for mainstream corporate governance is that both the insider and outsider models create potential governance concerns for minority shareholders which need to be mitigated by an appropriate framework of governance. In the insider model, controlling shareholders can potentially exploit their high level of control and influence over the company in ways that might damage the interests of minority shareholders, e.g. through a range of techniques and activities which collectively are known as 'tunnelling'. In the outsider model, minorities may fear that the CEO and the board may be tempted to exploit their significant (executive) powers in a similarly self-serving manner.

These problems have been addressed by an array of governance practices such as:

- Appointing a largely independent board of directors, led by an independent chairman and mainly composed of independent non-executive directors, which oversees management and ensures that they remain loyal to the

interests of the company as a whole (including minority shareholders);
- Giving strong legal rights to minority shareholders, including for example the right to call shareholder meetings, initiate civil actions against directors, pre-emption rights which prevent dilution when new shares are issued, or shareholder votes on some key corporate actions and appointments;
- Adopting high levels of corporate disclosure and transparency, which facilitate the process of external company monitoring by outside shareholders and other stakeholders;
- Adopting executive remuneration policies that align management incentives with the interests of shareholders, e.g. through stock awards or share options;
- An active market for corporate control, which makes a company vulnerable to takeover or activist shareholder interventions if insufficient attention is paid by management to share price performance;
- A significant role for external actors and advisors – such as auditors, proxy advisors, activist investors, investment bankers and stock market analysts – in keeping corporate decision-making in line with shareholders' interests.

According to conventional wisdom, the effective implementation of such a governance framework should enhance investor trust in the company and reduce the cost of capital. Such measures are also seen as an important means of attracting domestic and foreign investment. Many of these governance features have been encouraged or made obligatory over the last three decades by a mixture of developments in corporate and securities law, listing rules and corporate governance codes (implemented on the basis of "comply or explain").

Together with the OECD (Principles of Corporate Governance) and advisory firms, the European Commission has also been influential in promoting the spread of these practices in corporations. Recently, however, researchers have started to uncover the existence of a fundamental trade-off between mainstream corporate governance and the ability of a firm to innovate. For example, Bianchini et al. (2015) measure the correlation between composite governance and innovation performance for over two thousand companies and find a surprising result: companies with 'better' corporate governance had on average a worse innovation performance. This effect was particularly evident for younger, less established companies. In addition, the authors found a strong negative association between innovation performance and the vulnerability of the company to takeover. One possible explanation for this is the dilemma between 'value protection' and 'value creation' in corporations (Bertoni et al., 2013). In a recent publication, Barker and Chiu (2018) boldly uncover the problem by observing that the insights from the resource-based theory of the firm "may conflict with the prevailing standards of corporate governance imposed on many securities markets for listed companies, which have developed based on theoretical models supporting a shareholder-centred and agency-based theory of the firm". The authors further argue that "there is a need to provide some room for accommodating the resource-based needs for companies in relation to promoting innovation" and suggest that the most practicable option would be the development of recognised exceptions that deviate from prevailing corporate governance standards.

Even in countries with a two-tier board structure and a significant 'co-determining' role for employees – as in Germany, the Netherlands and various Nordic and central European economies – the emphasis is still on 'protecting' less well-placed stakeholders from the potential abuses of those with their hands on the levers of corporate power. In essence, the fundamental assumption at the heart of modern corporate governance is a lack of trust between the major company stakeholders. In our opinion, and with the support of most recent literature on corporate governance, we argue that governance is too narrowly defined in this debate. As authoritatively observed by Lazonick and O'Sullivan (2004), "a theory of innovative enterprise plays little if any role in the current European policy discussion on corporate governance". In other words, corporate governance scholars continue to focus largely on how the interests of outside shareholders and stakeholders are considered and safeguarded in listed companies, but not on the models of corporate governance that make companies (i) more innovative; and (ii) more oriented towards the social good. To the contrary, more comprehensive enterprise models are required to provide a framework for the analysis of the impediments to the healthy development of the company and the removal thereof.

Our conclusion is that lack of innovation, declining productivity growth and overall growth are not primarily macro-economic problems, to be tackled by tried and tested macro-economic instruments; they are prevalently micro-economic problems. So far, politicians and policymakers have had far too much respect for private sector management and have felt politically constrained in addressing corporate governance shortcomings: removing these self-imposed constraints will lead to interesting policy implications.

3.2 Searching for the hidden treasure: a comparative analysis of business models

3.2.1 The Shareholder Model

At face value, the Shareholder (or Anglo-Saxon Enterprise) Model appears to be a highly appealing way to conduct business, but its key characteristics are also its flaws as outlined below. The underlying rationale is clear: shareholders are the modern incarnation of the entrepreneur, putting their money at risk: hence, it is considered morally just and economically wise to put the pursuit of shareholders' interest at the forefront of corporate governance rules and practices. This in turn means that the return on equity (ROE) becomes the overriding corporate objective. The underlying (wrong) assumption is that endlessly rising profits per share are the key to a higher stock price and shareholder return. This assumption creates a number of impediments to innovation and growth.

First, all things being equal, the push to optimise profits per share acts as a drag on investment. Bookkeeping conventions dictate that R&D and start-up costs of investments come at the expense of reported profits. Moreover, the push to maximise profit-per-share makes it more attractive to acquire than to invest, since acquisitions are accounted for on the balance sheet, not the profit and loss account, and can be amortised over many years. As most acquisitions fail, much value is destroyed (Schilling, 2018). Finally, the key role of profit-per-share is behind the extent of stock buyback programmes, an expensive hobby with exploding stock markets, with consequences for the solvency of the company while not adding any value.

Second, the safest way to increase profit in the shortest possible time is cost-cutting, often synonymous with manpower reduction. This practice can however break up valuable internal and external, commercial and operational networks and destroy intellectual property in the broadest sense of the word, e.g. including tacit knowledge. Defence of margins on existing products contributes more to profit than introducing new products, which might take time and resources. Another way in which cost-cutting is sought is mergers: but again, most mergers fail.

Third, emphasis on personal leadership is rooted in the belief that only individuals can guarantee consistency in corporate policies and should then be held accountable. But this comes with a high price to pay, since the enterprise becomes fully exposed to all the biases and stereotypes of the leader, and to their overconfidence in predicting the future and judging people. Each new CEO feels entitled to impose radical change on the enterprise and non-performing CEOs are very difficult to dislodge, leading to a toxic combination. In many enterprises, particularly US-headquartered ones, the Chairman and CEO roles are fulfilled by a single person, which may lead to a lack of checks and balances. In fact, the literature often compares this so-called US model with the UK model, which entails the separation of the two roles. This spurred a lively debate in academia, which ultimately seems to have led many US companies to consider the separation: the percentage of S&P 500 companies whose chief executives also serve as chairman fell to 45.6% in 2018, compared with 48.7% the year before: this is the lowest percentage in at least a decade, according to the Wall Street Journal.[22] According to the same article, the percentage of Stoxx Europe 600 companies with the CEO and Chairman roles combined was as low as 9.2% in 2018, down from 11% in 2013.

Fourth, the need to meet the profit-per-share target communicated to the markets leads to the implementation of tight controls based on financial and operational indicators. Sticks and carrots are introduced for each division and business unit down to the individual employee. This provides strong incentives to negotiate reachable targets (so-called key performance indicators, or KPIs) with the next higher echelon at the expense of other units and creates fierce competition for resources to meet the targets. In the name of rationality, internal competition for investment budgets, talent and other resources is encouraged. All this results in low-trust organisations, which is far from helpful as the availability of inspired individuals and fruitful, proactive cooperation across organisational boundaries are key requirements for innovation and growth.

Fifth, and more generally, the Shareholder Model can create a sometimes-suboptimal short-termism within corporations. As observed, among others, by Robert Anderson IV (2016), the law of corporate governance is "heading for a showdown" after, in recent years, a growing chorus of commentators has argued that "short-term investors, especially short-term activist institutional investors, wield too much influence over corporate governance". The core theme of these articles is that there is a "stark difference" between the interests of short-term and long-term investors: "[s]hort-term shareholders prefer managers to maximise short-run share price, while long-term shareholders prefer to forego immediate gains in favour of maximising long-run shareholder value" (Hazen, 1991). This is even truer in the case of institutional investors. As Kahan and Rock (2007) put it, short-termism "presents the potentially most important, most controversial, most ambiguous, and most complex problem associated with hedge fund activism", giving rise to the related accusation that hedge funds induce managerial short-termism. The issue is reportedly worsened by the existence of legal provisions and corporate policies, especially in the US, which tilt the balance in favour of short-term shareholders. They include: dividends and share repurchases, motivated by institutions' desire to increase "short-term earnings" by cutting research and development; and the combination of leverage returning cash to shareholders. Karmel (2004) observes that during the 1980s, "the pressure for high overall return by institutional investors in U.S. corporations resulted in an unhealthy leveraging of U.S. corporations to meet that demand. Funds were borrowed to pay dividends to shareholders, in the form of ordinary cash distributions, share repurchases, or takeover premiums"

(Anabtawi, 2006). Grossman (2010) further argues that myopic markets end up penalising managers for long-term investment, pressuring them to govern for short-term objectives.

Moreover, in a world dominated by the Shareholder Model, SMEs can suffer from the high staff turnover often occurring at large companies. The latter are constantly uprooting their organisation and cutting manpower, and SMEs struggle to find representatives with a mandate to close a deal. In organisations in which the avoidance of risk is a condition for survival this search could be frustrating. SMEs are never sure whether the negotiating positions adopted by their counterparts are chosen in the best interest of their companies, which is to be respected, or aimed at helping them meet their personal targets. Worse, SMEs know that their counterparts are under considerable pressure to meet their targets: a below-average bonus is in many listed enterprises a kiss of death, accompanied by a looming threat of dismissal. This in turn leads SMEs to pull out all stops to get their way. The relationship, given these constraints and fears, ends up suspended in an endless negotiation game. Attempts to build trust in the interest of both parties are in vain, and even past evidence of solid, trust-based cooperation loses importance. Unilateral changes in the contract should be expected. The epitome of pressure exercised by large listed companies vis-à-vis SMEs is the retrospective demands for discounts: no obligation to concur of course, but at the expense of future orders.

In summary, the favoured policies of listed companies often destroy economic value in the name of the shareholder: put bluntly, the Shareholder Model serves financial markets and not the economy. The emphasis on control and transfer of risk constitute high hurdles for innovation and enhanced productivity. And the consequence of adopting this model can end up worsening the relationship between large and small companies.

3.2.2 The Stakeholder Model

Like the Shareholder Model, the Stakeholder Model has considerable, albeit superficial appeal. Who would be against appropriate protection of shareholders and employees? And who wouldn't, given their legitimate interests, be in favour of fair treatment of suppliers and customers? Intuitively, companies that feel a responsibility to the communities in which they operate deserve support. However, the basic problem is that companies operate in a force field of conflicting demands expressed by a variety of more or less powerful interest groups. They must cope with many interrelated issues and continuously shifting coalitions around these issues. In more detail, companies that have embraced the Stakeholder Model are vulnerable in that they have to engage interest groups with and without legitimate claims. Stakeholders seek to institutionalise their position to strengthen their bargaining power. Also trade unions, employers' associations, municipalities and special interest groups have different channels to make themselves heard. Trade unions, for example, negotiate collective labour agreements, are represented in works councils and are in the position to put pressure on governments and supervisory bodies for legal steps and regulatory measures. They also make inroads into the company by nurturing contacts with senior managers; and finally, the human resource department often acts as their informal internal lobbyist. Stakeholder theory has also been criticised for being somewhat nebulous, to such an extent that it eventually leaves corporate managers with no clear objective and deprives them of the possibility to act strategically in their self-interest (Miles, 2017; Sternberg, 2004; Jensen, 2002). Other scholars (Key, 1999) have stated that it does not properly link different actors of the firm, nor does it link internalities and externalities. Also, Brandt and Georgiou (2018) observe that considering the interests of multiple stakeholders does not equate with being socially (let alone environmentally) responsible. On the one hand, broad social concerns and stakeholder considerations are not necessarily the same, and, indeed, stakeholder theory is not an underlying concept of corporate social responsibility. On the other hand, when it comes to long-term social and environmental sustainability considerations, it must be recalled that the relevant stakeholders (future generations) are often unable to make their voices heard within the boundaries of the corporation, and as such are mostly absent from the incentive scheme of the manager. The stakeholder approach is then nothing more than a strategic approach to doing business.

In a nutshell, stakeholder corporations often drown in endless quests for consensus-building and incur substantial transaction costs. Yet, the stakeholders of the future are not represented, which helps to resolve conflicts by postponing the tackling the issues of the day and by shifting the absorption of costs to later. This brings in a form of 'collective' short-termism, as opposed to the individual short-termism triggered by the Anglo-Saxon model. In a major misalignment between corporate incentives and the long-term requirement for pro-innovation, pro-sustainability corporate conduct, stakeholders end up exercising power without responsibility and accountability for the broader impact of the corporation's activities. They invariably claim to act in the best interest of the company, helped by the feeble resistance of many corporate directors. Overburdened managers who must juggle with many dossiers on a single day are no match for rested, focused negotiators who know their single dossier inside out. The standard push-back by directors focused on the need for profitability is inadequate, as it inevitably leads to an unwinnable debate about the right level of shareholder return on investment. The need to maintain access to stock markets over time is too abstract even if it were true. The obligation on the part of the company to generate enough economic value to pay for all expenses, to invest and to cover the real cost of capital constitute far more solid ground for discussions with stakeholders (see the next chapter for more details).

    The consequences for innovation, productivity and growth of the company are again profound. Stakeholders are inherently conservative as any technical and organisational disruption implies a challenge to the delicate balance of power and is likely counter to their members' interests. Most of the time it is a question of exercising veto power as most stakeholders lack the expertise to suggest viable alternatives. Thinking in terms of interests does not stop at the corporate boundary. The Stakeholder Model permits the practice where divisions and large business units act as powerhouses. The Board is well advised to obtain the support of divisions and business unit management for far-reaching proposals. Board proposals that seriously undermine the position of power of a division are guaranteed to trigger conflict. Proposals are often amended to accommodate divisions in the mistaken belief that such a concession will smoothen implementation. The original intentions of the proposal become compromised and its potential value is not achieved.

The position of power of various divisions is to a large degree dependent on their contribution to overall corporate profitability. This in turn often depends on a limited number of large customers that have integrated the corporate products in their offering to their customers and are therefore interested in improvement of quality and/or a lower price and not in innovation. Competition between divisions is part and parcel of corporate life, so as innovation requires permeable organisation boundaries many initiatives are short-lived. For all these reasons, the Stakeholder Model deserves its reputation for slow, inconclusive decision-making and the avoidance of risk.

3.2.3 An alternative: towards a European Enterprise Model

The most advanced European companies have moved beyond the standard models described in the previous chapters. Companies like Novo Nordisk, Statoil and Svenska Handelsbanken easily outshine their Anglo-Saxon competitors GSK, BP and Barclays in this respect. There is of course no way that financial markets will give up their grip on listed European companies which, with very few exceptions, have embraced the Shareholder Model, but companies that consider a stock market listing should be forewarned: this includes established private companies, but also small, fast-growing companies. The tide seems to have turned, as the number of listed companies comes down, the enrolment of students in MBA programmes declines, and public awareness of well-documented examples of corporate cynicism increases. Banking scandals have become part of life, large pharmaceutical companies come increasingly under fire for their pricing policies and the halo of the technological giants is gone. In the 'trust game', there is a need for more responsible business conduct, and the legal system is called on to provide adequate incentives to this end.[23]

Astute observers point to the fact that companies that are guided or bound by shareholder interest are not in the best position to contribute to long-term challenges such as those posed by global warming (Dahlberg and Wiklund, 2018). What we define here as the 'European Enterprise Model' is a broad church, as it should be, as different technologies and markets require different approaches, but some general principles emerge in sharp contrast to the other two models.

First, the European model draws heavily on the way many family companies are positioned and managed. Modern companies derive their licence to operate from society at large: this stimulates the exploration of possible futures and the prospects for the corporate products and services. Change without immediate need is a tall task but comes with huge rewards.

Second, many European companies make the creation of economic value the leading principle in guiding decision-making. The difference over time between all forms of income and all kinds of expenditure should exceed the cost of capital, dividends and interest payments. The aim is to generate free cash flow for future investment and strengthen the balance sheet of the company: only a strong balance sheet can address the concern that companies need to be able to capture future cash flows. A strong balance sheet is also required to take the risks inherent in entrepreneurship.

Third, this distinct emphasis helps to identify four different sources of economic value, each supported by specialised managers and by a tailor-made form of decision-making: the reduction of value destruction; better use of available assets and workforce; emphasis on investment *lato sensu*, including plant, equipment, and ICT but also organisational development and training; and changes made in the portfolio of business models supported by the company. A major step forward is that each member of the organisation contributes to one aim, each in a unique way. This way the company can be approached in a holistic way. This requires far-reaching delegation of responsibility and accountability to the different management teams in charge of a specific form of value creation.

In order to pursue its mission, such an organisation has dispersed leadership, not unlike the unique mandates of national, provincial and local institutions in well-designed multi-level governance systems. It can only be managed based on principles, not prescriptive rules. Its culture is characterised by fairness, internally and in dealings with suppliers, customers and partners (see above, Chapters 1 and 2 and below, Chapter 10). Only then can trust grow, and the cooperation fully move in the direction of productivity growth and sustainable development.

How widespread is this enterprise model? Schroeter (2007) recalls the words of famous American economist Charles Kindleberger, who observed that "If European integration is to be really achieved, there must be European corporations". In his investigation, Schroeter finds evidence of distinctive traits of a European enterprise, despite the ongoing contamination with the American model, characterised by more evident organisational patterns such as the multi-divisional structure (the so-called M-Form). Even today, large mergers such as *Bayer/Monsanto* pose challenges in the reconciliation of shareholder capitalism with more European ways to organise and conceive of business conduct and structure. Cassis, Colli and Shroeter (2016) have shed light on the transformation and contamination of European capitalism due to the advent of more risk-oriented forms of capitalism from across the Atlantic. Again, the push towards a European Enterprise Model may be further nurtured by Brexit, since the British corporate governance model has traditionally remained closer to the American one than the continental European one (Armour, Deakin and Konzelmann 2003). Williams and Conley (2005) spoke of a "third way" to capitalism already more than a decade ago, emphasising how the European model had already made progress towards enhanced corporate social and environmental responsibility of firms.

The prospective European Enterprise Model, however, is not fully represented in the current EU corporate governance model, despite the fact that a vibrant debate has emerged since the late 1990s among academics and other stakeholders (in particular trade unions) on the need to rebalance shareholder capitalism with more stakeholder representation and a more diffuse model of governance. For example, the so-called Davignon Working Group in 1997 argued that workers must be closely and permanently involved in decision-making at all levels of the company, and paved the way for the creation of the European Company Statute, or *Societas Europaea* (SE). Yet corporate governance was only put firmly on the European regulatory agenda a couple of years later, with the Financial Services Action Plan of 1999. A decade later, in the midst of the financial crisis, the De Larosière report commissioned by the European Commission concluded that corporate governance constituted "one of the most important failures of the present crisis". But little if anything has been tried since then to effectively reform the corporate governance model in Europe, let alone tailor it to SMEs, which constitute the overwhelming majority (more than 98%) of European businesses.

Horn (2011) sees a clear pattern in which the importance of workers in European enterprises, emphasised since the Green Paper on Employee Participation and Company Structure of 1975, has gradually been replaced by an almost exclusive emphasis on market efficiency. For example, she quotes the words of the then Commissioner for the Internal Market Frits Bolkestein, who claimed that the objective of regulation was merely "to set up a framework which then enables the markets to play their disciplining role in an efficient way" (Bolkestein, 2003). She further argues that during the 1980s and 1990s, "rather than advocating a 'positive' harmonisation approach, the Commission's approach has become increasingly based on identifying and subsequently eliminating obstacles to the free movement of companies and capital. Whereas corporate control used to be very much located in the domain of company law, subject to 'positive' harmonisation, it has become increasingly regulated under aspects of capital and financial markets law". The long, tortuous passage of the EU Takeover Directive was a prime example of this shift, with a final result that places decisions related to the company in the case of a takeover exclusively in the hands of shareholders. Later, the 2003 Company Law Action Plan and key decisions of the Court of Justice of the EU contributed to this shift towards the 'marketisation' of European corporate governance.

3.2.4 Key differences between enterprise models

The key differences between the three models are summarised in Table 2 below, which highlights the distinctive features of the European Enterprise Model, in particular as concerns the emphasis on principles, the dispersed leadership, the focus on quality and the culture of cooperation.

Table 2. Key differences between the Shareholder, Stakeholder and European Models

	Shareholder Model	Stakeholder Model	European Model
Source of legitimacy	Shareholder	Stakeholder	Society
Worldview	Financial	Political	Economic
Modus Operandi	Analytical	Continuity	Holistic
Overriding objective	Shareholder ROI	Eclectic	Creation of economic value
Steering Variable	Profit per share	Multiple	Free cash flow
Principal source of finance	Stock market	Banks	Diverse
Leadership	Individual	Committee	Dispersed
Culture	Individual competition	Competition between units	Cooperation
Management	By rule	By principle derived rules	By principle
Decision-making	Procedure driven	Horses for courses	Quality driven
Control	Command & incentives	Formal commitments	Professional standards
Attitude to risk	Transfer and control	Steering clear	Facing uncertainty

Source: Kalff (2017).

3.3 Policy implications

The discussion above has profound consequences for the relationship between corporate governance and the achievement of the vision of a more competitive and sustainable society, in particular in Europe. It also has significant consequences for economic policy as a whole. For example, since the 1980s, governments have privatised many state companies such as utilities, railways, social services, health care, and to some extent education. This is sometimes defined as the first wave of regulatory governance and was greatly inspired by faith in the market mechanism, and some of its direct corollary, such as the shrinking of government regulation ('less is more'). Governments were encouraged by the belief that markets were best suited to provide services on a large scale: this even led to a significant rise in the reliance on private sector to self-regulate even in critical domains of policymaking, such as the supervision of banks' sizeable exposures (Balleisen, 2009; Renda, 2011). After 2008, further decentralisation and the need to cut costs to bring government spending under control went hand in hand. Governments, unduly impressed by private sector efficiency, were unwittingly instrumental in rolling out the Shareholder Model in many sectors. Today, disappointing results and unrealised savings should inspire member states to explore the merits of alternative models.

Member states carry a direct responsibility for the enterprise model used by state-owned enterprises, and therefore for the value destruction that has taken place under their watch. Many opportunities to turn the tide have been squandered over the past decade, the most eye-catching being the chance to put banks on a different footing in the interest of the real economy. In particular, the stock market listing of banks makes them highly vulnerable.[24] Many supervisory and management boards played a large and negative role in the failure of their institutions. Governments replaced *fonctionnaires* but left the positioning, structure and culture of large banks intact. With the integrity of the financial system at stake, politicians, regulators and central banks should feel obliged to take a second look.

Another responsibility of the member states is the upgrading of corporate governance codes as in many countries these codes are enshrined in law. The well-established practice to leave the upgrading and the adjusting of the code to the private sector and rubberstamp the results amount to no less than an abdication of responsibility.

Finally, member states finance and cherish business schools that, with very few exceptions, accept the primacy of financial markets and are committed to the teachings of shareholder business doctrines. They should feel compelled to diversify business education: the academic literature appears ready to accept non-mainstream views, and the primacy of the Shareholder Model appears disproportionate in current curricula.

Below, we offer a few ideas for future policy initiatives that would help in remedying some of the problems outlined in this chapter, bringing to light the merits of the European Enterprise Model, our third hidden treasure.

3.3.1 Protect and stimulate diversity in corporate governance

The alleged superiority of the shareholder model of corporate governance can safely be considered to belong to the past. The rise of a variety of possible corporate governance arrangements, which can be subsumed under a broad notion of a European Enterprise Model, provides a new possibility for businesses and member states to experiment with forms of governance that are more oriented towards stability, fairness and sustainability. In this respect, the variants of the European Enterprise Model are very much aligned with the need to rediscover the good faith requirement in the civil law of contracts (Chapter 1), as well as the need to avoid the excessive financialisation of the economy (Chapter 2). Ideally, competition between models of corporate governance could be promoted and stimulated by a more neutral regulatory framework, which creates the preconditions for greater social responsibility among corporations.

3.3.2 Promote the development of the European Enterprise Model as an alternative for the Shareholder and Stakeholder Models

The Commission can make a major contribution by capitalising on Brexit to return to the drawing board to redesign the European Company to align it with European characteristics, needs and vision. At present the European Company is a hybrid creature, drawing on two very different legal traditions. It is remarkable that despite its shortcomings, 50 large companies have already signed up. A revamped European Company could provide a suitable framework for tailor-made governance choices to which each company can add elements of the European Enterprise Model. To facilitate this, the Commission should sponsor research into the impact of different enterprise models on innovation and economic development.

The European Commission should also revisit work undertaken in the past and develop a European Company model for SMEs. While awareness of the cost of the Shareholder Model is growing, politicians are tempted to dust off the Stakeholder Model as an alternative: these voices are heard even in the US. This, however, would be a very serious mistake: ignoring for the moment that the Stakeholder Model was swept away by the Shareholder Model in only a couple of years, the Stakeholder Model is unsuited for modern economies. A European Company 2.0 would be an attractive alternative for the Shareholder Model and would help to avoid the trap of the Stakeholder Model. It would also provide an historic opportunity to put co-determination on a modern footing. Where work councils at present are relegated to rubber stamping directors' decisions, a new body could become a true strategic partner in a context where financiers, the boards and the employees are all bound by the obligation to put the interest of the enterprise first.

3.3.3   Establish a revamped Societas Privata Europaea

Since the adoption of the SE legislation in 2001, the idea of creating a European Company form targeted at SMEs has been on the political agenda. In 2002, a High Level Group of Company Law Experts organised by the European Commission proposed the creation of the European Private Company, or *Societas Privata Europaea* (SPE). The Commission adopted an SPE proposal in 2003, followed up by a proposal for a Council Regulation on the Statute for a European private company: however, the proposal was heavily criticised, among others by the European Trade Union Council and its members, which fear that this legal form could be used by companies to avoid national rules on worker involvement. Also the issues of separation of home and host country, minimum capital requirements and taxation issues remain controversial between member states. The idea continued to develop over the years and after a positive feasibility study by the Commission's Company Law Action Plan, the European Parliament requested the

Commission to draw up a legislative proposal for the SPE in February 2007. In June 2008, the Commission presented its Proposal for a 'Council Regulation on the Statute for a European private company',[25] which was broadly (although not unconditionally) welcomed by the Committee on Legal Affairs of the European Parliament. However, the proposal spurred a heated political debate based on the significant national differences, in particular as regards employee participation, as well as on fears that the favourable legal framework for the SPE could be strategically exploited by large companies. (Roth & Kindler, 2013, p. 23; Teichmann & Fröhlich, 2014, p. 537; Conac, 2015, p. 221). This discussion led to the adoption of a significantly revised proposal by the European Parliament in 2009, and ultimately to the failure to reach a political compromise in the Council at the end of that year.

The Commission then proposed additional supranational legal forms, such as a European single-member company (*Societas Unius Personae*, or SUP). However, based on the Commission's 2012 Company Law Action Plan, the SUP mainly serves the purpose of facilitating the establishment of subsidiaries in other member states. As observed by Gelter (2018), "the relative lack of formalities, which might be its strength by making the SUP an appealing legal form, is again a weakness of this proposal, given the opposition from Member States favoring a more regulatory corporate law".

As of today, a genuinely European governance model tailored to SMEs is still missing. Establishing it would be a very important step towards the creation of an ad hoc legal system in which smaller businesses can thrive throughout the EU, both as stand-alone organisations and in their relationship with large companies.

3.3.4 *Diversify management education to cater to the requirements of the shareholder model*

Business guru Peter Drucker famously commented a few years ago: "if you find an executive who wants to take on social responsibilities, fire him, fast". Most of the business community, especially in the United States, has followed this mantra for decades. In Jon Benjamin's *The New Republic*, an MBA student and Dean's Fellow at the MIT Sloan School of Management argued that "MBA programs are not the open forums advertised in admissions brochures", and that when dealing with any business issue, MBA classes normally wave away society-level implications, assuming the principals' overriding goal—profit maximisation. In a *Financial Times* article, Sarah Murray observed that "while there is growing consensus that focusing on short-term shareholder value is not only bad for society but also leads to poor business results, much MBA teaching remains shaped by the shareholder primacy model".

The primacy of the Shareholder Model in today's business schools has been subject to extensive literature in economics and management. One specific case is that of the "agency theory" put forward by Jensen and Meckling (1976), which quickly reached the top of the ranking of the most quoted papers in major economics journals. As recently observed by Salter (2019), "the most significant management implication of this elegantly argued theory — that long-term value maximisation for shareholders needs to be the primary metric for assessing the performance of business enterprise — also found a great deal of support in the financial and business communities and among faculty members in many leading business schools, including my own" (i.e. Harvard Business School). Jensen also famously observed (in 2002) that "any organization must have a single-valued objective as a precursor to purposeful or rational behavior … It is logically impossible to maximise in more than one dimension at the same time … telling a manager to maximise current profits, market share future growth profits, and anything else one pleases will leave that manager with no way to make a reasoned decision. In effect, it leaves the manager with no objective". Even more recently, Spencer (2019) observes that mainstream economic theories have "condoned more than created 'bad' management", and that the transformation of management will require wider reforms in, and importantly beyond, business schools. Rönnegard and Smith (2018) recall that "business schools teach as part of the 'Theory of the Firm' that profit maximisation is the purpose of the corporation in society and that it is the duty of managers to pursue this end on behalf of shareholders as their agents". West (2011) adds that this is not only true of business schools but also law schools. Several authors suggested that a disproportionate focus on the Shareholder Model by business schools was a contributory factor in the 2008 financial crisis (Rönnegard and Smith, 2018).

Against this background, business schools are teaching, with few exceptions, the same theory of the firm that led the whole economic and financial system to the brink of collapse, and the whole economy along an unsustainable path. If a new variety of models of corporate governance is to be promoted in Europe, this too will have to change.[26]

4. Innovation:
Europe's most hidden treasure?

The dominant rhetoric among EU policymakers is that despite being a leader in basic research in several scientific domains, the EU lags behind the US and other countries, such as Japan and Korea, when it comes to innovation; and its lead over China is gradually shrinking. Very often, industry leaders and high-level politicians have denounced Europe's innovation deficit, and pointed at the impossibility to restore sustainable growth absent a shift of gear in this key dimension of economic performance. Among the key factors that are often associated with these concerns, the most recurrent are the lack of entrepreneurial, risk-loving culture in Europe's ageing society; the corresponding lack of widespread venture capital investment; an overall business environment that does not easily accommodate failure; a too precautionary approach in regulation, which ends up stifling innovation; a lack of openness towards immigrants, who end up having few chances to prove their worth at opening and running new businesses; and a massive amount of red tape, which forces SMEs into too burdensome compliance behaviour and investment. Based on all these arguments, both the Lisbon Strategy in 2000 and the Europe 2020 strategy at the beginning of this decade were launched with a clear intention to boost Europe's innovation performance, in particular by setting the target of spending at least 3% of EU GDP on research and innovation.

While these arguments all have some merit, a closer look reveals a more nuanced picture. First, not all European countries are performing badly on innovation: on the contrary, many of them, including Scandinavian countries, the Netherlands and Germany score very highly in global innovation rankings. Table 3 below shows the Global Innovation Index 2018 ranking, which sees Switzerland on top, followed by the Netherlands and Sweden, and with the UK, Finland, Denmark, Germany and Ireland in the top 10.

Table 3. Global Innovation Index 2018 rankings

Global Innovation Index 2018 rankings

Country/Economy	Score (0–100)	Rank	Income	Rank	Region	Rank	Efficiency Ratio	Rank	Median: 0.61
Switzerland	68.40	1	HI	1	EUR	1	0.96	1	
Netherlands	63.32	2	HI	2	EUR	2	0.91	4	
Sweden	63.08	3	HI	3	EUR	3	0.82	10	
United Kingdom	60.13	4	HI	4	EUR	4	0.77	21	
Singapore	59.83	5	HI	5	SEAO	1	0.61	63	
United States of America	59.81	6	HI	6	NAC	1	0.76	22	
Finland	59.63	7	HI	7	EUR	5	0.76	24	
Denmark	58.39	8	HI	8	EUR	6	0.73	29	
Germany	58.03	9	HI	9	EUR	7	0.83	9	
Ireland	57.19	10	HI	10	EUR	8	0.81	13	
Israel	56.79	11	HI	11	NAWA	1	0.81	14	
Korea, Republic of	56.63	12	HI	12	SEAO	2	0.79	20	
Japan	54.95	13	HI	13	SEAO	3	0.68	44	
Hong Kong (China)	54.62	14	HI	14	SEAO	4	0.64	54	
Luxembourg	54.53	15	HI	15	EUR	9	0.94	2	
France	54.36	16	HI	16	EUR	10	0.72	32	
China	53.06	17	UM	1	SEAO	5	0.92	3	
Canada	52.98	18	HI	17	NAC	2	0.61	61	
Norway	52.63	19	HI	18	EUR	11	0.64	52	
Australia	51.98	20	HI	19	SEAO	6	0.58	76	

Source: Global Innovation Index 2018.

While the comparison with the US is always methodologically difficult (one must consider that several states of the US, starting with Massachusetts and California, would rank above the best EU member states if compared one to one, see Granieri and Renda, 2010), this finding suggests that there are no structural elements that would prevent the whole of Europe from outperforming other large blocs on innovation. Looking at the most innovative cities, Europe is even better positioned: Barcelona, Berlin, Munich, Milan, London, Paris, Amsterdam, Copenhagen, Stockholm and many others provide proof of European dynamism, by providing ideal platforms and ecosystems to test socially relevant innovation. In a recent report by Philips Lighting and SmartCitiesWorld, Barcelona was listed as a prime example of a city undergoing a "smart transition" having created 47,000 jobs by embedding IoT solutions across the city, as well as saving €42.5 million on water use and generating €36.5 million annually through smart parking. Similarly, London has become a testing ground for IoT technology, almost equalling Singapore in this race to the future. In the *Cities in Motion* index compiled by Barcelona-based IESE Business School, and which presents performance scores for 165 cities across 80 countries based on an exhaustive list of economic and social indicators, London, Amsterdam and Paris rank in the highest positions alongside New York, and Helsinki, Berlin, Stuttgart, Antwerp and Prague rank among the highest in the Social Cohesion indicators.[27] Europe clearly dominates the top spots in the ranking, with seven west European cities in the top ten positions. Europe's dominance becomes even more evident if one looks at the top 50: more than half of the cities are European. Table 4 below shows how Europe performs compared to other regions in many city-related indicators.

Table 4. Cities of the world, various indicators

Ranking by city	CIMI 2018 (IESE)	Global Cities Index 2018 (A.T. Kearney)	Global Financial Centres Index (GFCI) 2018 (Z/Yen)	Global Power City Index 2018 (MMF)	Quality of Living City Ranking 2018 (Mercer)	Global Liveability Index 2018 (Economist Intelligence Unit)	Sustainable Cities Index 2018 (Arcadis)
1	London	New York	London	London	Vienna	Vienna	London
2	New York	London	New York	New York	Zurich	Melbourne	Stockholm
3	Amsterdam	Paris	Hong Kong	Tokyo	Munich	Osaka	Edinburgh
4	Paris	Tokyo	Singapore	Paris	Auckland	Calgary	Singapore
5	Reykjavik	Hong Kong	Tokyo	Singapore	Vancouver	Sydney	Vienna
6	Tokyo	Los Angeles	Shanghai	Amsterdam	Düsseldorf	Vancouver	Zurich
7	Singapore	Singapore	Toronto	Seoul	Frankfurt	Toronto	Munich
8	Copenhagen	Chicago	San Francisco	Berlin	Geneva	Tokyo	Oslo
9	Berlin	Beijing	Sydney	Hong Kong	Copenhagen	Copenhagen	Hong Kong
10	Vienna	Brussels	Boston	Sydney	Basel	Adelaide	Frankfurt

Source: Cities in Motion Index 2019.

Second, and relatedly, Europe seems to be performing relatively well in terms of the creation of start-ups. According to a report presented by Atomico, a venture capital firm started by Skype founder Nicholas Zennstroem, $19 billion were invested in European start-ups in 2017; the Global Innovation Index published by Cornell University, INSEAD and WIPO reported that 8 out of 10 of the world's most innovative markets are now located in Europe. Companies like Google, Facebook, Apple are launching incubators to reap the benefits of this cultural change: Google now has campuses in Berlin, London, Madrid and Warsaw, which launched start-ups that raised over €260 million in capital and created more than 4,600 new jobs; Facebook's Startup Garage in Paris is the world's largest start-up campus. Where Europe seems to have a problem is in scaling up, rather than starting up: this is why the European Innovation Council is being set up, to help existing small ventures access the whole of the single market and even go global.[28]

Third, it is a myth that Europe is always more precautionary than the US; and it is also a myth that the precautionary principle always kills innovation. While Vogel (2010) and others have reported Europe's more precautionary approach based on a limited number of specific, selected cases, a ten-year-long research effort that culminated in the publication of a thorough report (Wiener et al., 2010) found that the reality is more complex, and there are important cases in which US regulation is considerably more precautionary than that of the EU.[29] More recently, Wiener et al. (IRGC, 2017) reiterate that "it is not EU precaution versus US reaction, or *ex ante* versus *ex post* legal systems, or civil law versus common law, or uncertainty-based versus evidence-based regulatory systems". Moreover, since the early publications of Nicholas Ashford (1986) and later Porter and van der Linden (1995), scholars have shown overwhelming empirical evidence that regulation is often an enabler, not a killer, of innovation: especially stringent regulation and standards, properly designed, have stimulated new products, processes, and work practices that would not otherwise have occurred (Ashford et al., 1985; Porter & van der Linden, 1992; Pelkmans & Renda, 2014; OECD, 2016; Ashford and Renda, 2016). However, transformative, disruptive innovation often comes from sources beyond the incumbent producers or providers, which implies that care must be taken in order to prevent incumbents and special interests from unduly influencing either the industrial or the regulatory policy process.

Fourth, Europe's diversity, freedom of movement of people and cooperation between member states is potentially an unrivalled source of innovation. The number of professionals working in other EU countries is on the rise, the Erasmus programme contributes to increased mobility across borders, and EU cities are becoming increasingly diverse. Recent research has confirmed that cultural diversity, when supported by inclusion policies, significantly promotes innovation. For example, the Boston Consulting Group found that increasing the diversity of leadership teams leads to more and better innovation and improved financial performance;[30] a study for Bertelsmann-Stiftung (2018) finds that businesses that hire people of diverse cultural backgrounds are better positioned to develop ideas for new products, services and processes;[31] McKinsey (2018) examined proprietary data sets for 366 public companies across a range of industries in Canada, Latin America, the UK and the US in order to explore the relationship between financial results and the composition of top management and boards, and found that companies in the top quartile for racial and ethnic diversity are 35% more likely to enjoy financial returns above their respective national industry medians. However, Europe does not seem to be fully capitalising on its diversity, in particular since many member states are still extremely reluctant to attract talent from abroad, be that another EU country or a non-EU one. Ambitious past initiatives such as the Blue Card Directive, which aimed at establishing an easy-to-use, universal visa programme for highly skilled workers, have not produced the desired results, and the review of the Blue Card was a priority for the Juncker Commission.[32] Currently, the EU is not able to attract a large share of highly educated residents, as shown in Figure 11 below.

Figure 11. *Distribution of foreign-born residents with low versus high level of education, by OECD destination country, 2015-2016, in %*

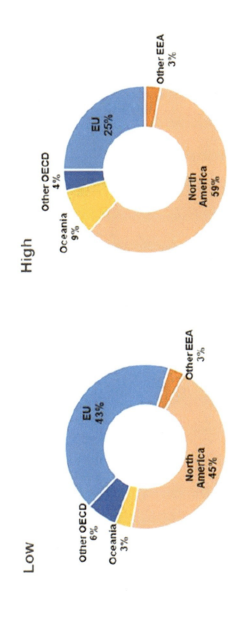

Source: *Database on Immigrants in OECD countries (DIOC), 2015-16. Note: EU refers to EU-28 without Croatia due to missing data. For Iceland, Japan, New Zealand and Turkey, data are from DIOC 2010-11. For the EU, only non-EU immigrants are included*

Due, *inter alia,* to mounting anti-immigration sentiments, the revision of the Blue Card Directive has proven to be a daunting task. Among the major blocking issues: the scope, the harmonisation of the EU Blue Card scheme on the EU level, the recognition of professional experience, the minimum wage threshold, the long-term mobility, the labour market test and the eligibility for the long-term resident status. Other issues such as equal treatment, permitted period of unemployment, procedural deadlines and recognised employers' schemes, are also awaiting compromises among political leaders in Europe. As a result, despite the changing attitude towards foreign talent in the US, Europe is currently not in the position to fully uncover this hidden treasure, further nurture its entrepreneurial community, and boost its innovation performance.

Fifth, academic literature is thoroughly revising the concept of innovation, reaching the conclusion that not all innovation is equally relevant for society. Entrepreneurship and innovation are means, not ultimate policy goals: and innovation is useful to society when it helps in achieving societal goals (Konnola et al., 2016). This means that public policy, besides striving to create a suitable environment for entrepreneurship, should seek to incentivise those entrepreneurial ventures and innovation efforts that help in addressing unresolved societal challenges. The emerging debate on the crisis of Silicon Valley, with *The Economist* even announcing the forthcoming "death of the Valley" (as opposed to the widely acknowledged problem of the 'Valley of death'), focuses in particular on the fact that Silicon Valley tech companies have lost contact with real societal needs, and increasingly develop inventions that are good for 'deep pockets', further exacerbating inequality. The Valley is now criticised as being too expensive, chaotic, and tough for small companies as big tech giants pay their employees so generously that start-ups struggle to attract talent.[33] Most importantly, the 'Silicon Valley model' focuses on the commercialisation of relatively mature technologies for specific markets: this model is considered hardly suitable for emerging societal challenges, which require a more orchestrated, disruptive, ecosystem-led approach to problem solving and innovation (Satel, 2018).

Finally, there is emerging consensus among academics that Europe does not have a problem with *innovation*, but rather with the *diffusion of innovation* (Ashford and Renda, 2016). Public policy in support of innovation should then look beyond the 'innovation deficit', to encompass the 'diffusion deficit' that prevents new technologies and business models from reaching the market or becoming affordable for the majority of consumers. The Staff Working Document published by the European Commission in 2015 on "Better Regulation for Innovation-Driven Investment" acknowledged the key role of public policy in removing obstacles to the commercialisation and diffusion of existing technologies, which lack a sufficiently large market in Europe.[34] Rodriguez-Pose et al. (2017) observe that "many European firms, regions and countries have problems in absorbing and exploiting new knowledge from an economic point of view and are not particularly able to turn knowledge generation into innovation. This is especially true in the more peripheral regions in the EU where R&D is often spatially fragmented, concerns mainly public, not private R&D, and is concentrated disproportionally in scientific disciplines like Social Sciences and Humanities". The authors, members of the RISE advisory group to Commissioner Moedas, advocate a public policy that focuses on enabling diffusion through nurturing the innovation ecosystem. These include increasing the absorptive capacity of local firms; promoting the presence of 'related variety' in regions, which enhances local knowledge spillovers and diversification; a suitable set of formal and informal institutions, as embodied in high quality of government and bridging social capital (Cortinovis et al., 2016); agents of change offering better support for private R&D; building on 'pockets of excellence'; and dealing with global value chains and digitalisation.

4.1 A misrepresented gap?

Against this background, the gap between the US and the EU appears to be at once exaggerated due to the outstanding performance of selected, extremely large tech giants in the US (and also China); and exacerbated by Europe's problems in harnessing all its potential. More precisely, the gap may be exaggerated due to the exorbitant performance of the top tech firms in the US, which led Apple and Amazon to break the roof of $1 trillion in terms of capitalisation, and the rest of the economy. The market cap of the top 5 S&P 500 companies is slightly greater than the market cap of the bottom 282 S&P 500 companies.

As of 1 July 2018, one stock alone was responsible for more than a third of the market's year-to-date (YTD) performance: Amazon, whose 45% YTD return had contributed to 36% of the S&P total return of 3%, including dividends. Goldman Sachs also calculated that the return of the Top 10 S&P 500 stocks of 2018 amounted to 122% of the S&P total return in the first half of the year. Amazon, Microsoft, Apple and Netflix were responsible for 84% of the S&P growth in 2018: without the FAANGs, as estimated by Bank of America, the S&P 500 return in the first half of 2018 would have been -0.7%.

Figure 12. Excluding FAANG stocks, index returns would have been negative in 1H2018

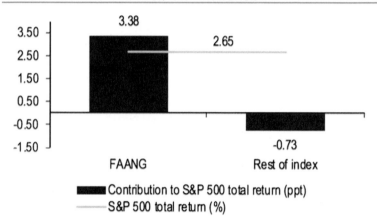

Note: FAANG = FB, AAPL, AMZN, NFLX, GOOG/GOOGL
Source: S&P, BofA Merrill Lynch US Equity & US Quant Strategy

Below the so-called FAANGS, 95% of the most advanced US companies (part of the S&P500) have not improved their productivity in the past decade. Van Ark et al. (2018) observe that "technology and especially digitisation have led to inflated early expectations of faster productivity growth. While new digital technologies have rapidly diffused across the economy, their absorption and translation into better business performance has been quite slow and uneven". This leaves the prospects for the future of US capitalism uncertain, despite an overall sustained productivity growth; and further raises the issue of whether European capitalism is (or should be) different (as we observed above in Chapters 2 and 3).

The gap between the US and the EU is, of course, also exacerbated by several contradictions and imperfections in policies and strategies undertaken by the EU and its member states. These must be overcome for Europe to achieve leadership in large-scale, socially relevant innovation, our proposed hidden treasure. Several causes can be identified.

- The European Commission has highlighted the need to improve the creation and diffusion of high-quality new knowledge and innovation in Europe. Technology transfer between universities and businesses seems to encounter significant obstacles and is only partly addressed by existing EU policies (Renda et al., 2019, forthcoming). Knowledge diffusion between business and academia remains lower in the EU than in the US, as public-private co-publications per million-population stand over 35 points lower than in the US.

- Too often policies are not aligned with the goal to promote socially relevant innovation. For example, Ashford and Renda (2016) show the existing misalignment of policies that should promote decarbonisation at various levels of government in the EU. The role of the state is essential in these cases, given that investment in sustainable technologies and market solutions creates positive externalities, which are not reaped by investors absent a specific intervention to correct the market failure. This is to be coupled with the poor performance of carbon pricing in Europe's ETS framework. The EU's stated goal to mainstream the Sustainable Development Goals into all aspects of EU policymaking (European Commission 2016, 2019) is currently far from being implemented: suffice it to think about the lack of orientation towards SDGs in the semester; and also the relatively 'unsustainable' footprint of many of projects funded by the first years of the 'Juncker plan'.[35]

- Demand-side policies such as the strategic use of public procurement to promote socially beneficial innovation are under-developed. This is due, *inter alia*, to the lack of coordination of public procurement at the EU level (Renda et al., 2014), as well as the fact that procurement, even when it is most innovation-friendly, rarely looks at more disruptive innovation products and services, and concentrates on incremental ones (Czarnitzki et al., 2018). In addition, the diffusion of SME-friendly procurement is still very uneven in the EU, as shown by recent studies for the European Commission.[36] The often-evoked financing problem of SMEs would at least be mitigated if governments at all levels helped in offering facilities for testing prototypes, or acted as launching customers.

- Innovation funding is still very complex and burdensome for SMEs. Scientists and product developers spend up to 30% of their time preparing requests for subsidies, supported by a whole cottage industry of subsidy experts, although the last Multiannual Financial Framework has seen some marked improvements in this respect, reducing the time spent for Horizon 2020 projects to an estimated 5%-10%.[37] The European Commission also estimated that it costs Horizon 2020 applicants €636 million annually to write proposals, for a total of €1,908.9 million during the first three years. Of these costs, it is estimated that €1.7 billion was spent on writing proposals that did not obtain funding, including €643 million for non-funded high-quality proposals alone.[38]

- The transition from innovation to the creation of economic value could be made smoother if applications for funding included an 'early market test', such as commitments by private parties to bring a project to a next level of development if and when certain R&D milestones are achieved. So far, the bridging of research and innovation in Horizon 2020 has led to mixed results: as reported by Simonelli (2016), the share of SMEs among total applicants, funded applicants and granted funds were all higher in the previous Framework Programme (FP7) than in the Horizon 2020 calls completed in 2014, the first year of Horizon 2020.

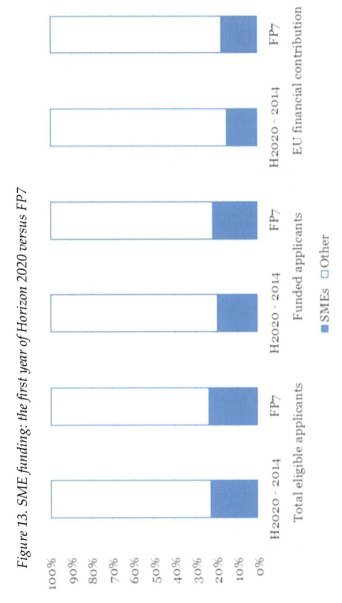

Figure 13. SME funding: the first year of Horizon 2020 versus FP7

Source: Simonelli (2016), based on data from eCorda.

Possible explanations to the limited involvement of SMEs in Horizon 2020 can be found in some barriers still hindering their participation. The CEPS Task Force on Innovation and Entrepreneurship, which concluded its work in 2016, pointed out that SMEs: i) are often unaware of the (complex system of) existing support schemes; ii) face substantial obstacles in drafting convincing proposals due to limited time and resources and inadequate access to skills and knowledge (including linguistic skills); iii) have considerable difficulties in finding partners and in building and managing international consortia; iv) have limited access to finance to complement EU funds when required (e.g. in Innovation Actions and SME Instrument). Other, more general problems relate to the excessive focus on quantitative goals, rather than on checking that SMEs actually participate in the research and innovation activities. For example, Simonelli (2016) analyses the new 'SME instrument' introduced by Horizon 2020 and finds that the lion's share of applications received so far have been submitted by single entities, a finding that is in line with the concern that the instrument might end up discouraging cooperation since it does not allow the submission and/or implementation of two or more projects at the same time by the same applicant. In the future, this instrument could be accompanied by strategic procurement tools such as the Small Business Innovation Research (SBIR) and Small Business Research Initiative (SBRI), which produced positive results both in the US and in European countries such as the Netherlands (and to some extent, the UK) (Granieri and Renda, 2010).[39]

The role of pro-innovation regulation, the "innovation principle" and "innovation deals" has been limited. So far, the adoption of the "SME test" and of the "innovation principle" at the EU level has not been fully satisfactory. This is also because these screenings tend to become last-minute concerns and box-ticking exercises in the overall policy process (Renda and Simonelli, 2019). Similarly, the attempt to translate the Dutch "green deals" into "Innovation Deals" has produced less than a handful of meaningful applications to date, and the instrument itself seems to be affected by an excessive emphasis on 'less is more'; a rather toothless set of possible remedies in case the deal is successful (only "clarification" of rules is contemplated); and an overall design that is ill-suited for more disruptive, systemic innovation. In fact, due to their negotiated nature, innovation deals can suffer from an "incumbency" problem, and as such would lend themselves more easily to incremental innovation, rather than substantial market reshuffling.

4.2 Towards a mission-oriented approach to innovation

In the era of digitally-enabled, open innovation, socially relevant breakthroughs require a massive transformation of many industries, the use of both money (spending programmes) and policies, a joint effort of the public and the private sector, and a contribution from citizens and users in co-creating solutions (Soete et al., 2017). No leap forward can be achieved without the unique contribution of different parties: therefore, much more needs to be done to forge coalitions. Such coalitions should be established on the basis of the contributions each member makes to the project, and would ideally also include non-EU partners.

We believe that the power of mission-oriented coalitions could be exploited further, through better governance and enhanced consolidation: this is why we include them in our hidden treasures. The European Commission has experimented with such coalitions in the past two decades, generating all sorts of platforms and corresponding acronyms: KETs, FETs, KICs, JUs, JTIs, RIs, EIPs, RIAs, and many more. However, on only a few occasions has the participation of different communities (researchers, entrepreneurs, students, policymakers, local administrations, investors, etc.) led to the expected, or desired, results. One good example is provided by the Knowledge and Innovation Communities, which incorporated research, innovation and also education components, and have in some circumstances led to remarkable, inclusive results (e.g. ClimateKIC and InnoEnergy, more than the others). But overall, the lack of a clear set of milestones, the lack of discretion in simplifying procedures and selecting a portfolio of projects with varying levels of risk-reward, and a lack of citizen engagement have undermined the full success of these initiatives.[40]

Moreover, in two recent evaluation exercises, the European Commission has found added value in large institutionalised partnerships that aim at advancing the EU's agenda in specific sectors, addressing specific societal challenges. Partnerships such as CleanSky2, Shift2Rail, SESAR, FCH2, IMI2, BBI, ECSEL have been generally successful, but have also faced a number of challenges that would need to be effectively addressed in the future governance arrangements. Among the common challenges are the need to include a wider range of stakeholders either in the governance structures or in submitted proposals; the limited interaction between the Governing Boards and their advisory bodies; alignment with policies at EU, national and regional level; the choice of the Key Performance Indicators used to measure specific impacts; the need to include indicators related to the global competitiveness of the relevant industrial sectors; the participation of SMEs; the low participation rates of the EU-13 member states; and the need to improve and enforce communication activities and, in particular, to ensure effective dissemination of project results.

Figure 14. Evolution of existing Joint Undertakings

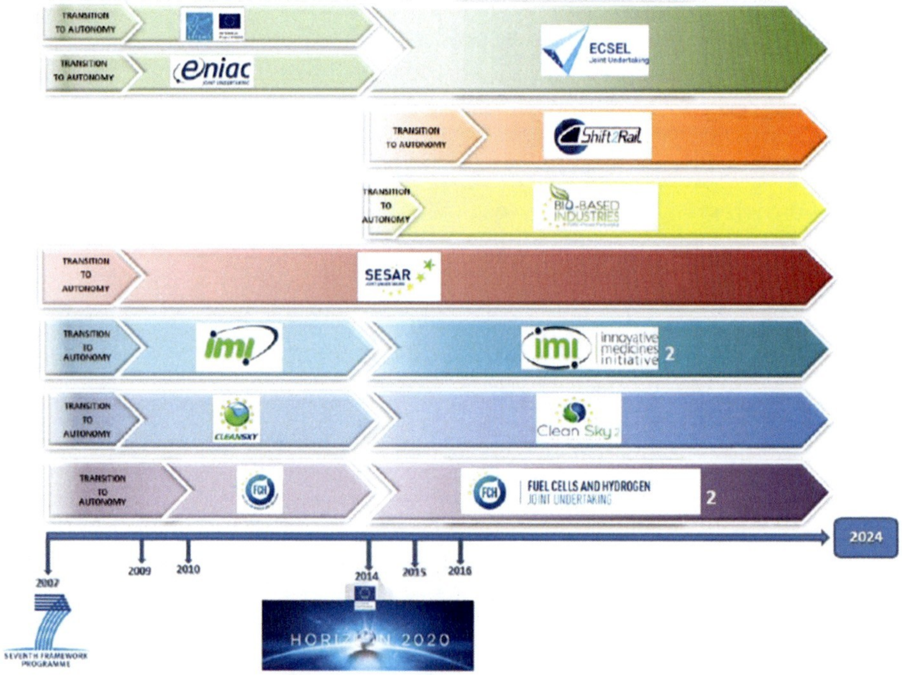

Source: European Commission Interim Evaluation, SWD(2017) 338 final.

Figure 15. Article 185 Partnerships launched to date

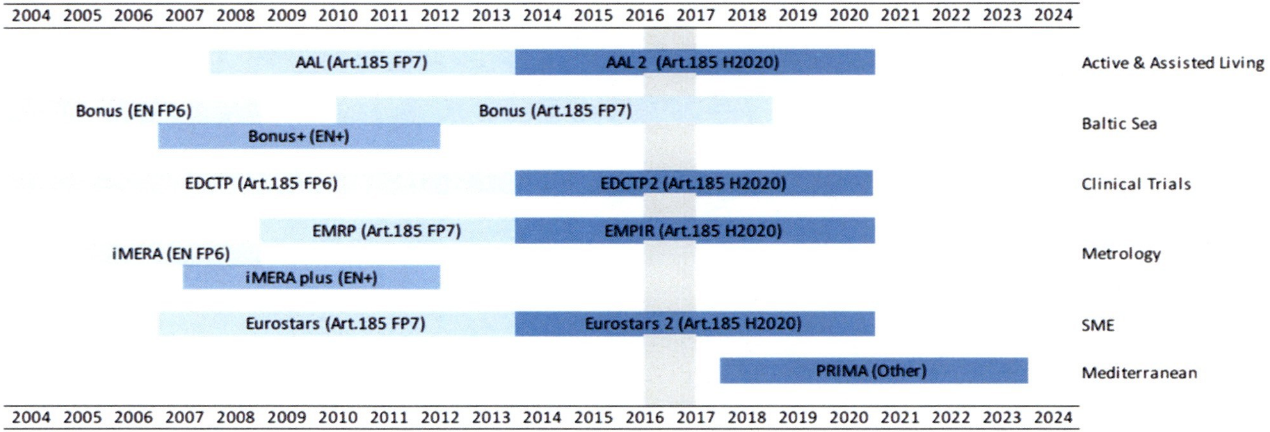

	2004	2005	2006	2007	2008	2009	2010	2011	2012	2013	2014	2015	2016	2017	2018	2019	2020	2021	2022	2023	2024
Active & Assisted Living			AAL (Art.185 FP7)								AAL 2 (Art.185 H2020)										
Baltic Sea	Bonus (EN FP6)			Bonus+ (EN+)					Bonus (Art.185 FP7)												
Clinical Trials		EDCTP (Art.185 FP6)								EDCTP2 (Art.185 H2020)											
Metrology		iMERA (EN FP6)	iMERA plus (EN+)		EMRP (Art.185 FP7)					EMPIR (Art.185 H2020)											
SME				Eurostars (Art.185 FP7)						Eurostars 2 (Art.185 H2020)											
Mediterranean														PRIMA (Other)							

Source: Meta-Evaluation of Article 185 Initiatives Report of the Expert Group.

Article 185 initiatives have been shown to contribute to a more integrated and coordinated R&I programming in Europe; at the same time, they require a dedicated implementation structure, which in and of itself involves a considerable investment in administrative management and governance. The financial commitment expected from the EU and its partners is also much larger than any of the other options, given its longer life cycle compared to other options and the administrative burden of establishing and implementing these partnerships.

A meta-evaluation of existing 185 Partnerships in 2017 highlighted, *inter alia*: the need to use Article 185 as a strategic opportunity to enable policy cooperation between MS and the EU; the need to develop a coherent process for identification and selection of initiatives, the need to define an exit strategy from the outset; important margins of improvement in term of efficiency, especially through the creation of a single structure, preferably a public body, to serve all of the active Article 185 initiatives; the need to re-orientate the Article 185 more towards outcomes and impacts; the need to acknowledge more the needs and priorities of less research-intensive countries in shaping these initiatives, and to accommodate better and more actively the priorities and needs of the less R&D intensive countries; the need to exploit synergies with Structural Funds; and the need for the Commission to play a more proactive role without compromising member states' ownership. The meta-evaluation also called for more coherence and a reinforced international dimension.

Against this background, the European Commission, backed by experts such as Pascal Lamy, Mariana Mazzucato and two groups of advisors (RISE and ESIR), decided to propose the transition towards a more consolidated group of Partnerships and a limited number of Missions in five domains.

As regards Partnerships, a major (and highly needed) simplification is expected with the transition from Horizon 2020 to Horizon Europe in 2021.

The budget increase foreseen (from €80 billion to more than €100 billion) and the consolidation of the 'partnership' form are extremely good news for the future of European innovation, and bring back to the forefront of the debate another of Europe's hidden treasures: the ability to promote and achieve innovation through large coalitions and public-private initiatives.

Figure 16. The new landscape of Partnerships in Horizon Europe compared to Horizon 2020

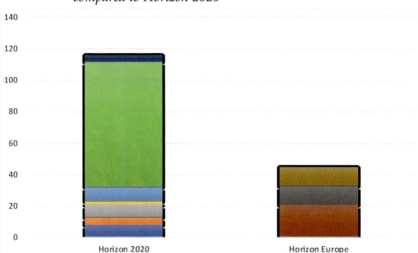

Source: European Commission.

The new Partnerships will be flanked by a brand new type of initiative, the so-called Missions in which selected agencies, with agile governance, will be called on to merge education, research innovation and industrial policy into large, dynamic coalitions that will seek maximum impact, generate spillover effects, provide input to policies, and reach out to the general public to co-create solutions. Nested in the Sustainable Development Goals, the forthcoming Missions should follow a constant cycle of road-mapping, consultation, planning, experimentation, monitoring, evaluation, learning and feedback into the road-mapping exercise (see ESIR second memorandum, Soete et al., 2018). This should be a constant cycle, that spins as fast as the Mission allows, and should be fed by as many researchers and entrepreneurs as possible. The five areas selected for Missions include "Adaptation to climate change including societal transformation", "Cancer", "Healthy Oceans, Seas, Coastal and Inland Waters", "Climate-Neutral and Smart

Cities" and "Soil Health and Food", and will be led by well-known figures, who will act as Chairs of the respective Mission boards. These Missions are expected to boost the impact of EU-funded research and innovation by mobilising investment and EU-wide efforts around measurable and time-bound goals concerning issues that affect citizens' daily lives. Each Mission board will consist of 15 experts, including the chair.

Partnerships and Missions are a 'once in a generation' opportunity for Europe's unique approach to innovation, and may be coupled with other initiatives between member states and industry, called Important Projects of Common European Interest (IPCEI), as perfectly exemplified by the recently launched "Battery Alliance" and Microelectronics projects (see box below). These industrial policy projects must also be scrutinised under EU state aid rules. The 2014 Communication on Important Projects of Common European Interest observes that where private initiatives supporting innovation fail to materialise because of the significant risks such projects entail, member states can jointly fill the gap to overcome market failures and boost the realisation of innovative projects that otherwise would not have taken off. In order to qualify for support under the IPCEI Communication, a project must: (i) contribute to strategic EU objectives, (ii) involve several member states, (iii) involve private financing by the beneficiaries, (iv) generate positive spillover effects across the EU that limit potential distortions to competition, and (v) be highly ambitious in terms of research and innovation.

Box: the "IPCEI" in batteries and microelectronics

Batteries

Batteries will represent a high proportion of the value added in cars of the future. Since the car industry is a major player in the European economy, it is essential to retain as much value creation in Europe as possible. However, currently, the EU has no capability to mass produce battery cells, and relies for this on foreign, mainly Asian suppliers. Batteries can also be a major source of jobs, economic growth and investment for the EU.

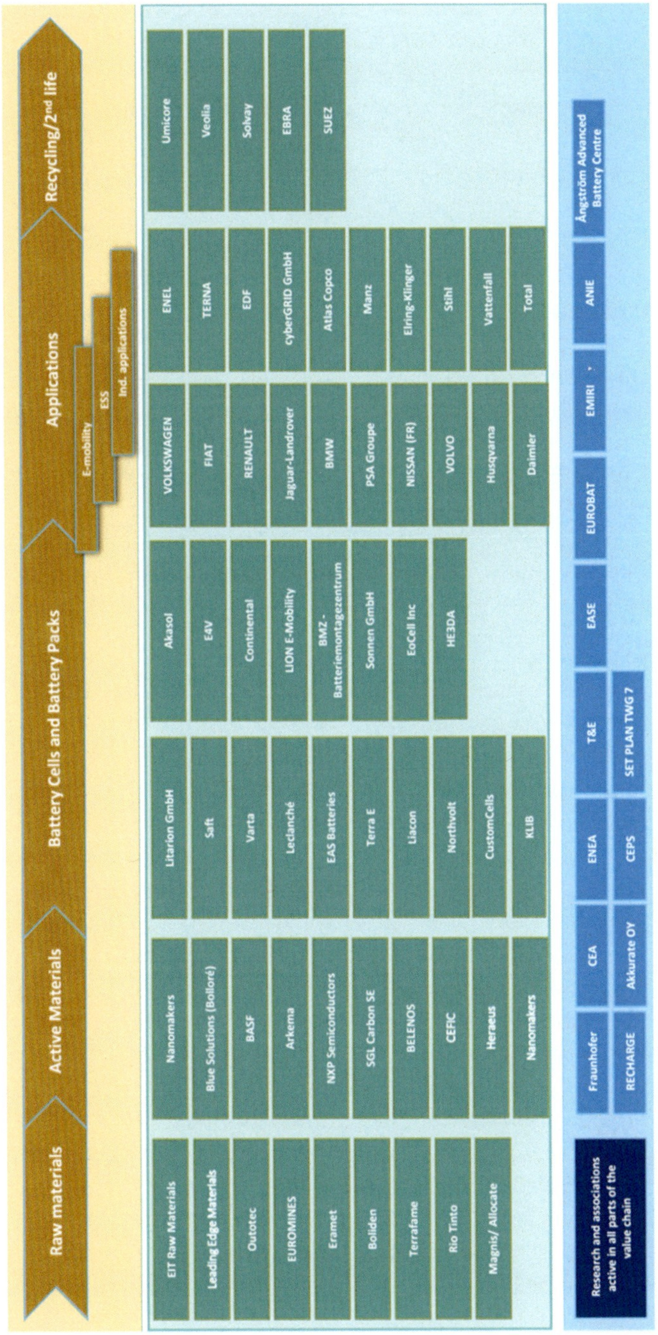

Figure 17. The European Battery Alliance

Raw materials	Active Materials	Battery Cells and Battery Packs	Applications (E-mobility / ESS / Ind. applications)	Recycling/2nd life
EIT Raw Materials	Nanomakers	Litarion GmbH	Akasol / VOLKSWAGEN / ENEL	Umicore
Leading Edge Materials	Blue Solutions (Bolloré)	Saft	E4V / FIAT / TERRA	Veolia
Outotec	BASF	Varta	Continental / RENAULT / EDF	Solvay
EUROMINES	Arkema	Leclanché	LION E-Mobility / Jaguar-Landrover / cyberGRID GmbH	EBRA
Eramet	NXP Semiconductors	EAS Batteries	BMZ-Batteriemontagezentrum / BMW / Atlas Copco	SUEZ
Boliden	SGL Carbon SE	Terra E	Sonnen GmbH / PSA Groupe / Manz	
Terrafame	BELENOS	Liacon	EoCell Inc / NISSAN (FR) / Elring-Klinger	
Rio Tinto	CEFC	Northvolt	HE3DA / VOLVO / Stihl	
Magnis/Allocate	Heraeus	CustomCells	Husqvarna / Vatterfall	
	Nanomakers	KLIB	Daimler / Total	

Research and associations active in all parts of the value chain									
Fraunhofer	CEA	ENEA	T&E	EASE	EUROBAT	EMIRI	ANIE	Ångström Advanced Battery Centre	
RECHARGE	Akkurate OY	CEPS	SET PLAN TWG 7						

For this purpose, a European Battery Alliance (see Figure 17) was launched in October 2017 by Vice-President Šefčovič, gathering the European Commission, interested EU countries, the European Investment Bank, key industrial stakeholders, and innovation actors. The immediate objective is to create a competitive manufacturing value chain in Europe with sustainable battery cells at its core. According to some forecasts, Europe could capture a battery market of up to €250 billion a year from 2025 onwards. Covering the EU demand alone requires at least 10 to 20 'gigafactories' (large-scale battery cell production facilities).

Two years later, in 2019, cross-border, large-scale integrated consortia are being established in EU countries across all segments of the EU value chain: raw materials (Sweden, Finland, Portugal); chemicals (Belgium, Poland, Germany, Finland); battery cells production (Sweden, France, Germany, Italy, the Czech Republic); battery pack, software, machine tools and engineering (Germany, France, Spain, Slovakia); and recycling (Belgium, Germany). According to InnoEnergy, €100 billion have already been announced as being invested in flagship projects covering the entire supply chain. Public authorities – namely, the European Commission, member states and the EIB – are joining forces to support this venture.

Microelectronics
Investment in research and innovation in microelectronics carries a considerable element of risk, and therefore public support is appropriate and necessary to incentivise companies to carry out these ambitious research, development and innovation activities. Microelectronics are considered by the Commission as a Key Enabling Technology, which are technologies that have applications in multiple industries and will help tackle societal challenges. The Commission thus concluded that the IPCEI on Microelectronics notified jointly by France, Germany, Italy and the UK was in line with EU state aid rules, and kick-started the process of its creation. The IPCEI (see Figure 18) is expected to unlock an additional €6 billion in private investments in the microelectronics sector. This was the first integrated IPCEI in the field of research, development and innovation approved by the Commission since the adoption of the Communication in 2014. The IPCEI on Microelectronics involves 29 direct participants from the four member states. Direct participants could receive from their respective national administrations a total of up to approximately €1.75 billion in funding. More specifically, France has sought approval to grant aid to provide funding of up to €355 million, Germany up to €820 million, Italy up to €524 million and the UK up to €48 million.

Figure 18. The IPCEI on Microelectronics

Project management				
1 Energy efficient chips	2 Power semiconductors	3 Sensors	4 Advanced optical equipment	5 Compound materials
CEA-Leti 🇮🇹	3-D Micromac 🇩🇪	CEA-Leti 🇮🇹	AMTC 🇩🇪	AZUR Space Solar Power 🇩🇪
Cologne Chip 🇩🇪	AP&S International 🇩🇪	CorTec 🇩🇪	Carl Zeiss 🇩🇪	CEA-Leti 🇮🇹
Globalfoundries 🇩🇪	CEA-Leti 🇮🇹	Elmos Semiconductors 🇩🇪		Integrated Compound Semiconductors 🇬🇧
RacyICs 🇩🇪	Elmos Semiconductors 🇩🇪	Fondazione Bruno Kessler 🇮🇹		IQE 🇬🇧
Soitec 🇮🇹	Infineon 🇩🇪	Infineon 🇩🇪		Newport Wafer Fab 🇬🇧
ST Micro-electronics 🇮🇹	MURATA 🇮🇹	Robert Bosch 🇩🇪		SPTS Technologies 🇬🇧
X-FAB 🇮🇹	Robert Bosch 🇩🇪	ST Micro-electronics 🇮🇹		OSRAM 🇩🇪
	SEMIKRON 🇩🇪	TDK-Micronas 🇩🇪		Sofradir 🇮🇹
	ST Micro-electronics 🇮🇹	ULIS 🇮🇹		Soitec 🇮🇹
	X-FAB 🇩🇪	X-FAB 🇮🇹🇩🇪		ST Micro-electronics 🇮🇹

Name in "*italic*" = SME

Source: European Commission.

Based on trust and an ongoing relationship between leading academics and universities, governments, administrations, businesses and civil society, coupled with funding from various sources, these large coalitions can achieve something that is seldom obtained by other large superpowers: giving adequate, consistent direction to research and innovation, steering them towards societal challenges and future sustainable development. Upcoming governance choices and strong results-orientation will be essential for these coalitions to deliver their full potential, as well as address important problems that have already emerged such as excessive focus on incremental innovation, the lack of sufficient diffusion of innovation, and the difficulty in scaling up the most promising new firms. This is why a new debate on the need for a new, modernised EU industrial policy is emerging. If these problems were effectively addressed, Europe's concerns about the need to boost venture capital and follow in the footsteps of Silicon Valley would become a distant memory, replaced by a new, more socially relevant way of designing and implementing innovative ventures.

4.3 Policy recommendations

Against this background, Europe may be disregarding a possible hidden treasure for innovation, which would be extremely precious in restoring a path to future growth. At a time when the United States is drowning in various forms of inequality, and many EU companies are starting to display a relatively encouraging productivity trend, Europe could be on the verge of what Harberger (1998) called "yeasty growth",[41] but it needs to create the right ecosystem to accompany this possible *renaissance*. Van Ark et al. (2018) subscribe to this view but opine that Europe's productivity glass may still be seen as either half full or half empty. Europe's hidden treasure can be summarised with an old saying, according to which "if you want to fast, go alone; if you want to go far, go together". And indeed, Europe seems to display lower levels of inequality compared to the US (Gros et al., 2018). However, it needs to get rid of several obstacles to the diffusion of technology across firms and society. These obstacles include the persistence of "zombie firms" in many markets (Veugelers, 2016); the existence of powerful incumbency interests that often stand in the way of innovative business models (OECD, 2015); the lack of policy alignment towards innovation and grand societal challenges (Ashford and Renda, 2016; Renda, 2017); the reluctance to attract talent from other EU countries, as well as the rest of the world; the difficulty in involving SMEs in fruitful collaborative projects (Simonelli, 2016); and the failure to fully embed innovation in the policy process (Renda, 2017).

Despite these layers of dust, Europe has the potential to "go together" in innovation and is actively pursuing it. Beyond the veil of Europe's inferiority complex about innovation lies a wealth of opportunity. Not only are European cities leading the world in innovation; but the more global challenges appear prohibitively difficult, complex and multi-sectoral, the less individual, venture-capital-backed solutions *à la* Silicon Valley will be fit-for-purpose. This requires some fixes to current policies and programmes, which we outline below.

4.3.1 Blend instruments and consolidate programmes, especially for SMEs

The European Commission should devote time and resources to bring the right partners together and to cut a path through the forest of grants, loans and equity. The ongoing consolidation along Partnerships, Missions and IPCEI (among others) will have to be carefully monitored and possibly lead to further, strongly multi-level coordination, along with ongoing monitoring and evaluation at all stages of implementation. In addition, the technology transfer component between large and small companies should be strengthened, since otherwise the ambition to strengthen EU competitiveness in research, innovation and industry will fall prey to incumbent interests, losing agility and the potential to bring forward new competition in the generation of ideas and innovative solutions.

There are far too many funds, both in the private and public sector, with the mandate to finance innovative SMEs in one way or another. Consolidation is thus required to increase the maximum contribution, reduce management cost and improve the quality of the staff devoted to this crucial activity.

4.3.2 Beyond money: provide infrastructure and facilities to innovative SMEs

EU institutions and national governments should provide SMEs with more than money, and more than mere advice. SMEs very often need infrastructure for innovation: laboratories, ICT facilities, office buildings, even legal and IP support. An adequate level of assistance on these fronts would substantially lower the threshold for start-ups and open up the field for part-time entrepreneurs. The associated cost would be modest in comparison with the investment in infrastructure triggered by large investments in large companies.

In addition, the financing of innovative SMEs becomes far, far easier when a prototype is successfully tested in real-life settings. It falls on governments at all levels to provide such experimental settings. This form of investment has an extremely high return and involves government at the cutting-edge of technology and innovation. In fact, such an approach reduces the technical risk for investors, and helps government agencies reduce the commercial risk by acting as launch customers. This powerful demand-side tool to stimulate innovation may require a clarification of competition rules, in order to avoid a 'chilling effect' due to the often-false perception that these rules hamper support to individual SMEs by member states.

4.3.3 Bring innovation to the core of policymaking

As technology accelerates, alongside product and process innovation, policymakers will increasingly be affected by a 'pacing problem': technology and the market changing faster than legislators, and even more so EU legislators, are able to cope with. Thereby, legal rules often end up being too rigid, and hardly in line with what entrepreneurs and innovators need to be able to fully deploy their potential. The European Commission has tried to address this problem by increasingly looking at alternative forms of regulation, including less prescriptive regulatory frameworks, co-regulation, and market-based instruments. Part of the European Commission experimented with an "innovation principle" and "innovation deals", which however have produced few results to date, and would deserve a better design and formulation within the domain of EU better regulation (Renda and Simonelli, 2019), as well as a stronger involvement of civil society throughout the process. These tools await a better mainstreaming into the policy process, and clear guidance from the Commission: the issue at stake is not the reduction or elimination of regulation, but rather the redesign and recast of regulation in ways that can facilitate product, service and organisational innovation in the Union. Perhaps the creation of a permanent group, similar to the Group of Regulatory Innovation advisors established in Canada, would provide an interesting avenue to spur innovation embedding European values.

More precisely, the EU should establish new ways to connect the increasingly important domain of Partnerships and Missions for innovation to the policy process. In 2018, the second ESIR Memorandum proposed the creation of a joint board comprising the Chairs of all Missions, which would select, on a yearly basis, the proposed policy actions to be submitted to the European Commission Secretariat-General for inclusion in the yearly agenda of the Commission (and based on the new Inter-institutional Agreement on Better Law-making, also in the new three-year rolling legislative plan of the three institutions involved). Based on this scheme, there would be two major inputs to shaping of the EU yearly legislative and work programme: the ones validated by DG RTD, coming from mission agencies; and the ones proposed by the REFIT platform. The policy cycle activity, as well as the experimentation activities of the missions, would then lead to feedback into the overall Agenda 2030, which underpins the whole exercise, in the name of policy alignment and coherence.

Regardless of the mode of implementation, it is essential that innovation and the specific challenges faced by entrepreneurs do not remain an afterthought, however highlighted, in the EU policy process. Rather than devoting resources to checking impacts on innovation after a policy problem has been selected, after policy alternatives have been compared, and often even after a preferred policy option has already been chosen, the need to promote innovation should become an input into the policy agenda. Such inputs could also be linked to new forms of experimental policymaking, such as sandboxed or randomised controlled trials, which could be developed at the EU level to help SMEs test their new business models and innovative solutions.

Finally, funding instruments for research and innovation should become much more streamlined in the future: instruments such as large-scale partnerships, strategic value chains, IPCEI projects are hard to reconcile and frame into a consistent strategy, which in turn makes it difficult to assess whether public money is complementing or crowding out, private investment. The next Commission should engage in a further consolidation exercise, seriously rethinking the criteria and evidence base underpinning funding and governance decisions in this crucial domain. Likewise, the Commission should develop its mechanisms so as to obtain the right balance between grants, loans, equity funding, bottom-up and top-down funding processes. All this should be aimed at developing a more comprehensive evidence base for the overall design of the funding policy, rather than adopting ad hoc, uncoordinated decisions for each instrument and strategy.

4.3.4 Behind the curtains of open innovation: the EU needs a dedicated policy for SMEs

An important finding in our analysis is the need to ensure that open innovation does not become a trap for SMEs. The outsourcing of R&D solutions from large to smaller companies is, in fact, only apparently a brilliant solution for all. Rather, it may be accompanied by new forms of exploitation of large companies' superior bargaining power vis-à-vis smaller companies or individual entrepreneurs. As outlined above, in Chapter 1, while Europe can rely on a legal system that would in principle perfectly fit the need for trust-based relationships in complex innovation projects, the lack of suitable access to justice and redress for smaller companies can frustrate these attempts, often leaving SMEs in a corner, with few alternatives to remaining in the commercial relationship, despite the fact that conditions are unfair.

Not surprisingly, many SMEs still have fears about the widespread use of open innovation practices: for instance, many small companies worry about the unauthorised use of IP or the unfair sharing of costs and profits. We recommend that the European Commission launches a study into the use of open innovation by smaller businesses in Europe, and possible fears and solutions associated to these problems. Already five years ago, the Commission found that an "open" atmosphere can lead to the leakage of a company's core competences (European IPR Helpdesk, 2015): the misappropriation of this information may lead to the complete downfall of a company. Given the different bargaining position of larger and smaller companies, which can translate into economic dependency especially when large companies widely purchase R&D solutions from smaller partners to foster their widely known brands, and small firms undertake transaction-specific investment to best fit the innovation process of their counterpart, there seems to be room for strategic, hold-up behaviour to the disadvantage of smaller players.

This situation reaches extreme scenarios in the case of digital platforms, as will be explained in more detail below in Chapter 10. There, strong direct and indirect network effects lead to a significant accumulation of power in the hands of the platform owner (thanks to the 'winner-takes-all' effect); and often to a lock-in situation for smaller players that do their business through the platform. This situation has prompted action by the European Commission, in the form of the Platform-to-business (P2B) Regulation, which aims at remedying cases of unfair or non-transparent practices applied by online platforms to the businesses that act as their customers. However, once again the P2B Regulation, however welcome, does not adequately address the problem of redress. In this respect, SMEs involved in repeated interactions with large platforms would need to think twice before voicing their concerns about unfair practices, if anything for fear of being demoted, or de-listed. Analogous to what has been introduced by some countries (e.g. the UK) in the grocery sector, the possibility for smaller businesses to lodge confidential complaints with a central European authority would greatly improve access to justice in these delicate situations, thereby restoring trust in the system, and in open innovation arrangements (Renda et al., 2014).

Once again, as will be recalled below in Chapter 6, there remain gaps in the legal remedies and solutions available to SMEs in Europe, which are in stark contrast with the emphasis that is very often placed on the need to focus on SMEs as the real engine of growth in the Union. We recommend that EU institutions consider the creation of a dedicated authority in charge of policing unfair B2B commercial practices.

4.3.5 Learn from failures, and terminate projects that do not produce results

In managing research projects, EU institutions should become more inclusive (through the partnership and mission models outlined above), but also more agile. This means that multi-stakeholder partnerships should feature enhanced forms of portfolio management, in which projects that appear unlikely to produce results are promptly terminated, freeing resources for modified or entirely new projects. For example, whenever it appears clear that the basic assumptions that were part of the proposal are no longer valid, the project should be immediately abandoned: to provide an incentive to the parties involved, funds that have not been spent could be used for other, related programmes. In any event, the inevitable programme failures should be evaluated, financially, technically, organisationally and in terms of the quality of cooperation, in order to enable enhanced learning on the side of institutions that manage the projects (Luetjens and t'Hart, 2018).

The evaluation of grant and project proposals would also benefit from other practices. Applications for EU grants could be screened for interesting combinations of (parts of) programmes and possible blending of funds. The applicants involved should then be invited to submit a revised plan that will most likely be funded. And the evaluation of the technical parts of the proposals could become partly double-blind, as an experiment, in order to avoid that incumbency issues percolate through the evaluation process.

5. PATENTS: A NOT-SO-HIDDEN TREASURE, NOW AT RISK

Patents are essential to innovation, as they reward investment in R&D with exclusive rights for a specified period of time, and in exchange for disclosure of the technical solution backing the innovation. The 'social bargain' behind the patent system is aimed at promoting the generation and safeguarding the diffusion of innovation: this requires that inventors file an application claiming that the sought-after patent is a new solution, which implies a real inventive step. Chen (2015) uses historical panel data of the US and 14 west European countries from 1600 to 1913, finding a significant positive effect of patent laws on economic growth by using different models. More generally, since the 1950s economic studies have consistently found that patents foster innovation: notable recent studies include Arora et al. (2007), which found that firms earn on average a 50% premium over the "no patenting" case, ranging from 60% in the health-related industries to about 40% in electronics; Acemoglu, Bimpikis and Ozdaglar (2011), who observe that "patents improve the allocation of resources by encouraging rapid experimentation and efficient *ex post* transfer of knowledge across firms"; and Lévêque and Ménière (2006), who found that 88% of US, European, and Japanese businesses reportedly rely upon the information disclosed in patents to keep up with technology advances and direct their own R&D efforts.

5.1 Quality: where European patents lead

In this context, Europe is normally considered as having a very high quality patent system compared to other parts of the world such as the US or China. As reported by Chien (2016), industry surveys conducted since 2010 have consistently found the EPO to have the highest ratings among the five leading Patent Offices around the world. This perception is robust across the subgroups surveyed – companies, patent lawyers, and non-practising entities. In an earlier contribution, Drahos (2010) interviewed 140 examiners from all over the world between 2004 and 2008, and found that the EPO had the best reputation, including for its research capabilities and *esprit de corps* – the personal pride examiners took in the quality of their work. Van Pottelsberghe (2011) finds that the comparison of the patent offices in Europe (EPO), Japan (JPO) and the US (USPTO) shows that their operational designs differ substantially: the EPO provides higher-quality and more expensive services than the USPTO, while the JPO is in an intermediate position. In her empirical analysis, Chien (2016) finds that "at every stage in the patent lifecycle, the US system tilts towards a higher quantity patent system than does the EPO".

The difference between the EPO and USPTO in terms of patents awarded is striking and nurtured by a number of concomitant factors. First, patent (and more generally IP) protection in the United States is generally stronger than in Europe, where the social function of property (Foster and Bonilla, 2011) is rooted in many national constitutions, and where competition law typically trumps intellectual property when the two clash, as in the case of 'refusal to deal' cases (Renda, 2010).

Second, and relatedly, the patentable subject matter in the US has traditionally been much broader than in Europe, peaking in the 1980s when the Supreme Court and Congress championed the view that "anything under the sun made by man" could be patented (Granieri and Renda, 2010). This led, *inter alia*, to the expansion of patents on methods of doing business, as well as software patents, never fully endorsed at the EU level (and rejected after years of discussion of a proposed proposal on computer-implemented inventions) despite relative openness shown by the EPO. Since 2006 the United States has exceeded Japan and Europe in patent applications, mostly due to the rise of foreign patenting activity in the United States (Leydesdorff, Etzkowitz, and Kushnir, 2016). Increasing volume has led to a current backlog of 522,149 applications at the USPTO.[42] More recently, the Supreme Court decision in *Alice Corp. v CLS Bank International*, by increasing the benchmark for what can be considered 'patentable', had a direct effect on lowering the total number of patent applications.

Third, strong patent protection in the US led to the use of patents as both a 'sword' and a 'shield', to claim exclusivity, as a bargaining chip to license technology, to create a protective layer around a given product or service, or as an asset to accumulate and then use strategically when an opportunity arises. Patents are bought, sold, brokered, accumulated, left idle, used to blackmail rivals, and to threaten litigation for which costly insurance is regularly sold. Patent intermediaries and brokers such as Ocean Tomo and Yet2.com have seen their business grow, with limited impact on overall social welfare. All this created what Carl Shapiro (2001) defined as a "patent thicket", i.e. "a dense web of overlapping intellectual property rights that a company must hack its way through in order to actually commercialize new technology".

All in all, since the 1980s the USPTO has been flooded with a number of applications it could hardly manage. The backlog was so unsustainable that Berkeley Professor Robert Merges (1999) denounced, with an ironic quotation from Alice in Wonderland, the likelihood of seeing of "As many as Six Impossible Patents Before Breakfast". Since then, and even more after the *eBay v MercExchange* case (Castro, 2011), the diffusion of patent trolls and other strategic intermediaries have led the system close to collapse. Especially in the pharmaceutical and biotech sector, and increasingly in ICT, over-patenting has become a way to secure long-lasting protection and a remarkable breadth of exclusivity for many large corporations. For example, pharmaceutical company AbbVie, the patent holder for Humira, the world's best-selling drug, has filed 247 patent applications for the product in order to potentially secure at least thirty-nine years of patent protection for the drug (the primary patent for Humira expired in 2016). In March 2019, a welfare benefit fund filed antitrust claims against AbbVie and a number of its competitors, alleging that they created a "patent thicket" by applying for a number of patents for Humira since the drug was developed, as a means to block competition in the US market.[43] Pfizer, the patent holder for Lyrica, a drug used to treat neuropathic pain, has employed product hopping with over-patenting to potentially extend its market control beyond the mandated term of patent protection. Revlimid, developed to treat multiple myeloma (and which has also been indicated for treatment of other cancers), has been patented by Celgene, which has sought to expand its control of the market for up to 40 years by filing over 100 patent applications on the drug.

All in all, the patent thicket has become much denser: the solution proposed by the Obama administration took the form of the Leahy-Smith *America Invents Act* (AIA), which marked the move from a "first-to-invent" to a "first-to-file" patent system, and a one-year commercial use limitation for any patent applicant to use an invention prior to filing an application for a patent. The AIA is reportedly having damaging effects on innovation in the US (Campbell, 2016), leading to a reduction in patent quality and a surge in patent applications (as reported by the USPTO). In 2015, *The Economist* newspaper published an editorial decrying the state of the patent system, and condemning the "parasitic ecology of trolls" that has bruised the patent system. The magazine added that "today's patent regime operates in the name of progress, instead it sets innovation back".[44]

In China, conversely, the patent system is clearly on the rise, and the dramatic increase in quantity is slowly being coupled with an increase in the quality of the patents awarded. China occupied the second position a source of international patent applications filed via WIPO in 2017, and is projected to become the first by 2020. Domestically the system is booming: the State Intellectual Property Office of the People's Republic of China (SIPO) received 1.3 million patent applications in 2016 – more than the combined total for the USPTO (605,571), the JPO (318,381), the KIPO (208,830) and the EPO (159,358).

103 | Patents: a not-so-hidden treasure, now at risk?

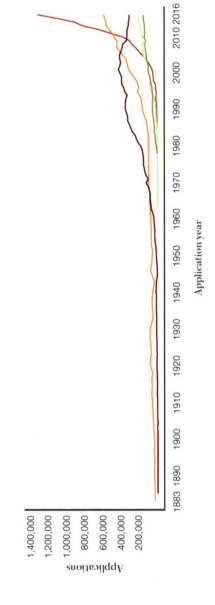

Figure 19. Total Patent Applications in the top 5 Patent Offices, 1883-2016

Note: The IP office of the Soviet Union, not represented in this figure, was the leading office in the world in terms of filings from 1964 to 1969. Like Japan and the U.S., the office of the Soviet Union saw stable application numbers until the early 1960s, after which it recorded rapid growth in applications filed.

Source: WIPO (2017).[45]

The rise of Chinese patents mirrors the strong emphasis placed by the government on innovation since 2012, the strong leadership of companies like Huawei and ZTE in global markets, and the increased strategic interest placed in sectors such as green tech, 5G and quantum cryptography (more on these in Chapter 10). But the quality of Chinese patents is still far from that of European patents. Virtually none of the applications originating in China are "triadic patents" (patents filed jointly in the patent offices of Japan, the United States, and European Union). Some 76% of the patents filed in China by Chinese nationals cover only minor improvements and changes; and that the rate of abandonment of patents is exceptionally high: in 2018, 91% of design patents granted in 2013 became invalid because their holders failed to pay maintenance fees. After five years, the rate of abandonment for utility model and invention patents were 61% and 37%, respectively (in the US, the same rate was 14% for patents). In the first half of 2019, the trend showed a decline in patent applications (649,000, down 9.4% from 2018), but an increase in the number of patents approved (238,000 invention patents granted from January to June 2019, up 9.9% year-on-year). Looking inside these patent applications, it is important to note that the overwhelming majority of filings comes from Chinese companies, but the success rate for these applications was only 26% in 2018, whereas it reached 68% for non-residents (in the US, the success rate is broadly equal, at around 50% for both categories).

5.2   Europe's long run towards the unitary patent

Europe has struggled a lot to develop a common patent system. The Commission has been advocating a Community (then Unitary) patent since the Lisbon Strategy;[46] but in reality, attempts to build a unified European patent system date back to 1959 (Granieri and Renda, 2010). In 2009, under the Swedish presidency of the Union, the Commission took a number of significant steps, such as the publication of a Draft Agreement and Statute for new Unified Patent Litigation System, and a Recommendation to the Council to open negotiations for the adoption of the Agreement creating the UPLS. Finally, at the end of 2012, agreement was reached between the European Council and European Parliament on the two EU regulations that made the unitary patent possible through enhanced cooperation at EU level. Today, all EU member states except Spain and Croatia participate in the enhanced cooperation for a unitary patent. 16 member states have already ratified the Agreement on a Unified Patent Court and there is good reason to believe that the new system will start with close to 20 states, in mid-2019. A study published on 14 November 2017 by the EPO found that the Unitary Patent could significantly enhance technology transfer in the EU through more trade and foreign direct investment (EPO, 2017). Behrens et al. (2018) estimate that the cost savings due to the introduction of a Unitary Patent might stem from lower translation costs, lower fees for publishing the patent (incl. agent fees), and lower renewal fees.[47]

However, now that the unitary patent and the related litigation system are finally becoming a reality, interest in the prospective benefits appears to be hitting a new low. A simple Google trends analysis of the words "unitary patent" (Figure 20, below) shows that the estimated interest is today one quarter of what it used to be in 2012, when the agreement on the unitary patent was reached.

Is the unitary patent a real hidden treasure? The estimates show that the unitary patents, if well designed, implemented and enforced, could be a game changer for innovation in the EU, especially if coupled with a streamlined, mission-oriented research and innovation policy with clear technology transfer rules (see above, Chapter 4). At the same time, there seems to be room to make the European Unitary Patent a strategic asset for the EU: as the US drowns in the crisis of its patent system, and seems far from developing a solution to its patent backlog; and as China still struggles with gigantic numbers and limited quality of the reviews, European patents could be used as a true 'quality seal', which guarantees novelty and a true inventive step. In other words, obtaining a European patent could become a way to escape the 'noise' generated by bad quality patents around the world, just like obtaining a certification of compliance could become an export product for new technologies such as artificial intelligence (see below, Chapter 10).

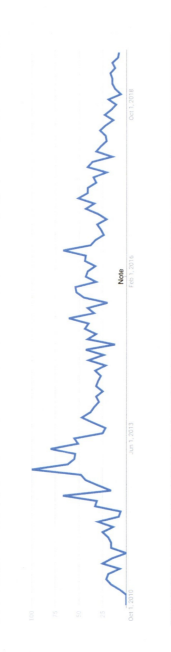

Figure 20. Google trends chart for "Unitary Patent", 1/1/2010 - 24/08/2019

However, just as the unitary patent enters its last mile, the European Patent Office seems to have experienced a deeply problematic phase over the past few years, also due to the fact that the Office was in deep financial trouble back in 2010. Since then, attempts to improve the efficiency of the patent examination process have been criticised as potentially leading to a drop in the quality of the review: recent cases in which this risk has surfaced include, *inter alia*, the *Perindropil* case.[48] In March 2018, a letter from nearly 924 patent examiners denounced a fall in patent quality, mostly attributed to an intentional push by EPO management to approve more, rather than better patents. Examiners complained that they are evaluated based on criteria, such as the number of 'products', which are not a correct lens through which to assess their performance. Moreover, renowned law firms recently criticised the drastic cuts in the time allocated to the examination of patents, which negatively reverberated on quality. The main concerns are that the new incentive system and internal directives at the EPO increasingly lean towards rewarding or even requesting rapid termination of proceedings and a correspondingly higher productivity. This, according to a prominent German law firm, resulted in penalisation of detailed and thorough assessment of cases.[49]

In conclusion, it seems essential to put measures in place to protect and relaunch a high-quality patent system in Europe: this could improve patent justice and certainty and restore the patent system in Europe as a catalyst of innovation efforts and investment. This move may imply an increase in the quantity and quality of staff, as well as a change in the performance evaluation criteria examiners are subject to. Below, we offer some policy recommendations to strengthen the European patent system in its role as a world-class 'quality seal'.

5.3 Policy recommendations

5.3.1 Time is of the essence: expand the resources available to the EPO to allow for fast, high-quality handling of applications

For large and small companies, when it comes to intellectual property protection timing is at least as important as cost. A number of measures could be implemented, which would improve the functioning of the European patent system in this crucial respect.

First, ideally the handling of patent applications in the EPO should feature a fixed term. As the granting of a patent is crucial for SMEs to attract finance and subsequently expanding, a fixed term greatly facilitates negotiations and planning, including in the context of negotiations with larger companies (see above, Chapter 4). In order to avoid losses in quality, this would require an expansion of the EPO divisions.

Second, the appeals process in the case of decisions that reject patent applications should be re-designed to offer more transparency and efficiency. At present, the appeals board is not bound by any deadlines, and procedures can last up to four years. This is again a matter of resources: in 2016 the Board of Appeals had as many as 23 vacant positions for Technical Members. These positions appear to have been filled in 2018, as the Administrative Council of the EPO approved 23 additional technically qualified member posts for the 2019 budget, and has positively noted the request for another 16 of such posts for the 2020 budget. In view of these developments, the Board of Appeals observed in its latest Annual Report that it is well on track to meet its five-year objective to settle 90% of cases within 30 months of receipt and to reduce the number of pending cases to less than 7,000 (EPO, 2019). However, due to a large increase in incoming cases, backlog and pendency will nevertheless continue to grow in the short term, and a careful monitoring of this issue is warranted if the EU is to keep its leadership in the quality of the patent system.

5.3.2 A more SME-friendly patent system

SMEs require a patent system suitable to their needs. A recent study by the EPO and EUIPO (2019) confirms that SMEs with prior IPR activities are more likely to grow than other SMEs. More specifically, SMEs that have filed at least one IPR petition are 21% more likely to experience a subsequent growth period, and 10% more likely to become a high-growth firm. Importantly, the likelihood that an SME experiences a high-growth period is 17% higher for SMEs that have filed at least once. Filing a European IPR petition therefore provides a positive indicator of an SME's readiness to scale up its business to the European level. This is even truer for SMEs that use bundles of trade marks, patents and designs.

There is a growing consensus that the Unitary Patent will lead to a more SME-friendly system. According to the European association of Chambers of Commerce and Industry (Eurochambres), the new patent system will prove more efficient than the current patchwork of national regimes and will significantly increase access to patents for SMEs. In this respect, it would further help if the EPO, while maintaining high standards of review, lowered the cost of patent applications and maintenance for SMEs, to be compensated by higher fees for larger companies.

Another area in which improvements are possible is in intermediation. There, the Commission should work with member states to stimulate competition among commercial patent lawyers, since in many member states oligopolies have been established, which increase the cost for SMEs. Alternatively, government agencies could provide application services as part of "soft support infrastructure" for SMEs (see above, Chapter 4). Such services are already provided by the Technology Transfer Offices of many universities: these offices could be consolidated to improve service levels and to introduce specialisation. Available evidence confirms that uncertainties related to the patenting process can affect the propensity of individual researchers and SMEs to make full use of the patent system and engage in licensing activities (Renda et al., forthcoming). The European Commission is reportedly working on creating a network of intermediaries formed by public or private entities involved in IP and/or business support, and will provide information on the European patent, on the availability of this funding scheme and will channel financial support to successful candidates among innovative SMEs. A coordination office will be set up to coordinate and monitor the implementation of the measure.

More generally, the European Commission has been working on supporting the use of the patent system by SMEs, which is considered to be "minimal" at present. This includes providing IP pre-diagnostic services to innovative SMEs and improving SMEs' access to patent protection, to secure better returns on investment for innovative and creative SMEs. As stated by the European Commission, "providing information on the business use of patents and providing financial support for European Patent registration costs, external legal advice costs, as well as patent litigation insurance costs will contribute to promoting access to other markets within the EU as well as growth amongst European SMEs". This support will be provided for the Unitary Patent only.

Finally, there is a need to work on SMEs' access to justice when it comes to IPRs. Evidence shows that while the cost of filing court proceedings to enforce IPRs, and in particular patents, is relatively low, the total cost of those proceedings is beyond the reach of many SMEs.[50] Moreover, in the case of controversies with large companies it becomes prohibitively costly for SMEs to sustain litigation for a long time. Once again, as in Chapter 1, we stumble against access to justice as a key problem that prevents a hidden treasure (the EU patent system) emerging and achieving its full potential to contribute to EU growth. Specific measures that can mitigate this problem include the introduction of court fees discount and reimbursements for SMEs, support measures to pay for lawyers' costs, lowering the 'loser pays ceiling' for SMEs and issuing guarantees/bonds required from SMEs seeking provisional measures such as injunctions.

6. Competition Policy:
Should Europe beg to differ?

6.1 A transatlantic divide

The European Union developed a body of antitrust rules long after the United States, but competition rules have existed in different forms and shapes in many European countries since the early 20th century. Antitrust in its modern conception was born on the other side of the Atlantic, with the first laws enacted in Canada (1989) and the United States (1890). The Sherman Act, still probably the most prominent and influential piece of antitrust legislation worldwide, was essentially a piece of tort law, passed by Congress to challenge the crystallisation of power in heavy industries such as oil and steel at the end of the 19th century. There was no competition authority (it would come only in 1914, with the FCT Act), and there was no plan to enforce antitrust law as part of administrative law. The underlying logic of US antitrust law was essentially that of the invisible hand, or "private attorney generals": by empowering individual firms and citizens to sue for damages caused by infringements of the Sherman Act, the public interest in competitive markets would essentially be served by the private interest in having damages compensated.

The scope of the Sherman Act remained intimately connected with this original rationale: subsequent refinements, with the exception of the 1936 Robinson-Patman Act, which was gradually discarded by courts, were in the direction of maximising the deterrence potential of antitrust rules by sharpening procedures and creating an overall, pro-plaintiff environment. Treble damages, opt-out class actions, one-way fee-shifting rules, the use of contingency fees to remunerate lawyers, as well as the discovery process, gradually distanced US antitrust from a culture of compensation, towards a culture of litigation (Renda et al., 2008; Renda, 2016).

Today, despite the existence of a public prosecutor (the Federal Trade Commission), US antitrust remains essentially a matter for private enforcement and FBI investigations (in the case of cartels): more than 90% of the cases are private, and almost all of them are settled before trial, very often confidentially. Companies routinely purchase before-the-event insurance, knowing that litigation will come. In terms of scope, the legislation became gradually sharper and more minimalistic, with a clear influence from the Chicago School of economics (overall, rather conservative in contemplating intervention in markets), even if later mitigated by so-called post-Chicago approaches (Crane, 2009; Hovenkamp, 2009). Today, scholars often consider the coverage of EU antitrust law as insufficient to guarantee competitive markets. Gutierrez Gallardo and Philippon (2017) observe that since the early 2000s US industries have become more concentrated and profitable and find evidence in favour of decreasing domestic competition among possible alternative explanations.

On this side of the Atlantic, and particularly in continental Europe, the evolution of competition legislation was completely different. Already in 1909, Germany adopted an Unfair Competition Act (*Gesetz gegen unlauteren Wettbewerb*, UWG), which was rooted in civil law and thus left to private enforcement. The UWG gave competitors the right to take action for injunctive relief and damages regarding unfair competition: the concept of fairness, based on the concept of *boni mores*, was completely separate from the notion of neoclassical economic efficiency that underpins antitrust intervention both in the US and (officially) in the EU today. Rather, it was related to the protection of competitors from defamation and misleading advertising and aimed at protecting a sound rivalry between enterprises based on reasonably good behaviour. In England, the common law system conceived of unfairness in a totally different way: on several occasions judges in England and Wales reiterated the difficulty of defining what is 'fair' and what is not; and to use fairness as a litmus test for any finding of tort.[51] In a nutshell, as observed by Wadlow (2007), the positions of civil and common law on fairness, fair trading and fair competition have traditionally exhibited "the polarity of irreconcilable opposites".

The largest divergence between the two approaches is the clear focus on the consumer in English law, reiterated in the US through landmark decisions. In Germany, the duty of fair trading imposed under UWG 1909 was primarily owed to one's competitors (interpreted in the broadest possible sense) and to the relevant business community at large, and was enforceable by them and by various trade associations dedicated to stamping out trade practices that their membership or their executive considered undesirable. The unfair competition rule spread through several countries in continental Europe and is present in the Civil Codes or Commercial Codes of several member states, generally as part of tort law, and normally focused on misleading advertising and conduct aimed at intentionally discrediting rivals (Ullrich, 2005). This more protective approach towards competitors also explains why, in continental Europe, legislation on comparative advertising took so long to be introduced, and still faces important challenges in its implementation.

The 'European difference' in the approach to competition was also clearly visible and influential when the Treaty of Rome was drafted. In particular, scholars have attributed the specific wording and overall meaning given to Article 86 (today Article 102 TFEU) to the influence of Ordoliberalism (aka the "Freiburg School"), mostly led by Walter Eucken and Franz Böhm in the 1930s, and partly developed in opposition to the Nazi regime (Larouche and Schinkel, 2014; Gerber, 1998; Akman, 2009; Patel and Schweizer, 2013). Not surprisingly, Article 102 TFEU explicitly includes *"unfair trading conditions"* and *"unfair prices"* within the prohibition. This would explain, at least partly, the persistence of diverging approaches and concepts in EU as opposed to US antitrust, which remain notwithstanding the similar wording of the provisions on abuse of dominance or monopolisation contained in Chapter 2 of the Sherman Act and in Article 102 TFEU. For example, EU antitrust enforcers regularly apply the 'essential facilities' doctrine whenever competitors cannot easily replicate an asset or an information set held by a dominant player; whereas this doctrine was never endorsed by the US Supreme Court (Renda, 2010). Moreover, EU antitrust still attributes a special responsibility to dominant firms, which in some CJEU decisions such as *Telia Sonera* even implied a *de facto* responsibility to ensure the profitability of smaller competitors (Petit, 2014).

Furthermore, the enforcement of EU competition law is dramatically different from that of US antitrust. While the overwhelming majority of cases are privately enforced (and settled) in the US, more than 95% of cases are publicly enforced by competition authorities in the EU, and do not end with requests for damage awards, but rather with administrative sanctions. A much lower share of cases is settled in the EU, and procedural rules for private enforcement are much less oriented towards deterrence, and much more towards corrective justice (Renda, 2016). This difference remains despite the adoption of a Directive on Private Antitrust Damages Actions (2014/104/EU, entered into force on 26 December 2014), later complemented by a Commission Recommendation on collective redress and a Practical Guide on quantifying antitrust harm in damages actions, and only very recently implemented by some member states.

Figure 21. Countries with rules on abuse of economic dependence, 2011

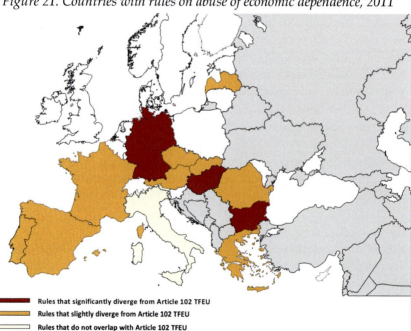

Rules that significantly diverge from Article 102 TFEU
Rules that slightly diverge from Article 102 TFEU
Rules that do not overlap with Article 102 TFEU

Source: Renda (2011).

But divergences do not end here. Outside of competition law, and outside of unfair competition, a different stream of legal rules emerged over time in the interstice between contract and tort law, to capture those cases in which despite the absence of a clear antitrust concern, one party in the contract can be considered as having a superior bargaining position, and/or the other party a position of economic dependence. Renda et al. (2011) map the emergence of these rules in EU member states, finding a wide variety of rules as shown in Figure 21 above. Very often, these rules are enforced by the competition authorities, as it the case for the *Bundeskartellamt* in Germany, and the AGCM in Italy.

Besides general provisions on significant imbalances in commercial relationships, which initially focused mostly on cases of industrial subcontracting, legislators in member states have also gradually focused on specific sectors, such as food and retail. In these sectors, small suppliers are often in a situation of economic dependence vis-à-vis large retailers, and generally refrain from suing their large counterparts in cases of unfair trading practices (e.g. de-listing, risk-shifting, unfavourable contract renegotiation, etc.), for fear of retaliation (Renda et al., 2014). Over the past three decades, many member states have tackled this problem, either by stretching antitrust law beyond the rather narrow boundaries of Article 102 TFEU, by relying on unfair competition laws, laws on abuse of economic dependence, rules on the abuse of "relative dominant position" (e.g. in France), contract law, or simply ad hoc legal provisions for the agri-food or the general retail sector (like the UK Grocery Act) (Boy, 2006).

The stark divergence between US and EU competition rules is mirrored by the divergence between the provisions on dominance contained in Article 102 TFEU and those applied, both within and outside the realm of antitrust legislation, at the member state level. But the real surprise is that, while until the middle of this decade the orientation of DG COMP was towards reducing this level of fragmentation by bringing back national competition rules to converge with the (narrower) scope of Article 102 TFEU, in line with what Regulation 1/2003 already had achieved for Article 101[52]; the past four years, in particular with Commissioner Vestager's tenure, have led to an important new set of developments.

6.2 A new 'age of fairness' in EU competition law?

Commissioner Vestager has made frequent reference to the concept of fairness as an inspiring principle of her mandate as Competition Commissioner. In her speeches, the word 'fair' appears to be far more recurrent than the word 'efficient'. Vestager also argued that the concept of fairness plays a "substantial role" in helping the Commission to prioritise cases. She even evoked in a speech the Code of Hammurabi, arguing it ensured "the market worked fairly by regulating the prices for things like hiring a ferryboat".[53] She also added that this "doesn't mean that just because something is unfair, it's automatically also against the competition rules". But her overall approach have left a clear impression that fairness is more central to the rhetoric and scope of competition law in Europe than it was in the past.

Fairness was high on the agenda also on the regulatory side, especially if one considers the recent proposed directive on unfair trading practices in business-to-business relationships in the food supply chain (COM/2018/0173 final, presented in April 2018); the P2B Regulation on promoting fairness and transparency for business users of online intermediation services, on which a political agreement was finally reached in 2019; and to some extent the Second Payment Services Directive (PSD2). Both initiatives acknowledge the need to capture, through regulatory measures, situations in which EU antitrust law cannot be invoked, but the imbalance of bargaining power nevertheless creates the need for restorative measures, or the prohibition of certain practices.

The latter proposal appears the most indicative of the change of approach in the Commission. In its impact assessment of the draft regulation, the Commission identifies as problems the multiplication of P2B unfair terms and practices, an enforcement gap and a fragmentation of the digital single market (De Streel, 2018). It proposes more transparency on the terms and practices of the online intermediation platforms and, in some cases, online search engines, as well as better dispute resolution mechanisms.

What seems to emerge from these developments is that the Commission has spotted a hidden treasure: rather than over-stretching traditional antitrust tools that have become increasingly difficult to apply, especially in the digital world, the Commission can tap into an extremely rich national experience that extends the reach of competition-related rules way beyond the remit of Article 102 TFEU: and rather than being an obstacle, this now seems to be an opportunity. In fact, in the US a similar, but far more timid development has led to the re-discovery of a provision, Chapter 5 of the FTC Act, which prohibits, among other things, unfair or deceptive acts or practices in the marketplace (Davis, 2019).

6.3 Should Europe be ashamed of protecting smaller competitors?

A mantra in each and every antitrust debate around the world is that competition rules are there "to protect consumers, not competitors" (Fox, 2003). Students of antitrust learn this on the first day, practitioners repeat it whenever useful and strategic. However, the meaning of these words changes depending on time, place and backing interests. Ultimately, the rationale behind this statement is controversial, for two main reasons.

First, there is still a heated and unresolved debate in the domain of competition law on whether antitrust rules should pursue consumer welfare, or total welfare. Some commentators have even argued that the first and foremost advocate of the consumer welfare standard, Robert Bork, improperly used the term, creating a false dichotomy with the total welfare one (Blair and Sokol, 2012; Werden, 2014). In reality, if one considers antitrust law as a public policy intervention triggered by a market failure, it would make sense to adopt a total welfare standard, in line with what happens for all efficiency-oriented public policies in the United States and, to a large extent, in Europe (Renda, 2018). Neoclassical economics traditionally disregard distributional impacts, which would otherwise be embedded in a consumer welfare standard (Hovenkamp, 2019).

Second, while the original emphasis on consumer welfare can be justified, and can be traced back to the years of the 'discovery' of consumerism, today the evolution of markets portrays situations in which, alongside cases of exploitative abuses in the form of high prices and welfare-decreasing discrimination, some of the most important cases are related to the exploitation of sheer size, economies of scale and network effects to preserve and consolidate dominance, depriving competitors of sufficient scale to operate viably in the market. When this happens on a sufficient scale, the protection of competitors becomes essential to ensure that the competitive constraints exercised by rivalry are preserved in the relevant product market: thence, the dichotomy between consumers and competition vanishes, and protecting competitors becomes a way to protect the competitive process, and therefore ultimately consumers.

Accordingly, different competition authorities have adopted diverging approaches to the 'consumer harm' standard in antitrust, and the latter has become so widely debated that some authoritative commentators even proposed its replacement with more easily interpretable alternatives. For example, Steinbaum and Stucke (2018) argue in favour of an "effective competition standard" as an alternative to the consumer welfare standard, explaining that the "price-centric" approach that flows from the consumer welfare standard misses important metrics such as harm to quality, privacy, innovation, and input providers, including workers[54]. In a widely read article that inspired the so-called Neo-Brandeisian antitrust movement, Lina Khan (2018) made a similar point by arguing that "the current framework in antitrust – specifically its pegging competition to 'consumer welfare', defined as short-term price effects – is unequipped to capture the architecture of market power in the modern economy". Glick (2018) takes sides with the Neo-Brandeisians, but rather than attacking the consumer welfare standard for its unacceptable outcomes, it argues that such an approach is "theoretically flawed and unrigorous from the start". More sceptical, equally authoritative views have been provided by Hovenkamp (2019) and Melamed and Petit (2019).

Third, regardless of the merits of competing approaches in antitrust, one could also observe that not only the underlying theoretical approaches, but also the economic structure of markets and individual preferences is different in Europe compared to the United States, and that the consumer welfare versus total welfare debate may not be a perfect fit for EU competition law, which may well look at the protection of smaller competitors (more important in Europe than in the US in relative economic terms, as shown in Chapter 2) in order to avoid that the accumulation of market power in a few hands ends up disrupting the otherwise-preferred fragmentation and pluralism as key features of truly competitive markets. In other words, if one considers that EU competition law is still deeply rooted in Ordoliberalism, then it may well be the case that approaches that are rejected in the United States become viable when it comes to Europe. Or, put differently, if it is true that Neo-Brandeisian antitrust is based on an untested assumption (i.e. that citizens prefer higher prices and more firms than lower prices and a more concentrated market), it is equally true that in Europe, citizen preferences may look different from how they appear in the United States. Should, then, Europe beg to differ?

6.4 Uncovering the hidden treasure: policy recommendations for the future of EU antitrust

Sound competition rules are essential for a smooth functioning of the market. In particular, in the age of open innovation and the platform economy, many SMEs depend on larger counterparties for access to the market, and in more industrial sectors also for more practical reasons, such as testing their prototypes technically and commercially and also to scale production, marketing and sales. They often lack the financial resources and specialised staff to deal with more than one potential partner at a time, and this further exacerbates their situation of economic dependence and the transaction-specific investments they have to face to establish a suitable commercial relationship with larger companies.

Whether this situation is becoming more widespread, and the imbalance of bargaining power more evident over time, should be subject to a specific investigation of the Commission. If the extent of the problem is as significant as it seems, this could mark the official introduction of B2B and P2B unfair commercial practices in the scope of EU competition rules and should be accompanied by an extension of the enforcement powers of DG COMP to include such practices.

Below, we provide some policy recommendations for the next European Commission.

6.4.1 Extend the scope of EU competition rules to protect SMEs against unfair commercial practices

SMEs are not adequately protected by existing competition rules, despite the ongoing debate about Europe's tendency to protect smaller competitors. As observed in the previous chapters of this book, the emergence of new organisational forms for innovation, from open innovation to platforms, can put SMEs in a position of unprecedented advantage, but also creates a risk of their being subject to abuse in their relationship with larger corporations. Accordingly, rules on abuse of economic dependency and abuse of superior bargaining power may not only be needed in specific sectors such as retail and digital platforms; rather, the Commission could consider proposing their introduction in all sectors, provided that they are accompanied by adequate provisions for access to justice, support for IP litigation, and a clear indication of the types of behaviours that are considered to be exploitative, discriminatory or simply unfair.

In this respect, some European countries (most recently, Belgium) have decided to extend the scope of the EU Unfair Commercial Practices Directive (UCPD), originally focused on B2C relationships, to also cover B2B settings. Recently, with respect to the P2B Regulation, the Commission observed that consumer law instruments were not considered appropriate to deal with B2B relations, since extending consumer law to P2B issues would be disproportionate. Moreover, the Court of Justice specifically dealt with the issue of the possible application of the UCPD in B2B settings in its ruling on the case C-295/16 *Europamur Alimentación SA*, but the case was mostly about jurisdiction issues, rather than on substantive policy.

The European Commission reported in 2015 that only "four Member States currently apply, with some modulation, the UCPD also to B2B relations", and that "the extension, at EU level, of the scope of the UCPD to B2B relations has been mooted in the past by some stakeholders mainly with a view to solving the problem of the practices of Misleading Directory Companies affecting mainly small enterprises and independent professionals", practices that are already forbidden by Directive 2006/114/EC on misleading and comparative advertising. Meanwhile, however, other countries are joining the list (recently, Belgium). The Commission should reopen this dossier, with a view to providing adequate protection to SMEs beyond digital platforms and large retail markets.

Finally, ensuring adequate protection and legal certainty for SMEs also requires suitable enforcement arrangements. In most countries that have enacted rules that capture imbalances of bargaining power in commercial or industrial relationships, the competition authority has been tasked with enforcement. Whether the same could be done in Europe, or a separate authority located outside DG COMP would be the best place to address these controversies, is an issue that we leave to EU institutions, and to future research.

6.4.2 Consider the adoption of an effective and sustainable competition standard in antitrust decisions

As recalled by Ezrachi (2018), "the promotion of consumer well-being and the prevention of consumer harm have long been established as the prime goals of competition law". The General Court observed in *Österreichische Postsparkasse and Bank für Arbeit und Wirtschaft v Commission* that "the ultimate purpose of the rules that seek to ensure that competition is not distorted in the internal market is to increase the well-being of consumers... Competition law and competition policy... have an undeniable impact on the specific economic interests of final customers who purchase goods or services". Mario Monti famously observed, when dealing with the *Microsoft* case, that "competition policy puts markets at the service of consumers... After all we say the consumer is king!"; his successor Neelie Kroes observed that "the Commission has made an important choice in putting consumer interests at the centre of our competition work"; and Commissioner Almunia also said that "all of us here today know very well what our ultimate objective is: competition policy is a tool at the service of consumers."

However, it is important to clarify that the focus on consumers does not mean legitimising conduct that thwarts competition to offer short-term relief in terms of lower consumer prices. Conduct such as predation, but also controversial cases of above-cost predatory pricing, can be configured as ultimately detrimental for consumers' well-being (Edlin, 2002; Elhauge, 2003). This is why the Commission and the Courts have often juggled with the concept of consumer welfare, in order to avoid that it becomes a straitjacket, or even an obstacle towards the realisation of the Commission's own vision of the single market. In some cases, e.g. in *Telia Sonera,* the Court of Justice even ventured into rather acrobatic interpretations of the principle of the "special responsibility" of dominant firms, another doctrine that is well established in Europe, and nowhere to be seen in the United States. Moreover, market integration is included as one of the overarching objectives of EU competition law, alongside economic efficiency: but which type of market integration should be placed at the forefront of competition law enforcement? And in what way would market integration interact with economic efficiency?

In the forthcoming reform of EU competition rules, it would be extremely useful if the Commission could clarify what is the role of antitrust in pursuing economic efficiency, fairness and market integration, and how will the interplay between these concepts be approached in the future. Note that this is a direct consequence of our reasoning in the first five chapters of this book: if Europe chooses to 'dance to a different drummer' in its economic policy, and pursue a more SME-centric policy leading to a less concentrated market structure and thus more choice for consumers, then its approach to antitrust will not resemble the one advocated by the Chicago School in the US, in which monopolies should not be stopped when they are essentially the result of fierce competition, a view that was perfectly summarised by the views of Judge Scalia in cases like *Trinko*.[55] The idea of loosening antitrust rules to promote more innovation has not proven its full worth in decades of antitrust history. Even in the US, an authoritative Chief Judge, Diane Wood of the US Court of Appeals for the Seventh Circuit, recently expressed concerns about the political consequences of monopolisation, and observed that the distribution of power "is essential not just in economic markets but for political stability". Not far from what the Freiburg School argued when thinking about competition and market structure.

6.4.3 *Refrain from political oversight of antitrust decisions*

Competition rules are, and should remain, essentially a technical field. Antitrust is not supposed to achieve industrial policy goals, and the independence of antitrust authorities was not only practised by the European Commission in past decades, but also preached to member states. The so-called ECN+ proposal of the Commission, tabled in 2017, is aimed at ensuring that competition authorities in member states "act independently when enforcing EU antitrust rules, i.e. without taking instructions from public or private entities". Directive (EU) 2019/1 to empower the competition authorities of member states to be more effective enforcers and to ensure the proper functioning of the internal market was eventually signed into law on 11 December 2018, and aims to ensure that national competition authorities have the appropriate enforcement tools in order to bring about a genuine common competition enforcement area.

However, when the stakes become too high, the temptation to take over competences otherwise allocated to technical bodies is always strong. This is currently the case, especially after DG Competition, led by Commissioner Vestager, decided to reject the proposed mega-merger between Alstom and Siemens. The French Minister for Economic and Financial Affairs Bruno Le Maire described European competition rules as obsolete, while German Chancellor Angela Merkel expressed doubts on the EU's ability to create global players. France and Germany published a joint manifesto to revive EU industrial policy around three pillars, which included the revision of European competition rules. The manifesto proposes the creation of a "Phase III" in merger review, which would amount to a political review of merger decisions, possibly by the Council (although the body tasked with the review is not specified in the manifesto).

This move, in our opinion, would be a fatal mistake. Europe does not need to subvert its credo on competition rules to return to meaningful industrial policy. And as already explained, achieving size by artificially creating large players that would end up capturing massive market shares is not the best way to serve the interest of European citizens, consumers and SMEs. In many sectors, consolidation across borders is of course possible, especially where there are no significant overlaps between national markets, and the merger thus simply contributes to 'bonding' the single market closer together by enabling businesses to cross intra-EU borders. At the same time, as will also be recalled in Chapter 10, in many sectors of the economy, and in particular those where digitalisation is happening fast, the creation of European giants is not the only way to create a dynamic and prosperous single market. Our claim is that EU institutions can chart their own path towards an approach to competition rules that is tailored to the legal and economic traditions of the Old Continent, rather than emulating the United States, or China.

7. TAXES: CAN EUROPE OUTPERFORM THE REST OF THE WORLD?

Taxation is one of the pillars of the modern organisation of the state. Through direct and indirect tax collection, governments internalise externalities, provide services of general interest, and achieve redistribution of resources among citizens and businesses. Principles such as fair and progressive taxation are widely acknowledged in all developed countries, and lay the foundation for social cohesion, economic prosperity and overall sustainability. In the context of the EU's single market, the reduction and elimination of barriers to cross-border trade and the protection and promotion of the 'four freedoms' created the need for cooperation between national authorities, mostly to avoid double taxation of enterprises. In addition, the need to coordinate taxation policy to create a level playing field in the single market has emerged as a necessity, alongside the need to avoid that companies, in particular multinationals, exploit loopholes and divergences in the EU tax system to artificially reduce their tax exposures.

Minimum standards have been achieved on the quality of tax code and tax rulings in the EU-27. However, as observed by the European Parliament in 2016, the current state of tax policy worldwide is increasingly characterised by massive evasion and avoidance, to the detriment of social justice. The 'Panama Papers' and the 'LuxLeaks' scandal have raised awareness of the need to fight tax evasion, tax avoidance and aggressive tax planning more effectively. In January 2016 the European Parliamentary Research Service published a study that assessed the loss of tax revenue to the EU through aggressive corporate tax planning to be between €50 billion and €70 billion *per annum*, which becomes three times bigger if one adds special tax arrangements, inefficiencies in collection and other practices. The Commission provided a much less conservative estimate, placing tax evasion and avoidance at €1 trillion per year. Most aggressive tax planning exploits loopholes and enforcement deficiencies in bilateral tax treaties and mismatches in cross-border accounting practices, openings abused in particular by multinational groups and resulting in profit shifting towards jurisdictions with lower tax rates.

Since June 2013, the Commission has been investigating individual tax rulings of member states under EU state aid rules. It extended this information inquiry to all member states in December 2014. This ongoing trend should not overshadow the overall good quality of tax administrations and rulings in the EU, which largely surpasses that of the US. The US continues to rank at the top of financial secrecy indices.[56] Since the 1920s, the US has adopted measures aimed at attracting foreign capital to the country: today, the US still refuses to comply with the emerging global standard of multilateral information exchange, the OECD Common Reporting Standards (CRS), and maintains its Fair and Accurate Credit Transactions Act (FATCA) model, rather than adhering to the CRS. As observed by Noked (2018), the experience so far raises numerous questions about the effectiveness of FATCA's reporting regime.[57]

Against this background, Europe seems to fare a lot better than the US when it comes to the reliability and effectiveness of the tax system. This treasure is however hidden due to the great heterogeneity of tax regimes and, most importantly, the overall lack of cooperation between member states, which leaves numerous loopholes that multinationals can exploit to reduce their overall tax exposure, and thereby also undermine tax justice in the EU. Years of calls and attempts to improve cooperation have merely created an appearance of cooperation. Only real legislative action, such as that started by the 2003 harmonisation of taxation of savings, can lead to effective progress. A clear perspective in the EU integration process towards more fiscal union is needed for this to happen. The recent 'leaks' may have advanced the debate about EU and global initiatives to tackle tax evasion, but this is only the beginning of a huge agenda.

7.1 Tax harmonisation in the EU: an historical account

A process for more cooperation amongst tax authorities started with the Monti Group, that was only recently re-launched, in the context of the debate around tax avoidance scandals, affecting both corporations as individuals. So far, it has led to soft, rather than hard actions, with the exception of the tax on personal savings.

The 1992 programme in the area of direct taxation produced two directives and an arbitration convention, while several other proposals had to be abandoned. The two directives deal with the abolition of double taxation of associated enterprises operating on a cross-border basis in the EU. The parent/subsidiary directive (90/435/EEC) exempts dividends paid between associated companies from taxation, the merger directive (90/434/EEC) eases cross-border company restructuring operations from a fiscal perspective. Both directives, while being useful, were narrow, and earlier attempts by the European Commission in 1993 to expand their scope failed. Moreover, the implementation by member states has given rise to doubts. The Arbitration Convention created a mechanism for the settlement of disputes between enterprises and tax administrations related to the level of taxation. The limited success of harmonisation in the field of corporate taxes demonstrated that the EU would first need to institute more cooperation between enterprises, if it wished to achieve more convergence in tax regimes.

An EU process for effective cooperation amongst tax authorities was initiated by the then Commissioner Mario Monti, with the creation of the code of conduct or Primarolo group in 1997, named after the UK Paymaster General, to bring about more convergence among corporate tax regimes in the EU. A code of conduct was agreed between the member states composed of a 'standstill and rollback' process to stop aggressive and harmful tax competition between member states and abolish the most distortive schemes. But the process stalled, and the 'Luxleaks' controversy of late 2014 indicated that not much had been achieved. Member states compete as much with each other as with third countries to attract foreign direct investment or facilitate business development and want to maintain their freedom to create the conditions to do so. Although this process is harmful in relation to less mobile factors of taxation, such as labour, and to other member states, it seems that this has not yet led to more tax harmonisation. While it could be argued that such a process stimulates fiscal discipline, the excesses revealed by Luxleaks indicate that it erodes tax revenues and should be seen as contrary to what the EU stands for.

7.1.1 The Savings Tax Directive

Progress was however made in the domain of personal savings taxation, with the adoption in 2003 of the Savings Tax Directive. This directive instituted a system of automatic exchange of information amongst member states about interest income obtained by their residents in other member states. It was the result of a long negotiation process, starting in 1989 with the agreement on the liberalisation of capital movements. Initially, it was envisaged to have full and automatic exchange of information, but certain member states, including Austria, Belgium and Luxembourg, wanted to maintain bank secrecy and requested a similar agreement with third countries, most importantly Switzerland and other small offshore financial centres. In the end, a transition period was agreed during which these three member states would transfer a part of the tax on interest income to the resident's home member state without revealing the identity of the beneficiary, which in the case of Austria ended only in 2014. The same arrangement continues to apply to Switzerland and Liechtenstein, and other offshore jurisdictions.

Seen in hindsight, the 2003 agreement was probably of merely symbolic importance. It only covered interest income and was not applicable to dividend income or capital gains, which in today's low interest rate environment are much more important. It was also calculated that the information shared about interest income had serious shortcomings, or that the revenues transferred from the countries that did not apply the automatic exchange of information was limited, meaning that the enforcement left much to be desired (Corry and Mather, 2012). However, it contributed to the overall acceptance of the principle of exchange of information in the EU, a trend that has spread more widely in the meantime.

The Savings Tax Directive was followed up by the 2011 directive (2011/16/EU) on administrative cooperation between tax authorities, and the October 2014 Council agreement that bank accounts have to be transparent for tax authorities of other member states, something that was unthinkable only a few years before. The latter agreement brings interest, dividends and other income within the scope of cooperation. Its importance is highlighted by the fact that it was adopted by unanimity in the Council, as is required for tax matters. It was also followed up more recently by an agreement with Switzerland on 27 May 2015 on the automatic exchange information on the financial accounts of each other's residents, starting in 2018, extending the scope of the agreement equally to other forms of income, and thus doing away with the previous agreement.[58] The latter agreement indicates that the trend towards more tax cooperation will also be increasingly applied with third countries, which is a priority of the G-20 as well.

7.2 Recent moves towards coordination among EU corporate tax administrations

After years of quasi-standstill, the EU managed to make progress in international and European tax coordination in the follow-up of the media campaigns on wide-scale tax avoidance and evasion by corporations and wealthy individuals. The G-20 mandated the OECD to implement a series of measures to address base erosion and profit shifting (BEPS) and set a minimum tax transparency standard, to be reviewed regularly, as a basis for more automatic exchange of information. This was translated at EU level into the Anti-Tax Avoidance Directive (ATAD), that was rapidly adopted by the member states, and in the action to blacklist non-cooperative jurisdictions around the world.

The basis was the Commission's 2015 White Paper 'Towards a fair and efficient Corporate Tax System in the European Union', which outlined five key areas for action, with the CCCTB as the end-objective. The current system, the European Commission states, is no longer fair, as taxes are not equally spread, and large corporations shift their profits to low tax jurisdictions, whereas others are subject to double taxation. It is no longer efficient either, as the tax bases are not adapted to the intangible economy, and tax systems favour debt over equity finance.

The ATAD was agreed in five months on 21 June 2016, which is an absolute record by EU standards, and even more remarkable as EU tax measures require unanimity among member states. The directive is limited in scope, but is still far-reaching, as it sets a limit on interest costs that can be charged (in high tax jurisdictions), prevents exiting tax rules and limits the use of controlled foreign company rules to avoid taxes. It sets general intra-EU anti-hybrid (tax constructions) and anti-abuse (of tax systems) rules. During the same period, the EU also agreed on a directive as regards mandatory automatic exchange of information in the field of taxation, addressed specifically at tax practices of multinational corporations.

Coordination between member states was also improved through progress in the completion of double taxation agreements. This is a precondition to achieving a more harmonised system in the context of the single market. By the end of 2014, the proportion of double taxation agreements among the 28 EU member states reached 96%, up from 58% in the year of the creation of the single market (1992) in an EU of 12.[59] Bilateral double taxation agreements do not require the EU, however, as they are concluded with third countries as well. But they institute a high degree of cooperation among the tax administrations of the countries concerned, albeit on a bilateral level, i.e. every agreement is different.

7.3 EU tax policy today: between a utopian Common Consolidated Tax Base, and state aid rules

The next step is to agree on a more EU-wide corporate tax system, and to do away with the distortions that have been so widely publicised. In 2016, the European Commission proposed re-launching the 2011 CCCTB project by splitting it into two separate proposals.[60] CCCTB would allow corporations to consolidate their profits and losses in a single country in the EU following a harmonised tax base. Profits would then be apportioned to the different member states, in view of certain operational criteria, such as revenues, factories, workers, etc., and taxed according to the local rate, thus implying a high degree of cooperation among the member states. The 2016 proposal formally drops the 2011 one, and also the consolidation, given the problems this still causes, but makes a common corporate tax base (CCTB) mandatory. It adds rules for calculating the corporate tax base, including certain provisions against tax avoidance and on the international dimension of the proposed system. A second proposal adds rules on consolidation, awaiting agreement on the first proposal. Given the lukewarm reception by member states when it was first proposed in 2011, it is questionable whether the European Commission will be more successful this time. It is also seen as a difficult fit with the overall priority of the Juncker Commission to limit intrusive harmonisation proposals.

The European Commission's competition watchdog DG COMP nevertheless reacted to excessively generous tax practices in certain member states under the powers of the EU Treaty to tackle illegal state aid. Subsidies given to enterprises that result in very generous tax treatment distort the single market, and can be considered as illegal state aid. In October 2015, the Commission concluded that Luxembourg and the Netherlands had granted selective tax advantages to Fiat and Starbucks, respectively. As a result of these decisions, Luxembourg recovered €23.1 million from Fiat and the Netherlands recovered €25.7 million from Starbucks. Later, in January 2016, the Commission concluded that selective tax advantages granted by Belgium to at least 35 multinationals, mainly from the EU, under its "excess profit" tax scheme are illegal under EU state aid rules. The total amount of aid to be recovered from the 35 companies is estimated at approximately €900 million, including interest, of which over 90% of the aid has already been recovered. In August 2016, the Commission concluded that Ireland granted undue tax benefits to Apple, which led to a recovery by Ireland of €14.3 billion (the amount was paid by Apple to the Irish tax authorities in summer 2018). In October 2017, the Commission concluded that Luxembourg granted undue tax benefits to Amazon, which led to a recovery by Luxembourg of €282.7 million. In June 2018, the Commission concluded that Luxembourg granted undue tax benefits to Engie of around €120 million. The Commission also has one ongoing in-depth investigation concerning tax rulings issued by the Netherlands in favour of the Inter IKEA Group, and one investigation concerning a tax scheme for multinationals in the United Kingdom.

7.4 Can code succeed where politics have failed?

Corporate taxation is one of the areas where the degree of harmonisation has not matched the level of market integration or the progress achieved in other areas. Under the banking union, for example, the ECB becomes the single supervisor of all large banks in the euro area, but the tax treatment of these banks, and of the products they sell, remains entirely national and diverse. These and other developments, such as the unique competence for the EU to negotiate investment treaties, will increase the pressure for further progress in the tax field, but this is likely to continue to advance slowly, more through improved cooperation rather than in outright harmonisation, as was the case over the last 20 years. While it is true that tax coordination has advanced over the last two to three years, it must be recalled that this was the result of widely publicised cases. The ATAD and state aid investigations by DG COMP tackle the most flagrant cases, but concrete progress will only be achieved with the adoption of CCCTB, which remains a distant dream. The latter would also level the playing field between SMEs and large corporates, and remains therefore a priority.

Recently, legislative progress was made thanks to the Anti-Tax-Avoidance Package, which besides proposing the introduction of anti-avoidance rules, also aims to prevent profit shifting by introducing public Country-by-Country Reporting (CBCR) through an amendment of the European Accounting Directive.[61] All EU parent companies with a consolidated revenue of more than €750 million as well as subsidiaries of non-EU companies with a consolidated revenue above this threshold would be required to publish relevant information on an annual basis, both on their webpage and in a public register of the European Commission. The required information includes a list of all subsidiaries, the pre-tax profit, cash taxes paid, the amount of stated capital, the number of employees and several other details. All of these items have to be attributed to the individual taxing territories in which the reporting company operates.

This emerging framework could easily be coupled with RegTech solutions in the future, as is already happening in the market. The availability of tech-enabled solutions will enable the creation of an automatic data-sharing sandbox, into which multinationals could (voluntarily) enter to start exchanging data with the administration for compliance verification purposes. This system would, of course, have to be adequately coupled with technical, semantic, organisational and where possible legal interoperability between administrations, something that the ISA2 programme is trying to achieve (purely on a voluntary basis) under the leadership of DG DIGIT, and the auspices of the Tallinn Declaration of October 2017 (Renda et al., 2019). The automatic collection of direct and indirect tax across the single market would enable easier cross-border compensation and detection of aggressive tax planning schemes. This, in turn, would help Europe uncover its most hidden treasure: a high-quality tax system, oriented towards competitiveness and distributional justice.

7.5   Policy recommendations

Europe is potentially looking at a significant opportunity when it comes to taxation. The US system features a triple challenge: a highly complicated tax code, a common-law-based legal system turning a complicated code into a quagmire, and reliance on draconian measures to enforce compliance, necessitated by an antagonistic attitude to the state in general and taxes in particular, let alone a highly politicised discussion on tax rates as fuelling inequality. Chatzky (2019) recalls that US President Donald Trump signed major tax legislation, notably reducing the top rate levied on corporations from 35% to 21% and lowering individual income taxes to bring the top marginal income tax rate down from 39.6% to 37%.[62] Following the publication of Piketty's (2014) book *Capital in the 21st Century*, several scholars have produced new estimates of long-run trends in wealth concentration around the world. Gros et al. (2018) show the different patterns of inequality in the EU and in the US, with the latter featuring a constantly falling share of labour income, and a constant rise of inequality since the 1980s.

7.5.1   *Rebalance the tax treatment of large and small corporations*

The EU should tackle existing differences in the treatment of large companies and SMEs. The European Parliament has observed that recent reforms at the national level "have shifted the tax incidence from wealth to income, from capital income to labour income and consumption, from multinational enterprises to small and medium-sized enterprises (SMEs), and from the financial sector to the real economy", adding that this "has had a disproportionate impact on women and low-income people, who typically rely more on labour income and spend a higher proportion of their income on consumption".[63]

7.5.2 Establish tax incentives for the Societas Europaea, and tailor it to SMEs

Adopting the form of a *Societas Europaea* (SE) allows important simplifications in the area of company law, decreasing the cost of the companies operating in the single market, eliminating a web of different jurisdictions and legal framework applying to different subsidiaries. However, the SE does not solve the complexity of taxation, due to the lack of common regulations and full implementation across member states. Nerudova (2007) observed that adopting the SE form does not provide any meaningful tax advantage, since the SE Regulation does not cover taxation, and thus maintains the applicability of national tax law. As such, an SE must be treated as a national company, and each of its subsidiaries or branches is subject to the tax law of the country within which it is situated.

The absence of tax provisions in the SE statute never corresponded to the will of the European Commission, as stated, among others, by Commissioner Bolkestein. Extensive articles existed in the original proposal dated 1970, and were later gradually removed. Werlauff (2003) suggested that integration-friendly institutions such as the European Parliament could have wished to see uniform taxation of SEs both with respect to tax base (the calculation of taxable income), and tax rate. As stated by Meiselles and Graute (2017), "the lack of appropriate tax rules significantly reduces the practical attractiveness of the European Company Statute". The lack of such provisions also weakens the SE statute, leading companies to adopt it mostly for tax advantages, exacerbating tax competition inside the EU. Hornuf et al. (2017), for example, show that the stock price reaction is positive when the decision to incorporate as a *Societas Europaea* involves moving the firm's registered office towards jurisdictions with significantly lower corporate tax rates. Evidence suggests that corporate taxes in the countries of origin were significantly higher (27.5%) relative to the country of destination (21.8%).

Tax provisions for the SE could also be tailored to SMEs, if a dedicated SE statute is introduced for smaller companies (see above,

Chapter 3). Over the next five years, the European Commission will have an opportunity to explore these reforms as a package, to ensure that European SMEs can profit from a more sustainable and balanced business environment, and are effectively shielded from both tax and regulatory disadvantages vis-à-vis larger corporations.

7.5.3 Effectively tackle aggressive tax planning in the EU

Tørsløv et al. (2018) find that almost 40% of multinationals' profits are shifted to tax havens globally each year, with and multinational companies can pay up to 30% less tax than domestic competitors, adding that "aggressive tax planning distorts competition for domestic firms, in particular SMEs". Importantly, of the approximately $600 billion in multinational foreign profits shifted to tax havens in 2015, 30% were moved to tax havens within the EU; and 80% of the profits shifted from EU countries end up in EU tax havens, primarily Ireland, Luxembourg and the Netherlands. These countries accounted for a total of $210 billion in profit shifting. Oxfam estimated that "France, Spain, Italy and Germany lost around €35.1 billion in tax revenues in 2015 alone".

That means, that despite significant progress in tax enforcement in the EU there still remains a massive problem in the fairness of taxation and the possibility for aggressive tax planning across member states. This erodes the solidarity principle, as well as the European social model, since companies, especially large corporations, are still able to engage in forum shopping when deciding where to pay their taxes. We recommend that EU institutions tackle this issue starting from a clear standpoint on the Country-by-Country Reporting (CBCR) rules, which are still stalled in the ordinary legislative procedure, and notably in the Council – the European Commission tabled the proposed legislation in 2017 and the European Parliament massively approved it (534 to 98), even mandating that the information be published as open data to allow anyone to use it. The official reason for not proceeding with proposed rules is that public CBCR "could damage investment, by imposing additional compliance requirements and costs on companies, and forcing disclosure of sensitive taxpayer information". In addition, some stakeholders have observed that public CBCR would ignore existing differences between accounting rules and the non-harmonised tax regimes in different member states and globally. Moreover, CBCR rules would only cover EU member states.

However, all these concerns are not insurmountable obstacles, if the principle of tax transparency is shared across the spectrum of stakeholders. Once again, in order to effectively lead the debate on fair and transparent taxation at the global level, the EU should first do its homework properly: as part of a package aimed at promoting sustainable and fair business in the EU, the move towards enhanced CBCR appears to be meaningful and likely to restore the basic conditions for the European social model, as well as those for European SMEs to thrive in the single market.

Finally, the move towards a CCCTB, re-proposed in October 2016 after a first attempt in 2011, could provide a more level playing field for all companies operating in the single market. Investments such as the deployment of RegTech for regulatory monitoring and compliance purposes can help Europe exploit the quality of its tax system, coupling it with efficient and effective enforcement. Expectations are that the CCCTB would lift investment in the EU by 3.4% and growth by up to 1.2%. But formal adoption by the EU's Council of Ministers is not expected any time soon.

8. A COMMITMENT TO ERADICATE CORRUPTION

North-western EU member states rank consistently among the top performers in the world in terms of corruption control. Taking the EU as a whole, even though there are gaps in performance, the bloc comes out ahead of most of G20 countries, as reflected in a range of indicators like the Corruption Perception Index, the Global Competitiveness Report, or the Worldwide Governance Indicators. This makes Europe a better place for effective policymaking as well as for doing business. However, on average, the EU is outperformed by the US. More should be done to reduce performance gaps between member states and ultimately improve overall EU performance.

8.1 The plague of corruption

Corruption is dishonest or fraudulent conduct entailing the abuse of public or private power for private gain.[64] It includes, *inter alia*, active and passive bribery of public officials (also including elected and appointed officials), active and passive bribery in the private sector, undue influence peddling, abuse of function, embezzlement, conflicts of interest and favouritism. Corruption has widespread economic and social implications.

Corruption reduces public finances and depletes public investment, thus hampering economic and social development. From a social standpoint, it erodes trust in government, institutions and democracy, harms the rule of law and ultimately endangers human rights. By reducing efficiency, it also increases inequality. In a wider sense, corruption impinges on policymaking and policy implementation, thus limiting the ability of a state to deal with e.g. global warming, environmental degradation, security and organised crime and, ultimately, to achieve sustainable development objectives. From an economic standpoint, corruption discourages private investments, increases companies' uncertainty about day-to-day operations, harms the functioning of the single market, and burdens firms, disproportionately SMEs, with additional transaction costs, potentially leading some to exit the market (Gupta et al., 2016). The negative effects go beyond the reported economic impact, as corruption also brings with it the hidden costs related to inferior decisions, such as the poor allocation of capital, the development of sub-optimal products and the appointment of the undeserving.

While a number of EU member states (mainly concentrated in north-western Europe) rank very high (and better than the US) when it comes to preventing and fighting corruption, some member states still perform very poorly. Corruption in the EU costs up to €900 billion per year[65] and affects both citizens and businesses. Interestingly, most EU countries feature state-of-the-art rules against corruption; therefore, uneven enforcement explains the large variance across member states. In this context, an EU action to combat corruption could reduce the distance between leaders and laggards, cut corruption costs and favour economic growth and cohesion.

8.2 An Evolving Regulatory framework

According to the Treaties, the EU does not have direct competence in the field of corruption; however, it has a general right to act in the field of anti-corruption policy to ensure a high level of security. More specifically, article 83.1 of the Treaty on the Functioning of the EU (TFEU) includes corruption in the list of "particularly serious crimes with a cross-border dimension" and allows the European Parliament and the Council to adopt directives in order to establish minimum rules for the definition of criminal offences and sanctions to combat such a crime on a common basis. In addition, in the context of the Stockholm Programme,[66] all EU member states (and, where appropriate, the Commission) were requested to improve the prosecution of corruption in the private sector; the Commission was also given the mandate to measure member state efforts in the fight against corruption, increase cooperation between member states and develop a comprehensive anti-corruption policy in cooperation with the Council of Europe Group of States against Corruption (GRECO). Table 5 provides an overview of the main EU instruments to fight against corruption. The EU is also in the process of establishing the European Public Prosecutor's Office (EPPO), an independent and decentralised prosecution office with the competence to investigate, prosecute and bring to judgment crimes against the EU budget, including corruption.

Table 5. Main EU instruments to fight against corruption

Instrument	Purpose
Convention on the fight against corruption involving officials of the EU or officials of Member States (1997)	Criminalising active and passive bribery
Council Framework Decision on combating corruption in the private sector (2003)	Criminalising active and passive bribery in the private sector (implementation across member states remains uneven)
Directive on the fight against fraud to the Union's financial interests by means of criminal law (PIF Directive 2017)	Criminalising active and passive bribery
The European Anti-Fraud Office (OLAF)	Tasked with detecting, investigate and stop fraud and corruption against the financial interests of the EU
European Partners Against Corruption (EPAC) and European contact-point network against corruption (EACN)	Platforms for experience-sharing and cooperation among anti-corruption practitioners from EU member states and Council of Europe members

Source: Authors' own elaboration.

Furthermore, other EU instruments are indirectly relevant to tackling corruption, as they incorporate anti-corruption elements. For instance, the EU Anti-Money Laundering Directive (the fifth update having been adopted in April 2018) is meant to increase the transparency of financial flows in the EU. The latest update is particularly relevant in light of the tax evasion and hidden wealth brought to light by the Panama Papers. In this context, the directive targets, among others, the letterbox companies set up for corrupt purposes. In the same vein, the 2014 Public Procurement Directive includes a number of anti-corruption measures. In fact, corruption related to public procurement generates very high direct and indirect costs: by way of example, direct costs were estimated at €2.2 billion when looking at only five sectors (road and rail, water and waste, urban/utility construction, training, and research and development) and eight member states in one single year (2010).[67] Against this background, first and foremost the directive increases transparency, which can be considered the worst enemy of corruption. It ensures equal treatment of bidders, allows for an objective evaluation of tenderers and ensures compliance with the contract and the tender proposal. It introduces, *inter alia*, minimum standards for an EU-wide definition of conflicts of interest, the obligation of EU countries to take appropriate measures to detect, prevent and tackle fraud, corruption and conflicts of interest, as well as mandatory e-procurement.

Finally, when it comes to monitoring the progress of member states, the annual country reports under the European Semester include detailed analyses of country risks and challenges related to corruption. Furthermore, in the specific case of Bulgaria and Romania, the Cooperation and Verification Mechanism, which has been in place ever since their accession to the EU, sets benchmarks and tracks developments in the areas of judicial reform and fight against corruption, with the aim of supporting ongoing reform efforts.

Box - Highlights of EU and US anti-corruption legislation

Is either the EU or the US a definitive leader in anti-corruption legislation? According to the Global Integrity Report,[68] the US has a stronger anti-corruption legal framework and enforces it more effectively in comparison to EU member states. However, the data available is relatively old (2006-2011) and not all member states are covered by the study, the focus being more on emerging and developing economies. Taking this into account and going into more detail, two Transparency International studies point out why a clear answer in this matter is difficult to substantiate.

The Anti Money Laundering Directive provides a good example of the good results stemming from EU-level interventions to tackle corruption. According to a 2017 study on beneficial legal frameworks in the G20 countries,[69] France, Italy, Spain have very good frameworks in place, with Germany following closely behind, while the US performs less well in this respect. All four EU member states have central beneficial ownership registers (in line with the fourth Anti Money Laundering Directive), thus addressing the issue of incomplete or difficult-to-access information, as is the case in the US where a central registry is absent.

The situation is reversed with regard to the implementation of the OECD's Anti-Bribery Convention aiming to curb global corruption. From this viewpoint, the US is a clear leader, followed by Germany.[70] The majority of EU member states, however, are experiencing significant enforcement difficulties. Transparency International reports little to no enforcement of the provisions of the Convention in 11 member states: Spain, Belgium, Ireland, Poland, Denmark, the Czech Republic, Luxembourg, Slovak Republic, Slovenia, Bulgaria, and Estonia.

8.3 Corruption indicators

Corruption indicators compiled by Transparency International, the World Bank, or the World Economic Forum point in a clear direction: the EU performs very well in terms of corruption control in comparison to most G20 economies. A consistent group of member states usually ranks among the top countries in the world and ahead of the US across all relevant corruption indicators. However, there are still member states where corruption is a rather significant issue that needs to be addressed (see Table 6).

According to the Corruption Perceptions Index (CPI) by Transparency International, in 2017 the EU included nine out of the 20 'cleanest' countries in the world. The US ranks 18th, ahead of Ireland but after Denmark, Finland, Sweden, Luxembourg, Netherlands, Germany, Austria and Belgium. However, a number of EU member states perform quite poorly. For instance, Italy, Slovakia, Croatia, Greece, Romania, Hungary and Bulgaria are all positioned below the 50th place in the ranking. The Worldwide Governance Indicators (WGI) provide a similar pattern with respect to the control of corruption in 2016. Ten member states rank higher than the US (Finland, Denmark, Sweden, Luxembourg, Netherlands, Germany, Ireland, Belgium, Austria, and France). While differences do exist inside the EU, the poorer performers still rank ahead of major economies like China, Russia, or India, according to this indicator.

Table 6. *Overview of corruption indicator scores across the EU and the G20 countries*[71]

Country	CPI 2017	Corporate ethics (GCI 17/18)	Public institutions: Ethics and corruption (GCI 17/18)	Control of corruption (WGI 2016)	Overall score
Finland	85	6.24	6.31	2.28	89.11
Denmark	88	6.08	5.74	2.24	86.62
Sweden	84	5.98	5.66	2.22	84.78
Luxembourg	82	5.76	6.01	2.08	84.08
Netherlands	82	5.95	5.95	1.95	84.00
Canada	82	5.61	5.46	1.98	80.68
United Kingdom	82	5.46	5.57	1.88	80.01
Australia	77	5.68	5.51	1.77	78.92
Germany	81	5.33	5.28	1.83	77.79
Ireland	74	5.59	5.48	1.63	76.91
Japan	73	5.68	5.31	1.51	75.74
Austria	75	5.44	4.93	1.54	73.84
Belgium	75	5.35	4.94	1.60	73.80
USA	**75**	**5.36**	**5.08**	**1.33**	**73.06**
France	70	4.94	4.73	1.37	68.80
Estonia	71	4.81	4.82	1.21	68.10
EU-27 GDP-weighted average	**69.32**	**4.77**	**4.55**	**1.24**	**66.51**
EU-27 average	**64**	**4.49**	**4.21**	**0.98**	**61.32**
Saudi Arabia	49	5.01	5.25	0.23	60.33

Portugal	63	4.31	4.14	0.96	59.92
Malta	56	4.21	3.92	0.72	55.62
Lithuania	59	4.19	3.77	0.67	55.41
Slovenia	61	3.97	3.65	0.80	55.15
Cyprus	57	3.95	3.79	0.82	54.76
Poland	60	3.92	3.60	0.75	54.26
Czech Republic	57	3.96	3.38	0.51	51.52
Latvia	58	3.75	3.27	0.49	50.36
India	40	4.57	4.38	-0.30	49.95
Spain	57	3.59	3.31	0.52	49.78
South Korea	54	3.55	3.65	0.37	49.52
China	41	4.16	4.38	-0.25	48.74
Indonesia	37	4.27	3.90	-0.39	45.55
Greece	48	3.74	3.16	-0.05	44.66
Italy	50	3.49	3.17	0.05	44.62
Turkey	40	3.56	3.87	-0.20	44.10
Croatia	49	3.44	2.86	0.19	43.61
Slovakia	50	3.35	2.76	0.24	43.32
Romania	48	3.41	3.04	0.00	43.04
South Africa	43	3.79	2.67	0.05	42.07
Bulgaria	43	3.54	3.02	-0.16	41.44
Hungary	45	2.90	3.01	0.08	40.43
Russian Federation	29	3.79	3.48	-0.86	37.42
Argentina	39	2.87	2.54	-0.31	34.91
Brazil	37	2.93	2.11	-0.44	32.20
Mexico	29	3.16	2.36	-0.77	30.57

Notes: Higher indicator values reflect a better performance. The EU-27 GDP-weighted average is calculated using 2017 GDP data provided by Eurostat. The overall score is a composite indicator built using the four corruption indicators presented in the table. The individual indicators have been normalised on a scale from 0 to 100 and then aggregated into a measure that reflects the average standing of each country. The values of the overall score range between 0 (weakest overall performance) and 100 (strongest overall performance).

Source: Authors' elaboration on Eurostat, Transparency International, the World Bank, and the World Economic Forum.

While the CPI and WGI focus particularly on corruption in government, the World Economic Forum, through its Global Competitiveness Report (2017)[72] and the underlying survey of business executives, better conveys the impact of corruption on business. In Finland, Ireland, Austria, Denmark, Germany, the Netherlands, Belgium, Luxembourg, Estonia and France, business executives perceive corruption as the least or among the least problematic factors for doing business from a list of 16 potential issues. Conversely, in the US, corruption raises more concerns, as businesses indicate corruption is the fifth most problematic factor from the same list. In fact, the US could also be at some disadvantage compared with the EU because of the number of elected law enforcement officers at the state and county level. For instance, the system of accountability through elections that applies to sheriffs leaves room for discretionary decisions and potential conflicts of interest (Tomberlin, 2018).

No major differences exist between the public and the private sector in terms of ethics and corruption when we consider the top performers from the EU alongside the US.[73] While north-western member states have a lead in rankings worldwide, scoring ahead of the US, the situation changes when EU averages are computed, with the US outperforming Europe. The heterogeneous level of corruption across the member states brings the overall average down, both when considering a simple average of scores, as well as when the measure considered is a GDP-weighted average of corruption. However, the EU tends to perform relatively well overall in comparison to most G20 economies. It is worth stressing, however, that differences do exist between US states as well. Alaska and California, for instance, are top performers, particularly with regard to lobbying disclosure, ethics enforcement agencies, and legislative and executive accountability; by contrast, Delaware, Wyoming and Michigan, being more prone to corruption, lag significantly behind in most aspects related to public sector transparency and accountability.[74]

> **Box - The "revolving door" phenomenon and associated corruption risks**
>
> A phenomenon contributing to the perceived levels of corruptions in the public sector is the flow of former public officials (particularly high-ranking) into private and non-profit sector positions that involve lobbying activities. This "revolving door" phenomenon raises a number of concerns such as the extent to which public officials are influenced in their decisions by a potential high-paying career, or the trading of policy information and strategic contacts in the executive and legislative branches. Washington D.C. is particularly affected by these practices. A study conducted for the 1998 – 2008 timeframe estimates that 42% of lobbyists in the US capital had prior government experience. Moreover, their activity represented roughly 60% of lobbying firm revenues (Draca, 2014). In the EU, the phenomenon has only recently been brought to public attention. Considering only high-ranking officials, 50% of former Commissioners and 30% of former Members of the European Parliament work for organisations in the EU lobby register.[75] From this perspective, the US could be more prone to corruption in terms of conflict of interest.

The EBRD-World Bank Business Environment and Enterprise Performance Survey (BEEPS) attaches numbers to the instances of bribery in the business sector. According to 2013-2014 data,[76] firms in Central Europe and the Baltics reportedly paid bribes ("informal payments to move things along") that amounted to less than 1% of total annual revenues, down from almost 6% in 2008-2009. This figure is lower than the one reported in Russia, where informal payments amounted to 1%. Surveys of small, medium, and large enterprises at the global level, as UNODC notes, show that the smaller the company the more corruption is perceived as a significant obstacle.[77] In addition, people working in SMEs are more likely to report that they were asked for bribes from the local government than those working in large enterprises.

SMEs are particularly vulnerable to corruption given their size as well as limited financial and bargaining power.[78] From a financial standpoint, informal payments in dealing with local government, for instance in exchange for permits, put a disproportionate burden on SMEs compared to large enterprises. Despite this, bribes can be unavoidable in certain cases, as the refusal to pay can result in market exit. From a bargaining point of view, SMEs lack the influence of large enterprises, which hinders their ability to oppose acts of corruption or better negotiate their position. Furthermore, special links between larger enterprises and the public authorities, whether legal or illegal, can have detrimental effects on the activities of SMEs.

8.4 Corruption and public opinion

A recent Special Eurobarometer (2017)[79] shows that corruption is considered unacceptable in most EU countries. More than two thirds of Europeans believe that corruption is widespread in their country, especially among political parties, politicians and national public institutions. Less than 50% of Europeans think that the level of corruption in their country has increased over the last decade; however, most of them believe that more should be done to tackle corruption. Nevertheless, Europeans exposed to corruption do not report it and this is most likely due to the following reasons: (i) they do not know where to report corruption; (ii) they think corruption is difficult to prove; (iii) they believe corruption is not really punished; and (iv) they argue there is a lack of protection for those reporting corruption. There are large differences between EU countries on all dimensions.

With respect to businesses, the last Flash Eurobarometer (2017)[80] on the topic emphasises that while 40% of EU companies consider corruption to be a problem when doing business, it is not the main problem. Over two thirds of EU companies confirm that corruption is widespread in their country and that close links between business and politics are a matter of concern, especially when it comes to public tenders. However, compared with previous surveys, the number of companies believing that corruption in national/regional public procurement is widespread is declining. Corruption affects SMEs the most and has diverse impacts on different economic sectors (e.g. it is more frequent in the construction or healthcare sectors). Companies tend to be pessimistic about the way corruption is tackled in their country. Once again, differences between EU countries are very wide.

8.5 Implications for future EU policy

The 2014 EU Anti-Corruption Report published by the European Commission[81] acknowledged the detrimental effect of corruption on the economy and society as a whole. It also showed that while all EU member states have the legal instruments and institutions in place to prevent and fight corruption, enforcement is insufficient in a number of countries, leading to unsatisfactory results and generating direct costs in the region of €179 billion to €990 billion per year.[82] The report also emphasised that there is no 'one size fits all' solution to this problem and identified key areas of risk in the Union. Interestingly, by accounting for the broad diversity among EU member states, the initial commitments to publish follow-up EU Anti-Corruption Reports every two years has been replaced by more "versatile approaches" entailing the analysis of corruption issues in the European Semester country reports as well as the introduction of anti-corruption experience-sharing programmes.[83]

8.5.1 *Leverage the European Semester to promote anti-corruption initiatives*

The European Semester should be the active tool of the EU anti-corruption strategy, consistently and continually featuring corruption challenges in the country reports and in the specific country recommendations. As an additional way of bolstering credibility, the EU could resume talks and set a timeline for joining the GRECO as a full member. Progress should be monitored and made public. There is a significant gap between the perceived level of corruption and the actual level of reporting. To increase trust and to encourage citizens to report acts of corruption, the EU could provide more coverage to the progress made by member states in adopting and enforcing rules against corruption. Prominent cases illustrating the progress made could be included in the country reports, alongside the risk analysis, as part of the European Semester. Together with this, the EU-wide collection of data on corruption offences could be a useful tool and efforts could be made in order to harmonise the data available at the national level. In addition, better protection for whistle-blowers should be guaranteed, including clearer and safer reporting channels as well as prevention of retaliation.[84]

8.5.2 Tackle the enforcement gap

Enforcement is the key issue to be tackled. A comprehensive legal framework is in place both in the member states as well as at the EU level. Variations in performance across countries are mainly due to implementation issues. As such, in order to bridge the existing gaps, member states could improve their national rules and, more important, effectively enforce the frameworks already in place. This will require a considerable increase in the budgets for law enforcement, prosecution and, potentially, specialised courts. These investments would curb not only the reported economic cost of corruption, but also the hidden cost of inferior decisions. In this context, as the world's 300 metropolitan economies account for about 50% of global GDP[85] and corruption follows power and money, there is an increasing need to better equip regional and local administration with rules and instruments to fight against corruption. For instance, city-level anti-corruption units could be introduced.

Anti-corruption strategies could be designed by taking into account the particular case of SMEs. As SMEs often interact with local and regional authorities, this is the level where they are also most prone to corruption. As mentioned, member state governments should ensure that national corruption strategies are effectively implemented at the local level as well. Considering the importance given to SME competitiveness as part of the EU innovation and growth agenda, the EU could encourage member states to take appropriate measures and devote sufficient resources to the right levels of government in order to support the fight against corruption. In addition, SMEs should have access to clear information about rules and regulations in place in order to protect themselves against corrupt acts.

8.5.3 Leverage public support

The EU could capitalise on the public support for the fight against corruption as well. A clear EU-wide strategy against corruption could raise public support for the Union alongside effectively lowering corruption. This is a unique chance to bolster the position of the EU at a time marked by Brexit and populist movements gaining momentum.

9. TRADE AND THE SINGLE MARKET: EXPLOITING SYNERGIES FURTHER

The competitiveness of business in Europe is strongly and permanently stimulated by the combination of EU trade policy and the single market. Both are well-known features of European economic integration, but it is the combination of the two which is a treasure in search of greater recognition. For all practical purposes, the two form a couple, with overlaps in policy areas, commonness in strategy and very frequent interaction in many ways. The two are inextricably linked, so much so that the Commission (2006) wrote: "Globalisation is collapsing distinctions between domestic and external policies".[86]

This chapter assesses EU trade policy, its links with the single market, and its actual and potential contribution to economic growth, jobs, productivity and the competitiveness as well as resilience of European business.[87] The focus on business competitiveness, however, should not be interpreted as a lack of interest in the social protection of workers or a lower priority for inclusive development. In fact, it is entirely possible to combine these legitimate concerns with a permanent stimulus of competitiveness. In the long run, it is wise for the EU and its member states to maintain a balance between these two aspects so that the EU economy can engage in 'responsible globalisation' for its workers as well as for stakeholders in developing countries. Moreover, in line with what we have observed throughout this book, social and environmental protection is needed to strengthen the sustainability of Europe's economic policy over time: trade measures and the single market must become more consistent and aligned with this sustainability goal (Ashford and Renda, 2016).

The first section of this chapter summarises the many economic benefits of an EU open to the world economy, while also paying attention to temporary losers having to adjust. Subsequently, the EU regime enabling this economic openness will be set out. The second section elaborates the close connections between EU trade policy and the single market, with the deepening of the latter helping the EU's trade and investment strategy, in turn creating powerful incentives for permanent improvements of competitiveness as the basis for EU's prosperity. The third section sketches the nature and substance of EU trade policy, emphasising critical trends of multilateralism and bilateral trade agreements over the last few decades. The fourth section concludes, with recommendations for EU trade policy and the single market underpinning it.

9.1 Economic benefits and costs of EU open trade and investment policy

Opening up the (European) economy for trade and investment generates many and sizeable economic benefits, but it also requires adjustment, in particular of firms losing out in terms of competitiveness for several reasons. The broad thrust is that the economic benefits tend to be far larger than the costs of adjustment; benefits are also permanent whereas adjustment costs are typically temporary. However, both need careful attention. The present contribution is not the place to go into the rigorous economics of trade and investment. Figure 22, based on Petersen (2016)] shows the so-called static effects of lowering barriers to trade, supplemented by the dynamic effects when productivity improves due to exposure to globalisation.

This diagram shows that the static effects work via two channels: reducing trade barriers lowers the price of imported goods and services while such reductions also increase cross-border trade. Trade barriers consist of tariffs (nowadays, after decades of reductions, often quite low or even zero) and usually much higher 'trading costs' due to disparities or non-recognition of regulation and certification between two or more trading partners. The lower import prices work their way through (higher) purchasing power and lower prices of inputs via increased domestic demand to higher production (and, with a time lag, to higher investment) and hence more jobs. Greater imports due to lower barriers and more demand for inputs similarly increase output and jobs.

Figure 22. Trade Liberalisation and economic growth

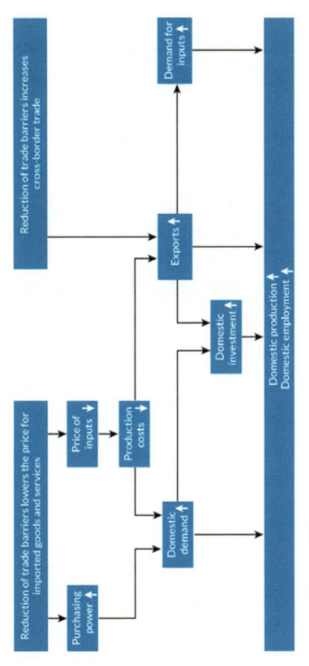

Source: Petersen (2016).

The dynamic effects refer to changes in production technology and/or better intra-firm solutions (e.g. learning from competitors or pushed by import competition) as well as innovation, for example prompted by a desire to be better capable of penetrating foreign markets via trade and/or investment. Dynamic effects can be cost reducing, too, but might also imply quality changes and new ways of doing things, all of them helping economic growth in various ways.

The literature on the economic effects of trade and foreign direct investment (FDI) is extensive. Below we provide a few critical highlights of the benefits in quantitative and qualitative form; we then discuss temporary adjustments for specific groups, in particular for those dubbed 'losers' from globalisation).[88]

First, trade is a very important source of job creation. EU trade with non-EEA countries generates some 31 million jobs, which is around 14% of EU employment; this is 12.5 million jobs more than in 1995.[89] Each €1 billion of extra-EU exports adds 14,000 jobs. Though too often ignored, extra-EU *imports* also generate jobs, in two ways. One way is via logistics, wholesale and retail as well as supporting financial and professional services. The other way is a result of European and global value chains: one consequence of such value chains is that components and other intermediate goods (and services, where relevant) are imported for use in production, much of which is exported again: extra-EU imports as a share of EU exports in 1995 amounted to nearly 9%, and this share increased by half to reach 13% in 2015. Value chains have the effect of spreading the benefits of extra-EU exports all over the EU, because what e.g. Germany or Italy exports incorporates intermediate goods and services from many EU countries. It is therefore misleading to pay attention solely to final export data.

The long-run EU benefits from exposure to globalisation include dynamic effects. Among the many available estimates, a prudent one for the EU found that a 1% increase in economic openness yields a 0.6% increase in labour productivity, but other studies have found a much higher impact.[90] Another benefit from imports is what is known as the 'pro-poor bias', generated especially by imports from emerging economies led by China. EU imports from China and other industrialising developing countries consisted of a high share of 'mass consumer goods' at lower retail prices than those prevailing in Europe. For China in 2014, this amounted to EU imports of no less than $124 billion of such goods implying an increase in the purchasing power of poorer consumers (as they rely heavily on such cheap consumer goods) of possibly up to €600 per year.[91]

A real powerhouse in EU trade policy is the increasing web of free trade agreements (FTAs) between the EU and its international trade partners. These agreements are not just about imports and exports, but contain a plethora of provisions, regulatory cooperation measures and conditionalities, which the EU increasingly uses to ensure that its principles and safeguards are also applied outside its borders. In 2006, when the EU resumed FTAs after a moratorium of seven years, the existing FTAs covered some 25% of extra-EU trade; in 2015, this had increased to some 36% (these additional FTAs were deeper and more comprehensive, too); if the 2015 FTA strategy of the EU is completed, FTAs in the future would cover as much as 66% of all extra-EU trade; however, the latter figure appears unlikely since it includes, among others, the suspended negotiations for a Transatlantic Trade and Investment Partnership, suspended for the time being.

FDI, both inward and outward, is also crucial for EU trade. Depending on the type of goods or services, outward FDI can substitute for exports or complement trade by altering exports of final goods to exports of components and imports of final goods. Due to the spread of global value chains, the difference between the two is no longer clear-cut – even if final goods are exported from the EU, much of the value added may in fact originate elsewhere inside or outside the EU, and – when outside – often from foreign affiliates of EU companies.

FDI is a key component of business and competitiveness strategies of European enterprises. At the same time, inward FDI is huge as well because the EU is a magnet, precisely because of its big single market. The investment regime of the EU is amongst the most liberal of the world. The EU is the largest FDI source and recipient in the world for decades, measured by FDI stocks. Without counting intra-EU FDI, the EU accounts for 36% of all FDI in the world, dwarfing any other economy (even the US, the largest FDI investor in the EU by far). Although it is good to observe that dynamic emerging economies have themselves become international investors, in particular in South-South relations, the public debate on FDI in Europe or in the US can be disproportionate to the realities in markets. Thus, Chinese FDI into the EU has become a major issue due to some spectacular takeovers (like robotics firm Kuka and pharma giant Syngenta – Swiss but with a strong presence in the EU) and in a dubious fashion (with investment funds dominated by state-owned enterprises). But 2016 Chinese FDI stock in the EU amounted to just €44 billion, compared to a stunning €2,350 billion from the US. Chinese FDI stock in the US is barely higher than in the EU, compared to EU FDI in the US of no less than €2,720 billion.

The EU is therefore a major and active 'globaliser'. For the most part, this is beneficial for companies, workers and consumers, and has generated extra economic growth and jobs while improving productivity, innovation and product variety. Nevertheless, one has to be conscious of the mechanisms generating such multiple gains. The more open an economy, the more the EU's comparative *dis*advantages are going to be exposed as well, which will sooner or later lead to shrinking market shares in such sectors and eventually job losses, closures or re-localisation of plants abroad. In some cases (and dependent on the business cycle), workers will find new jobs easily and adjustment costs are small or negligible, indeed, not necessarily different from jobs lost for many other reasons (including bankruptcies due to lost market shares or technological progress or demand shifts, etc.).

Of course, such a 're-allocation of resources' – as economists call this – yields a gross benefit for the economy at large as relatively inefficient firms exit the market and more efficient ones take over. But the *net* benefit depends on how many jobs are lost and not immediately replaced by new jobs for the displaced workers; wages might well be lower in the new jobs due to less experience in the other sector or lack of sectoral skills. The period of adjustment (e.g. in a crisis) as well as the uncertainty can be a rather painful experience which should be cushioned by welfare state social spending (paid by the much larger gains from trade). In addition, 'active labour market policies' (or ALMP) can greatly facilitate finding another job without losing too much wage premium from previous sectoral skills. However, regional differences in the prospect of finding other meaningful or skill-relevant jobs can add to the misery of the unemployed. In the extreme it might even cause hysteresis – a structural form of unemployment which may have the effect of eventually eroding individuals' competencies, thereby reducing further the prospect of finding a job in the near future.

The contrast between the EU and the US in this respect is quite sharp. Recent work by David Autor and co-authors,[92] and the debate triggered by Donald Trump blaming China for their job losses and indeed their prospects for new jobs, has revealed that the US offers little cushioning with its minimal welfare state, and only minor and selective trade adjustment programmes (rather than ALMP).[93] In the EU, welfare states do cushion and for quite a long time, thereby reducing income uncertainty for workers and buying time for re-skilling and thorough job searches. However, this does not mean that all is fine in the EU because there are considerable discrepancies in social support and ALMP between member states. The EU has a European Globalisation Adjustment Fund:[94] however, this Fund suffers from minimal funding and considerable eligibility questions. Eligibility is very hard to decide because usually there are several reasons why workers suffer a massive lay-off: moreover, why would globalisation be a more exceptional reason than far more crucial reasons for job losses, namely, technology and digitalisation? It remains critical for the EU to pursue 'responsible globalisation', both at home (via ALMP and the welfare state) and abroad (in terms of corporate governance and 'decent work'). The latter is supported by the EU's manifest preference to pursue 'sustainable development' in FTAs and, where possible, in the WTO via plurilateral agreements or other means.[95]

9.2 How EU trade policy and the single market hang together

There are three crucial ways the EU single market *acquis* and policies hang together with EU trade policies.

First, there is a *consistency requirement between internal and external* policies. There is a *common* EU trade policy because independent *national* policies and powers would distort and/or prevent the EU single market from being fully established and functioning properly. Thus, the Treaty of Rome incorporated a customs union – no longer national tariffs, but a common external one – and implied common quotas, if any. Over time, exceptions to common quotas – namely, national quotas for selected third-country goods (e.g. Japanese cars) – were removed. By 1993, the EU single market was incomparably more ambitious than a customs union. Thus, for consistency, EU trade policy required EU-level powers in e.g. services (itself a huge conglomerate of distinct markets) and for a wide spectrum of regulatory issues.[96] Indeed, tariffs and quotas became a relatively minor part of trade policy (except perhaps in agriculture) and 'regulatory trade policy' took centre stage. The trade policy response in the Uruguay Round (ended in 1994) confirmed the shift to regulatory issues, with the new GATS for services, besides a series of agreements on e.g. TRIPs, TRIMs, TBTs and SPS issues,[97] subsidies, anti-dumping, etc.

Subsequently, the CJEU gave its opinion about the scope of EU trade policy (in 1994), holding that a shift to more EU-level powers in these fields was justified, but in complex ways the member states still had to remain signatories in selected services, in some TRIPs (but not others) and in investment issues (not part of the Uruguay Round).[98] This opinion revealed the inconsistency between the internal and external *acquis* (in terms of powers) which could only be overcome if all member states would be cooperative in each and every negotiation, at both multilateral and bilateral levels. Whether for purposes of credibility in trade negotiations or for pre-empting distortions or gaps in the internal market, this legacy of inconsistency from the past was unfortunate. It was repaired in the Lisbon treaty. All services as well as regulatory and investment treaty powers are now found at EU level and belong to EU trade policy. The lingering issues were dealt with in another opinion of the CJEU in May 2017: whereas portfolio investment and ISDS (arbitration for investment disputes) fall under shared competences, all six modes of transport, IPRs plus trade and development issues now fall under exclusive EU powers. This consistency requirement is not at all a trivial issue. Having no residual national trade policies in several domains creates a more predictable business environment in the single market for business in Europe, including foreign multinationals. The EU can now define and execute its EU trade policy strategically in all respects and will not be hindered by a lack of credibility when having to 'deliver' an agreement via ratification.[99] Seen from within, the EU is entirely free to deepen and widen its single market the way it deems fit, and subsequently assume (if desirable) a forceful position in bilateral negotiations and at the WTO. Last but not least, its internal experience and functional solutions may serve (and have already regularly served) as inspiration for WTO or bilateral policy options or regulatory approaches. This is indeed a hidden treasure because solutions deliberated between 28 member states in terms of regulatory and intra-EU liberalisation can serve as relevant *and tested* experiences for the WTO as well. It goes without saying that this tends to be beneficial and convenient for EU companies accustomed to these solutions.

Second, and beyond mere consistency between internal and external, the *qualities of the single market regime in the wider sense* (i.e. including good regulation and most common policies)[100] is a crucial factor for the EU's trade and investment strategy and for the substance of its trade policy. The three fundamental qualities of the single market regime refer to its: (a) *depth*, i.e. how far-reaching commitments are in intra-EU cross-border liberalisation, accompanied by EU regulation where justified, and competition policy; (b) *scope*, covering all the five freedoms, with few if any exceptions, and hence being very broadly encompassing;[101] and (c) *credibility* with market players, ensured by proper implementation and enforcement. The treaty regime gives the single market (in the wider sense) a central role in pursuing the socio-economic aims of the TFEU: it is the 'superworkhorse' which should deliver higher prosperity over time, conditioned by sustainability and other aspects. A higher prosperity that, with a splintered EU and a shallow, non-performing single market, would be impossible to attain. Now that free movements and free establishment are much better respected in the EU than a few decades ago, the quality of EU regulation in incentivising business to compete and invest becomes ever more crucial both for the single market and for trade policy.

> **Box - The quality of EU regulation and its meaning for EU trade policy**
>
> Single market regulation is very important for EU trade policy for two reasons. First, high-quality EU regulation combines effective solutions for market failures (its purpose) with the least possible costs in terms of resources for companies and citizens and/or in terms of lost options to act. Market failures prevent proper market functioning. Practically all market failures can be summarised with the acronym "SHEIC": safety, health, environment, investor/saver and consumer protection. Markets on their own will not provide SHEIC; this is the assignment for EU

regulation. SHEIC regulation is essentially 'risk regulation'. If EU risk regulation succeeds in overcoming market failures at the least possible cost, business can act responsibly without incurring unnecessary costs, thereby retaining its competitiveness. This is crucial for the EU in international trade and investment, both ways. However, at times EU regulation goes far beyond pure market failures, and seeks the realisation of long-term EU goals such as ambitious carbon-neutrality goals for 2050: in these circumstances, EU businesses may have to face higher costs than their counterparts in other regions of the world, and this has to be adequately reflected in a proactive trade policy that avoids the creation of a 'race to the bottom', or an emerging trade-off between short-term competitiveness and long-term sustainability.

Second, high-quality risk regulation is also a major trade issue internationally, whether in the WTO, in bilateral FTAs, in sectoral agreements or in regulatory cooperation. The higher the quality of EU regulation, the better it can serve as a template or example for international trade negotiations. Negotiations over CETA, the EPA with Japan, the FTA with Korea, TTIP, Mexico, Singapore, Mercosur and today's ongoing talks with Indonesia, Australia and New Zealand are all predominantly about risk regulation, much less about tariffs. The idea behind such regulatory trade talks is to minimise the 'trading costs' for business in accessing each other's markets, that is, the costs of answering to different regulatory requirements in various markets. These trading costs are much higher than average tariffs nowadays.

It is true that the preferences about risk reduction in regulation may differ between trading partners and this implies that the EU cannot always 'export' its regulatory experiences in their entirety. Moreover, sometimes, techniques and traditions of risk reduction might differ, too and these have to be accommodated somehow. Nevertheless, 'good EU regulation' is an asset in such negotiations, because its objective quality can be recognised and may well reduce 'trading costs' significantly. This is further enhanced by the fact that the EU has systematically relied on many thousands of European technical standards which are very often identical to world standards (74% for electrical and 34% for non-electrical goods standards).

Third, even when internal/external consistency is addressed properly and the fundamental qualities of the internal market (in the wider sense) have become ambitious, the *competitiveness of firms* inside the single market – say, vis-à-vis imports or locally produced goods or services from foreign companies – and outside, in the world economy, is also determined by many other factors beyond the immediate control of firms themselves and beyond the single market regime. Such factors may consist of national measures concerning 'Doing Business',[102] or a host of other aspects typically incorporated in so-called Competitiveness Indices.[103] It is therefore entirely justified to broaden the policy perspective even beyond the single market in a wider sense to other determinants of companies' competitiveness such as hard and soft infrastructures, the supply of a great variety of skills, the quality of higher education and training, incentives for innovation (other than typical single market aspects), regulatory and taxation aspects at national and local levels, local and national institutions (including the legal system and public administration) and additional aspects of the business environment. However, *for the EU level* of government, the question is whether and to what extent and with which 'tools' these aspects can be improved, given that they are mostly national and local prerogatives. Still, the gradually increased competitive rivalry in the single market for goods and services has induced a kind of soft emulation in terms of 'Doing Business' between member states, leading many of them to improve on such indicators.[104]

But even if EU member states all say that they willingly cooperate on a range of such issues, is there a recognisable relationship with EU trade policy? Nowadays there surely is, due to the need to continually climb the ladder of dynamic comparative advantages. Especially for advanced economies like the EU, and given the awakening of the BRICs and many other emerging economies, a search for greater EU prosperity in the long run is and will remain very demanding in terms of the domestic economy's capacity to stay close to the (shifting) technology frontier, to be repeatedly amongst the first movers of new or innovative goods and services, to be competitive and innovative in all kinds of services (especially those that cannot be easily outsourced), to deliver high quality based on high skills and design specialisation and to remain a high value added partner in global value chains. Clearly, market pressures go a long way towards inducing permanent exposure and incentives to anticipate and adjust, for companies, workers and indeed customers and consumers. But active and strategic policy making over a wide spectrum of determinants of competitiveness of firms are required as well. National reforms are also necessary, given the lingering restrictiveness of product markets and – to some extent – labour markets. However, such reforms would also – and directly – help the single market to function better, which would render EU firms more robust and able to withstand competitive forces emerging from further globalisation. With respect to reforms in services and labour markets, some progress has been made in the EU but selectively only. The implementation of the wide-ranging 2006 services directive was a significant contribution but recent progress has been insufficient.[105] A lack of reforms raises the cost of adjustment, which, in turn, prompts political economy resistance to openness, which, in its turn, tends to reduce EU companies' competitiveness in the longer run. EU trade policy makers are acutely aware of how urgent is the move towards greater dynamism and flexibility in the EU economy: they observe the rise of emerging economies, notice their high to very high growth rates, negotiate with them on quickly shifting agendas in accordance with their shifting comparative and competitive advantages and worry about the defensive reactions sometimes heard in Europe. Much better for the EU to systematically anticipate such changes and stimulate Europe's progress up the ladder of comparative advantages.

9.3 The nature, scope and trends of EU trade policy

With the gradual completion of EU trade policy during the 1980s and 1990s and its formalisation in the 2009 Lisbon treaty, this important instrument has been better and much more intensively used by the Union, decisively helped by the size and deepening of the single market as well. Therefore, nowadays, EU trade policy has become very rich and interesting. It is multi-varied in international application, much more comprehensive in scope, and meanwhile includes investment besides trade, is 'deeper' in that international or bilateral commitments have fewer reservations and applies to both goods and services.

For goods and services, the pursuit of EU trade policy is multilateral in the WTO, regional (mostly in Europe, in the future possibly with Mercosur and with ASEAN as groups), bilateral (mostly in FTAs and – in one case – with a customs union, namely Turkey) and unilateral. For investment, there is no international overarching multilateral treaty, although a tradition of BITs (bilateral investment protection treaties) has emerged resulting in emulated international BIT 'models'. Investment treaties have been negotiated at the EU level since 2010. The WTO has not changed much since its beginning in 1995, despite enormous efforts during the WTO Doha Round to deepen and widen commitments and scope, largely frustrated by some larger developing countries.[106] The EU is a strong protagonist of the WTO and the entire idea of a multilateral rules-based system, disciplining big and small economies equally. The EU's activism in trade policy can be mainly found in bilateralism. The principal reason is that effective multilateralism has become very difficult with the manifold exceptions for developing countries and the refusal to deepen the WTO regime by large players like India, Brazil and sometimes China. Since 2017, it has been frustrated by the disruptive policies of the Trump administration.

In 1999, the EU unilaterally declared a moratorium on FTAs in order to make it more attractive for other WTO partners to concentrate on multilateral trade liberalisation and facilitation in the Doha Round.[107] But the EU turned out to be alone in this. Because multilateral progress became so difficult even in the Doha Round and most WTO partners frantically concluded FTAs with closer partners, despite the Round, the EU terminated its moratorium in 2006. Since then it has concluded a series of new FTAs, deepened and modernised some existing FTAs and started negotiations with several countries on additional modern FTAs. The overall picture of EU FTAs is complex[108] for the simple reason that the EU is a magnet: it is a very big market with high purchasing power and hence attractive for all trading partners. The search for access to its big, single market led to what Pelkmans & Brenton (1999) have called a 'me too' drive:[109] once a country A obtains better access to the EU via a FTA, its competitors B and C also plead to acquire similar FTA treatment, a domino effect stimulated by a fear of losing competitiveness for their firms in the big European market. Thus, the EU strategy of seeking better access to the most dynamic markets (East Asia in particular) is topped up with other FTAs due to the 'me too' logic. As a result, the EU has now FTAs of different generations, of different depth, with narrow and much wider scope and with partners in four continents, with the fifth continent (Australasia) having begun negotiations in 2018. An overview is provided in Table 7.

Table 7. Overview of EU's FTAs in four categories

Intra-European	'old' FTAs	new FTAs	FTAs/EPAs with APC
EEA-3, Norway, Liechtenstein, Iceland (deepest FTA, in fact a single-market-minus)	Southern Mediterranean countries (Israel, Lebanon, Tunisia, Egypt, Algeria, Morocco, Palestine, Jordan)	South Korea (2011), deep and comprehensive	EPA with Eastern & Southern African States (asymmetric, better market access for Africans, plus development aid)
Switzerland (mimics the EEA-3 but not fully, and without solid governance)	Chile (now under upgrade talks)	Columbia, Ecuador & Peru (2013), deep and comprehensive	EU/South Africa FTA (2000), in fact with the SADC
DCFTAs (with Ukraine, Moldova, Georgia)	Mexico (upgraded to 'deep and comprehensive' in 2018)	Central America (2012) (Panama, Costa Rica, Honduras, Guatemala, Nicaragua, El Salvador)	Cariforum, Caribbean countries in the ACP
Stabilisation & Association Agreements Western Balkans (Albania, Former		Vietnam (2016)	Pacific islands in the APC, incl. New Guinea

Macedonia, Montenegro, Serbia, Bosnia & Herzegovina, Kosovo)	Singapore (2015) (to be ratified, after a lengthy CJEU case upheld the treaty), deep and comprehensive	
Turkey (a CU, with advanced regulatory convergence in EU technical regulation for goods)	CETA (2016) (to be ratified), deep and comprehensive	EPA with Ghana, Côte d'Ivoire & Cameroon
	Japan (EPA) 2017, to be ratified, with investment separate; deep and comprehensive	
	Mercosur (2019), deep and comprehensive	

Under negotiation: Australia & New Zealand; ASEAN countries Malaysia (on hold), Thailand (on hold), Philippines (on hold), Indonesia; India and 6 Gulf countries (both negotiations have been stuck for many years).

Notes: EEA = European Economic Area; DCFTA = Deep and Comprehensive FTAs in Association Agreements (Ukraine, Georgia, Moldova); CU = customs union; EPA = Economic Partnership Agreement (but with very different substance and obligations in the case of Japan than with ACP countries); SADC = Southern African Development Cooperation (South Africa, Swaziland, Botswana, Lesotho and Namibia).

Table 7 shows the dynamism of EU's bilateral liberalisation strategy and the active pursuit of sound (risk) regulation reducing regulatory disparities with trading partners. Both forcefully lower 'trading costs' for companies interested in accessing markets in these countries. Given that SMEs are often not familiar with non-European foreign markets and that the 'trading costs' of regulatory disparities in particular are relatively bigger for them, or indeed might be considered as prohibitive or too risky, the FTA strategy of pursuing 'deep and comprehensive FTAs' is beneficial for SMEs. It is likely to pull SMEs into exports to non-European markets and thereby renders such SMEs more resilient and possibly more productive too. The European Commission has set up several internationalisation programmes for SMEs and supports SME helpdesks in e.g. China.

However, it is good to realise that EU trade policy encompasses more than FTAs. First, under multilateralism there are other recent accomplishments than just the Trade Facilitation Agreement. Although the WTO is a consensus-driven organisation, there are additional options for those 'able and willing'. One option actively promoted by the EU are 'plurilaterals'. In plurilateral agreements, a smaller group of WTO members covering a large share of world trade in the relevant sectors of activity commit to 'WTO-plus' liberalisation and extends this opening up to all WTO members. Of course, this might invite 'free riding' which is only bearable if the trade share of the plurilateral is high (say, above 75%-80% of world trade in the relevant activity) and no major player remains outside. There are two plurilaterals which work: the GPA (government procurement, considerable commitments to opening up) and ITA-2 (on ICT equipment or components, with zero tariffs). Two other ones are blocked half way in the negotiations: one on services (going beyond GATS commitments)[110] and one on 'green goods'.[111] For services, the US is hesitant, not least because Washington and many other countries do want China in as well, but China's six offers so far are insignificant.

Second, there are many narrower or partial agreements which nevertheless lubricate trade or investment. One type of deals are bilateral MRAs,[112] which can lower the trading costs of certain types of bulky or higher-risk goods. Another type includes narrow sectoral deals such as aviation treaties (greater opening up of the skies of participating countries) or mutual recognition of aircraft safety rules and permitted manufacturing practices (as between the US and the EU) by their regulatory agencies. Yet another is the IMO,[113] having fully harmonised the technical rules and standards of 49 critical types of equipment for sea shipping. A final example also offers an alternative to often cumbersome regulatory trade negotiations: recently, in medicines and (higher-risk) medical devices the national regulators have formed world fora, including industry as observers, where detailed 'common guidelines' are formulated on a voluntary basis, which are subsequently introduced into national legislation or practices. This substitution of trade negotiators by regulators (for the EU, in the single market) pre-empts lingering problems inside countries during implementation of trade deals.[114] Moreover, national regulators tend to faithfully follow up their 'own' global guidelines at home, which results in very similar rules in many countries, drastically cutting trading costs. Another such non-WTO forum is the WP29 of the UN-ECE[115] on technical automotive safety and environmental car regulations, which is leading to harmonisation of a large part of the technical elements of type approval of cars and trucks. The US is only very partially accepting of UN-ECE harmonisation on automotive, unlike Japan and Korea (large producers worldwide) and the EU above all, which is its biggest proponent. In Freund & Oliver (2015), a simulation shows that – if the US were to align with the UN-ECE WP29 rules – a gain of no less than $20 billion of lower trading costs and further benefits would be reaped, a non-trivial share of which would be benefitting EU exporters.

Since 2010, the EU (rather than its member states) has been responsible for negotiating investment agreements. The member states have, altogether, negotiated some 1,300 BITs over the last five decades. Once aggregated at the EU level, this number would be far smaller but still sizeable. Most of these agreements concern the protection of foreign investors' property and their reasonable expectations of local government action, without of course affecting the local 'right to regulate'. Newer EU FTAs include investment as a separate chapter. However, EU member states were claiming that, under EU trade policy, powers on investment are 'shared' between the EU and national levels. In that case, a 'mixed agreement' is required with the risk that one single member state might block it under ratification. For this reason, FTAs and investment agreements are nowadays split, in order to protect the FTA as an exclusive EU competence.

The case of China is much more special, however. Already 26 member states have a BIT with China. This shows that investment protection as such is not a major issue. The real and very important issue with China is what is called 'post-establishment market access': once a company invests in China, it might find that the market it wants to operate in is closed legally and/or de facto in a number of ways[116] and the new EU/China Comprehensive Agreement on Investment (CAI) tries to address this problem in earnest.

> **Box - Brexit lays bare the interwovenness of the single market and trade policy**
>
> The treasure of the 'interwovenness' of the single market and EU trade policy is demonstrated in a dramatic though unfortunate fashion by Brexit. The 'red lines' for the UK government include the departure from the customs union (part of both the single market and of EU trade policy), a greater degree of regulatory autonomy ('taking back control') and the ending of the supremacy of EU law via CJEU rulings. Knowing that the costs of giving up a good deal of the benefits of market integration with its biggest neighbour – the EU-27 – would be high, the UK wishes to retain far-reaching access to the single market. However, as a 'third country' (after Brexit comes into force), such far-reaching access to the single market would assume an EU trade policy vis-à-vis the UK very similar to that of the EEA-3, or at least that of Switzerland.
>
> Such almost complete participation in the single market is incompatible with UK red lines. The EEA-3 and Switzerland are not in a customs union but in a FTA (in terms of frontier controls); however, both accept a very far-reaching degree of regulatory alignment, which goes against 'taking back control', while allowing very light customs controls based on risk, and enforcement regimes that, in the final analysis, almost perfectly echo what the CJEU has ruled, which allows various forms of recognition and deep cooperation and also ensures a 'level playing field' in areas such as labour regulations, environment and climate and state aid.
>
> Not being in the customs union, post-Brexit, gives the UK the freedom to develop their own trade policy and negotiate

'independently' bilateral FTAs. There is little doubt that opting to stay in the customs union and negotiate together with the EU would give the UK much more leverage and clout in commercial diplomacy, and, at the same time, largely remove the business costs of a disruption of EU-wide value chains in the single market.

9.4   Policy recommendations

After decades of gradual policy development, EU's trade and investment legal regime and strategy has become a very comprehensive and pro-competitive set of instruments which greatly benefits the European economy and permanently stimulates the competitiveness of companies operating in the single market. As a result, the EU has become a leader in 'responsible globalisation'. At the same time, there is concern for temporary 'losers', mostly at the member state level via ALMP and the cushioning of unemployed workers via the welfare state, and to a minor extent at EU level via a special Fund and regional programmes and subsidies. Brexit is a painful experiment revealing once again how crucial EU trade policy is for all member states and companies and how important are the links with the single market. It has also shown rather dramatically how interwoven companies' value chains are in a market without internal borders and how costly it is to even threaten to disrupt such competitiveness-driven business models.

The following selective recommendations should guide the EU trade and FDI strategy for the following legislature of the European Parliament and the new European Commission:

9.4.1   *Preserve EU's exclusive power in negotiating agreements*

The exclusive power at EU level to conduct today's rich and comprehensive trade and investment policy is a treasure that opportunistic national politicians ought not to challenge for parochial short-term and narrow purposes. Its value is found in its legal properties as well as in its economic effects – both static and dynamic, as shown before, in particular for the permanent competitiveness of EU enterprises – and its negotiation advantages with WTO trading partners.

9.4.2 Make trade negotiations more transparent

For the three EU institutions involved (Commission, Council and EP), this exclusive power can only be exercised in a satisfactory fashion if, and only if, policy proposals and overall trade strategy are as public as possible and negotiations remain as open as diplomatically feasible so as to avoid accusations of being subjected to undue business pressures or sectoral lobbies or political pressures from trading partners. The European Parliament and stakeholders should remain involved on a regular basis.

9.4.3 Don't listen to the sirens of protectionism

Given Trump's aggressive mercantilist trade strategy, risking damage to the US economy in several ways while undermining the functioning of the WTO, it is often heard that the world economy has moved into protectionist times. This is wrong. Trump has no followers anywhere. The EU response to Trump, both bilaterally and multilaterally, of upholding the WTO and improving some of its rules while negotiating a limited WTO-compatible FTA with the US is the best possible, so far.

9.4.4 China as EU's greatest trade challenge

By far the greatest challenge of EU trade strategy is China. The FTA strategy going back to 2006 is focused on dynamic East Asian economies, for the simple reason that growth prospects there are the highest. China is by far the most dynamic East Asian economy and it is by far the largest economy in that region. It follows that the EU strategy can only succeed if China is fully incorporated. The economic potential of this approach is great and many European businesses are keen. The EU's formal policy position is that China and the EU must first agree on the CAI, with a firm set of legal commitments on 'national treatment' and other aspects of post-establishment market access. For China, rightly or wrongly, this is considered as very intrusive, prompting significant and pervasive legal and policy changes. Once agreed, the EU would be ready to negotiate a FTA, as suggested by president Xi Jinping, under the condition that China would implement the profound reforms it has proposed itself in November 2013. These deep reforms would benefit the EU (and indeed other partners) but first of all private business in China itself. For that reason, many specialists in China also advocate these reforms. This two-stage EU approach is more realistic today because of Trump's trade war with China, bringing China and the EU closer together. China and the EU are the two trade giants in the world liable to assume leadership, if possible joint leadership (Hu and Pelkmans, 2017).[117]

However, China's trade partners – besides the EU, also the US and Japan as well as several others[118] – insist that China profoundly alter its very restrictive trade and FDI policies and cement this in the WTO via legal reforms. The trilateral support of the US 301 case at the WTO about China's discretionary practices to force involuntary technology transfer with numerous foreign companies investing in China forms a break with the past diplomacy of soft cooperation with China, also for the EU. The EU should carefully balance its China strategy in a *jin-jang* fashion: EU/China trade and investment has yielded enormous gains for both partners and this must be recognised and upheld, whereas China should no longer continue its highly interventionist practices (with little, if any, legal redress for companies) and pursue the deep reforms it proposed itself; it should also push relevant reforms in the WTO together with the EU. Overarching this, the EU and China have to assume joint trade leadership in earnest, and not just verbally, forging alliances to counter and neutralise US trade aggression as much as possible.

9.4.5 Relentlessly pursue the reform and modernisation of the single market

It is crucial, if EU trade policy is to remain effective for EU prosperity, to continue to pursue single market reforms that deepen and modernise the single market. This is most urgent for services, in particular reducing restrictions on professional services and those in construction and retail (Pelkmans, 2019). There is a double rationale for such reforms: overall, they stimulate higher growth in the EU for all, and they tend to lower costs and/or improve quality of services as inputs in value chains, in turn supporting the competitiveness of business in Europe vis-à-vis EU imports and for EU exports to world markets. Reforms for modernisation of the single market are manifold. They encompass hi-tech related aspects such as digital and new technologies (see below, Chapter 10), but also the widening of the social agenda at EU and member state levels (harmonisation where artificial legal constructions allow extreme wage disparities – undermining the support for the single market; more ambitious upskilling of workers, especially in Mediterranean countries and weak regions in Central Europe) for a 'fairer' single market.

At first sight, the 'fairer' single market might be considered as a typical intra-EU issue, without much relevance for EU trade policy. But this would be mistaken. Precisely because of the economic openness of the EU and the interwovenness of the single market and EU trade policy, workers and labour unions justifiably perceive the single market, to some extent, as a reflection of globalisation. Since the EU prides itself on pursuing 'responsible globalisation', it should begin at home with a fairer single market, whether in subcontracting arrangements for value chains, labour-intensive services linked to digital platforms or tackling the tax evasion by multinationals. Such reforms are critical for the continued support of workers, indeed of numerous EU citizens, for a deep single market and for an EU trade policy seeking to 'harness globalisation' – the title of a Commission communication on its trade strategy, see European Commission (2017).

10. Leading the World in Technology Rules and Standards

Digital innovation has already significantly impacted the way we live. The internet revolution has led us into growing social interaction online, as well as a massive digitalisation of telecommunications and media, and later many other sectors such as energy, manufacturing, transportation, healthcare, agriculture. The first information revolution is now paving the way for another, even more pervasive set of changes, represented by the emergence of a whole new 'stack' of technologies: high-performance computing (including the new generation cloud infrastructure, edge or fog computing, and soon quantum computing); 5G connectivity; the internet of things, with already ten billion connected devices globally, and an estimated one trillion by 2035 (Gros et al., 2018); decentralised architectures such as the merging of peer-to-peer networks and the cloud, and where possible distributed ledger technologies (DLTs); and the rise of artificial intelligence as a pervasive, general-purpose technology that is poised to substantially revolutionise our working and private life (Renda, 2019).

10.1 How the digital transformation can help uncover many of our hidden treasures

While a full account of the potential and reality of these technologies would fall outside the scope of this book, it is extremely important to illustrate how digital technology can eventually help Europe uncover and leverage all its hidden treasures. In fact, digital technology is at the same time one of Europe's hidden treasures and a boost to all the others. For example, the emergence of smart contracts will increasingly affect contracting in online environments, in particular in complex relational contracts that require information sharing for compliance and verification purposes; embedding civil law in smart contract arrangements would then become both a question of political will, as well as a matter for standardisation and procurement when public authorities are involved (Cornelius, 2018). Blockchain/DLT and AI are expected to profoundly affect, among other sectors, corporate finance by enormously improving enterprise resource planning, streamlining procedures and improving accuracy of accounting and internal processes; and providing new opportunities for crowdfunding through initial coin offerings.

Digital technologies are also affecting corporate governance, leading to more distributed, decentralised, 'platformised' structures than the original 'Coasean' firm, based on hierarchy; blockchain promises to further disrupt the original architecture of corporations by creating decentralised trustless governance systems (Fenwick and Vermeulen, 2018). Innovation is changing and accelerating thanks to the digitisation of all markets, and this, in turn, creates tensions in the way the EU regulates data flows, as well as text and data mining activities, as will be discussed below: the role of governments, in this context, becomes essentially that of facilitator, but also entrepreneur, in charge of giving direction to innovation, steering it towards tackling societal challenges. Patent strategies change in the digital sphere, veering towards open patents and requiring new tools for technology transfer, and being fundamentally challenged by the artificial intelligence age. EU competition policy seems to be better equipped than most homologous pieces of legislation around the world when it comes to tackling issues such as algorithmic collusion and discrimination, as well as market power and unfair practices in platform-to-business relationships. The future of corruption control, as well as taxation policy, seem to be deeply linked to developments in blockchain/DLT technologies, and in particular RegTech solutions. Finally, trade policy is increasingly looking at digital goods and services and sees blockchain technologies as a possible engine of trust in complex global supply chains, in the Chinese Digital Silk Road, and even on the UK-Ireland border.

In other words, all our hidden treasures will be fundamentally affected by the digital transition. Uncovering them and bringing them to life means that the impact of digital technologies has to be fully taken into account, and that private governance through technologies does not develop as an alternative paradigm to EU law, but rather as a complement to it, and possibly a boost to its effectiveness, and to EU competitiveness. Importantly, digital technologies do not just change individual sectors, or bring new products and processes to the marketplace: the development of an entirely new "technology stack" (Renda, 2019) makes it possible to experiment with new forms of governance, which were previously considered to be prohibitively costly or inefficient. Accordingly, it also triggers a rethink of the single market in its very structure and *modus operandi*.

10.2 Digital technologies and their contribution to economic performance

The potential contribution to economic performance of new digital technologies can hardly be underestimated. Scholars and commentators are now convinced that the "Gordon paradox" (i.e. the fact that we see technology everywhere, but not in measures of productivity) is a thing of the past, and that new digital technologies will finally start massively contributing to productivity worldwide, including in the EU. Recent reports by Accenture/Frontier Economics, McKinsey and PWC conclude that technologies like AI will be game changers for total factor productivity and growth, by gradually rising as a third pillar of production, together with labour and capital. Chen et al. (2016) estimate the cumulative economic impact of AI from 2016 to 2026 as lying between $1.5 trillion and $3 trillion (0.15% to 0.3% of global GDP). Furman and Seamans (2019) review some of the most interesting literature on the impact of AI on the economy, which mostly finds that AI and robotics have the potential to increase productivity growth but may have mixed effects on labour, particularly in the short run. They also conclude that many economists believe that "AI and other forms of advanced automation, including robots and sensors, can be thought of as a general purpose technology (GPT) that enable lots of follow-on innovation that ultimately leads to productivity growth"; the fact that AI has not (yet) translated into large productivity gains, according to Brynjolfsson, Rock and Syverson (2017), is due to a "lag between technological progress and the commercialization of new innovative ideas building on this progress which often rely on complementary investments" (Furman and Seamans, 2019) – a lag, these authors claim, that is particularly notable in the case of GPTs.

The prospect of unprecedented productivity gains, and the certainty that "winter is not coming" for AI (Renda, 2019), have led countries around the world to launch dedicated strategies for the new family of digital technologies, and in particular on AI. The US and China are currently trapped into a digital arms race and making dominance in AI and related technologies (notably, quantum computing) the top strategic priority for the next decade. This, in turn, had led investment to skyrocket. Especially in the fields of high-performance computing, 5G/IoT and artificial intelligence, Europe risks being left behind by the scale of investment (including in the defence sector); the less precautionary approach to regulation; and the weaker importance attached to protecting users and citizens in countries such as China.

For example, the EU currently provides about 5% of supercomputing resources worldwide but consumes one third of them, and member states have long been in dire need of expanding their supercomputer capacities. [119] A look at quantum computing patents and investment is also revealing. As shown in the Figure below, the US and China are in a race to patent quantum-related technologies, although the EU is the region in the world with the highest number of research publications in this field. China is particularly interested in quantum cryptography, which has immense implications for military operations. In June 2019, in an attempt to catch up with these developments, the European High-Performance Computing Joint Undertaking (EuroHPC) selected eight sites for supercomputing centres located in eight different member states to host the new high-performance computing machines,[120] for a total investment of €840 million. The Barcelona supercomputer called MareNostrum 6, in particular, will be faster than the fastest US-based supercomputer (200 petaflops against 140), and may see the light by 2025.

Figure 23. Patents on quantum computing technology

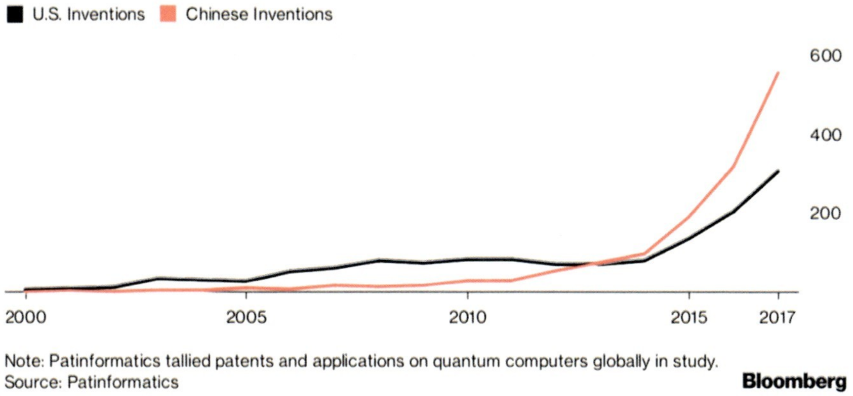

■ U.S. Inventions ■ Chinese Inventions

Note: Patinformatics tallied patents and applications on quantum computers globally in study.
Source: Patinformatics

Bloomberg

In the coming years, the race for developing a full digital technology stack will become even more hectic, as testified by the recent skirmishes between the US and China over 5G connectivity and wireless equipment. The most intensely competitive battlefield is probably artificial intelligence, given its pervasive, dual-use nature and the relevance it will have for all sectors of the economy. In this space, the debate at EU level is increasingly loaded with hopelessness: Europe has lost the B2C race; Europe does not have any of the technology giants; the data train has left the station, etc. There is some element of truth in these statements, but also excessive pessimism, which may become an alibi for policymakers not to take action to reverse the trend.

More specifically, it is true that the B2C domain is currently dominated by large US tech giants such as Google, Facebook, Amazon, Apple, Twitter, Microsoft and Netflix, though this dominance is increasingly challenged by Chinese giants such as Alibaba, Baidu, Tencent and Huawei. The two superpowers hardly fight in each other's backyard (at least when it comes to platforms); yet they compete at arms' length in global markets. The US tends to dominate on the software and applications side, but Chinese companies dominate the infrastructure domain, and will increasingly need to serve non-domestic markets once its middle class has consolidated and related markets are saturated.

In all this, it is widely acknowledged that Europe will not be able to compete on an equal footing with the United States and

China in terms of the sheer size of investment in new technologies. The Communication on Artificial Intelligence, adopted in April 2018, acknowledges the investment gap and highlights a possible alternative strategy for Europe, mostly based on a combination of competitiveness and ethical rules. In other, related fields such as 5G wireless communications, the internet of things, online platforms, high-performance computing and blockchain, the Commission has shown similar intentions, but so far relatively poor implementation. In yet another set of high-tech areas, such as genetics and genomics, the EU has remained almost silent despite the fact that the policy debate that emerged over the past few years was ethically loaded.

Could Europe play a leading role in the setting of rules and ethical principles for the development and commercialisation of new technologies? As things stand, the answer cannot be positive. If one looks at the overall technology stack that is emerging as the so-called Web 3.0, Europe appears to be lagging behind other regions of the world in many crucial respects: not only the size of investment in R&D&I, but also in terms of fixed and wireless broadband deployment (very high capacity networks, as well as 4G); level of per capita investment in e-communications infrastructure, relative presence in 5G standards; level of investment in AI, blockchain, the IoT; uptake of new technologies among consumers, as well as among firms; relative development of high-tech skills and competencies; ownership of patents in key enabling technologies; readiness for the quantum supremacy age; and even skills available in the public administration. All this weakens Europe's potential authoritativeness when it comes to credibly proposing (let alone imposing) global standards.

In all this, the recent entry into force (in May 2018) of the General Data Protection Regulation is considered by many as a possible exception, which may chart a new course in EU technology policy. By requiring strict standards of data protection, as well as restrictions on profiling, a right to data portability and to receive a meaningful explanation of how algorithms reached sensitive decisions, the GDPR seeks to establish a global standard in the high-tech world, and to chart a new course in technology policy, making it more user-centric after many years of rather drastic laissez faire vis-à-vis data protection.

The GDPR has been implemented only recently, and significant uncertainty still exists as regards its success in terms of improved protection of end users' right to data protection, as well as in terms of actual levels and modes of compliance. Accordingly, it is probably too soon to draw conclusions, but a few lessons can already be learnt. First, the GDPR has shown that courage pays at the EU level: the decision taken a few years ago on the need for a regulation on data protection has made the GDPR a path-breaking text in a world dominated by relatively lenient data protection rules. Second, Europe has successfully conquered the front pages of the international press, as well as grabbing the attention of top company CEOs through leveraging its ability to draft consistent, comprehensive rules, as well as its large and relatively rich internal market. Third, and relatedly, the EU has discovered that well-conceived, sound technology rules can potentially translate into effective export products, although there is no certainty that this is actually happening with the GDPR. Assuming that the GDPR will eventually be a success, can the EU replicate this experience in other, related fields? One attempt, as already mentioned, is underway in the field of artificial intelligence, and this link is so explicitly made inside the European Commission that the slogan "AI is the new GDPR" is becoming increasingly popular. At the same time, Europe has no consolidated tradition in the ethics of AI, which would help it build credibility in a field in which it has certainly neither research and innovation leadership (with some exceptions), nor a very established infrastructure.

10.3 Five reasons why Europe has a real opportunity to lead in digital technologies "for good"

Europe can credibly claim to possess five potential opportunities when it comes to setting global standards on emerging technologies. The first is its solid, comprehensive legal framework, which appears more complete and more consistent than the one available in the United States and China. The second is the size of the single market, which remains for now (but not necessarily for long) the richest market in the world: this gives Europe the possibility to dictate conditions to those that want to acquire or preserve market shares in Europe. The third advantage is Europe's potential leadership in the global quest for sustainable development, at a time in which the

United States is backtracking from human rights and SDGs, and China is not yet ready to lead. Fourth, it is false to state that the data train has left the station: the data needed to advance towards sustainable development through digital technologies still has to be created and collected, and data collection will not stop in the future, but rather will increase exponentially. Fifth, while Europe keeps complaining that it does not have tech giants, and that value extraction by online platforms is impoverishing the EU's traditionally strong industrial sectors, technology is coming to the rescue, allowing for new forms of governance that can mirror, more specifically, the EU's traditional way of approaching economic policy.

All five are still to be considered as potential advantages: it is up to EU institutions and member states to leverage them, exploit the current opportunity, and avoid being doomed to irrelevance in the coming years.

10.3.1 *Europe has the most comprehensive legal framework on digital technologies, but needs to improve it in many respects*

No country has the quantity and quality of legal rules on emerging technologies that the EU has. The new e-Communications Code is now following a very comprehensive e-communications framework launched in 2002, and only slightly reviewed over the past sixteen years, while the US 1996 Telecommunications Act was gradually being set aside by piecemeal regulation in the United States. The net neutrality rules in place since 2016 appear stable and balanced, whereas in the United States they are still contested and have been changed very frequently in the past half-decade. Most importantly, the NIS directive, the Cybersecurity Act, the reformed copyright regime, the Audio-visual Media Services Directive, the e-Commerce Directive, the GDPR, the e-Privacy Directive and the new Platforms–to-business Regulation (see above, Chapter 6) and on the free flow of data are paving the way for a very comprehensive framework, in which the new technology stack could find a high level of regulatory quality and certainty. In addition to existing rules, interpretive communications and soft law may be needed to promote legal certainty in domains such as artificial intelligence (e.g. the products liability directive, the machinery directive may have to be clarified or even adapted). Beyond being very comprehensive, the framework is also very protective of users' rights: the GDPR, in particular, appears as a lone bright spot in a world dominated by aggressive use of personally identifiable information for marketing purposes. Yet, the new President of the European Commission Ursula von der Leyen has announced regulatory measures on ethics and AI in the first 100 days of the European Commission.

Of course, Europe's legal framework is far from perfect, and needs significant reform and updates. In a recent publication, one of us called for "AI fitness checks" aimed at bringing the EU *acquis* up to speed with new technological developments (Renda, 2019), a proposal that was later echoed by the EU High Level Expert Group on AI (AI HLEG, 2019b). More generally, the legal framework for investment in infrastructure should be reformed to allow for more flexibility at the national level, against specific targets in terms of connectivity, as well as penetration of both fixed and wireless (5G) networks; and spectrum policy should be far more coordinated, and centralised when it comes to the key frequencies needed for 5G.

Most importantly, Europe should make sure that a suitable, consistent framework for data-driven innovation emerges throughout the continent, in order to facilitate data-hungry solutions such as those involving machine learning. This is a daunting task, given the need to strike a good balance between the free flow of data, the need to ensure national security (which is already an exception to the free flow of data), and the need to protect user privacy. The EU can strike a suitable balance by: adopting a full-fledged open data policy, which extends to publicly funded research as well as data held by public administrations; investing in, and endorsing, AI systems that do not make use of profiling based on personally identifiable data; and funding research and innovation projects on the condition that they include the use of privacy-by-design solutions; and establishing legal certainty on ethical rules for AI, including, *inter alia*, the transparency, explainability, accountability and liability of AI systems, so that developers will act in a less uncertain space. Moreover, at the sectoral level, the launch of 'industrial data spaces' could promote the sharing of data between competitors and new entrants, and at the same time ensure more a competitive environment by avoiding the accumulation of large datasets in the hands of a few large market players. Finally, and more generally, EU policy at the sectoral level should prioritise two aspects: ownership of data by players that create value through producing goods and services along the supply chain (e.g. farmers); and control of personally identifiable data by the end users.

10.3.2 Europe is still the richest market in the world

Europe is still the largest, richest single market in the world, although its leadership is increasingly under attack by the US and even more so by China. Europe's primacy as a market also means a lot in terms of policymaking: non-EU companies have a strong interest in serving Europe's half-billion consumers, and will accordingly try to adapt to whatever (reasonable) regulatory constraints policymakers introduce in order to ensure that digital technology conforms to the highest standards of user protection, respect for core EU values and fundamental rights. Not surprisingly, the GDPR was well received by many international players, and many of the largest digital companies are complying with it, regardless of whether they are headquartered inside or outside the EU. The GDPR has reportedly already exerted a significant impact on multinational organisations: if anything, the problem is compliance by smaller companies, who are disproportionately affected by some of its provisions. Some companies who may have initially viewed the regulations as a hindrance to the way they can communicate with their audience, will have now realised that the GDPR forced them to think more carefully about how to reduce the amount of data that is being transferred, or how to secure data in case of a cyber-attack or a major disruption of their servers or networks.

There are many ways in which the EU can leverage the attractiveness of its single market. Setting relatively strict rules is not going to be sufficient, if such rules are not fully enforced, and if they are not also applied to non-EU players that want to interact with European consumers. For example, in the case of the GDPR, the extent and mode of compliance with the rules introduced in May 2018 will determine whether, and to what extent, the legislation will have been a success. In this respect, a lot will depend on the role of data protection authorities at the national and EU level, as well as national courts. In other fields, similar problems may arise for future ethical rules on artificial intelligence: specifying that AI has to be transparent and non-discriminatory may be only a nice gesture, if no procedure is put in place to enforce these principles in a way that is compatible with the features of modern digital technologies: algorithms are constantly changed and updated, and simply requiring specific algorithmic features in legislation may not be easy, due to problems in verifying compliance.

A possible and necessary improvement in current EU policymaking includes the transition towards principles-based, experimental legislation that adopts both *ex ante* and *ex post* technological means of enforcement. The principles-based nature of legislation ensures that as technology changes, market players and citizens are aware that the same set of overall principles and values are embedded in legislation, and that they are invariable to technological change. In the case of AI, as recently advocated by Renda (2019), this core set of rules should include EU core values and fundamental rights, principles of responsible AI generally accepted in the community of AI developers, as well as additional principles that will determine the EU's specific approach to AI, which should include elements of complementarity between man and machine, responsibility in AI development, as well as sustainability.

The experimental nature of EU legislation is essential in order to ensure that innovative services and business models have a chance to be tested before being admitted to the market, and that legislation is stringent enough to steer innovation, but flexible enough to allow new business models to enter the market and improve societal welfare. The use of techniques such as RCTs, real and virtual sandboxes, ideation sprints, regulation through browser extensions and third-party algorithmic auditing can help Europe strike the right balance between the precautionary principle and the innovation principle.

Enforcement should also change: in data-rich digital environments, enforcement methods need to combine both *ex ante* and *ex post* techniques. *Ex ante* techniques include the obligation to leave audit trails in developing technologies, for future consultation by agencies and courts; the adoption of 'privacy by design' and 'fairness by design' tools and standards in the development of AI systems; the adoption of blockchain-based solutions to ensure decentralised control of compliance with legislation; and more. *Ex post* enforcement techniques increasingly require the use of bots to patrol internet traffic, the *ex post* auditing of algorithms, the imposition of strict liability rules and even compensation funds to ensure redress for users damaged by AI systems; and more.

Most importantly, securing the single market through stringent, flexible and well-enforced legislation is only a first step towards leveraging the power of Europe's 500 million consumers. In a world in which large superpowers are likely to adopt less stringent rules than the European ones, Europe will need additional tools to promote its laws and ensure that no 'race to the bottom' occurs in high-tech markets. These may include the use of certification (an 'EU seal' for high-tech products and services); the restriction to EU-certified products in public procurement; the introduction of specific safeguards in the use of high-tech products and services in trade agreements; and more. Only in this way, through a consistent set of rules and means to enforce them, can Europe aspire to becoming a global norm leader, offering market players a consistent, comprehensive environment in which new technologies are promoted, and users are adequately protected.

10.3.3 Filling the empty throne: Europe as a leader in socially and environmentally sustainable technology

It is often said, in the debate on new digital technologies and in particular on AI, that Europe lacks a 'vision' for the medium term. This, however, is not true. Europe already has a vision: Agenda 2030, based on the Sustainable Development Goals. In launching Agenda 2030 back in 2016, and in renewing its commitment in 2019, the European Commission announced its plan to mainstream SDGs (in their European version, most likely more ambitious than the global one) in all aspects of EU policy, including the European Semester, cohesion policy, better regulation, and sectoral legislation. In the negotiations on the future Multiannual Financial Framework for 2021-2027, the EU institutions referred extensively to sustainable development in earmarking funds for specific areas of policy while the new EU research and innovation programme, Horizon Europe, widely refers to the SDGs.

However, for some reason, when it comes to 'mainstreaming SDGs' in digital technology policy, there seems to be a reluctance on the side of the EU institutions. This may be due to the need to preserve control of specific policy areas in specific parts of the European Commission, without subjecting technology policy to the control of DGs in charge of social and environmental sustainability. But the overall result is very regrettable, for two major reasons. First, Agenda 2030 will be weakened if digital technology policy lacks coherence with overall EU sustainable development strategy. Second, the rules adopted for digital technologies will also be isolated, and ultimately weaker. AI is a perfect example in this respect: asking what rules are best to promote European competitiveness in AI only provides part of the answer; much more important will be to ask how can AI help Europe reach its 2030 goals. The latter include specific goals on decent work, reducing inequality, eradicating poverty and hunger, investing in human capital and eliminating gender bias; and on land use, water, the environment and energy among others. All these goals can be profoundly affected by AI developments, but the link is not being explicitly made, except by the global "AI for good" initiative launched by the United Nations.

Developing a comprehensive policy framework to enable the contribution of digital technologies to the SDG agenda would ideally place the EU as global leader both in the SDG arena, as well as in the technological one. Other global powers have fewer incentives to go down this road, and are currently either in denial with respect to SDGs (US) or in a conflicted position that prevents them from adopting economically, socially and environmentally responsible rules (China).

10.3.4 The data train has not (yet) left the station

Too often EU policymakers complain that European companies cannot compete since data are firmly in the hands of a few large tech companies, mostly based outside Europe. And indeed, current figures show that the bulk of Western world data (an estimated 92%) is currently stored in the United States, whereas only 4% is currently stored in Europe. If data, as many commentators say, were really the 'new oil', then there would be no possibility for Europe to compete on an equal footing with other superpowers. China is rising to the challenge by imposing data localisation requirements on all players that deal with Chinese consumers. In a nutshell, everyone wants data, and if possible on their territory, and there is a growing belief that restrictions to data flows, including the ones introduced by the GDPR for the purposes of data protection, may hamper the development of digital technology, and the competitiveness of legal systems that dare to go down the road of strong privacy and data security standards.

However, this is only a very static way of portraying reality. This is what has happened to date, but there is no reason to believe that it should happen in the same way, and to the same extent, in the future. In a word: the data train is still on the platform and has not left the station. Here's why.

First, in the B2C domain large online platforms have accumulated personal and non-personal data for several years, often without having to pay, and will most likely continue to do so on account of positive network effects, which tend to sustain and reinforce their position in the market. But to the extent that these data will be needed for services of general interest, or whenever these data will be found to represent a significant barrier to entry, public authorities will have the option of requiring access to specific datasets, or even imposing mandatory interoperability requirements on large technology giants. This would be a re-proposition of the essential facilities doctrine in a new fashion, with a specific approach that dates back more than two decades in EU competition law, to cases like *Magill, IMS Health,* and *Microsoft* (Renda, 2010). Based on this approach, whenever a dominant market player holds an asset of information that is essential for competitors to viably compete in the relevant market, and refusal to provide access to this information is likely to either lead to the exit, or even prevent the growth of, 'as efficient' or even 'not yet as efficient' competitors, then competition law may provide for compulsory access remedies. Much in the same vein, the German government is now imposing compulsory access obligations to tech giants for specific datasets. In a recent paper for the European Commission's DG COMP, Jacques Crémer, Yves-Alexandre de Montjoye and Heike Schweitzer echo this view by observing that "the ability to use data to develop new, innovative services and products is a competitive parameter whose relevance will continue to increase"; and clarified that "in a number of settings, data access will not be indispensable to compete, and public authorities should then refrain from intervention. In other settings, however, duties to ensure data access – and possibly "data interoperability" – may have to be imposed". The paper correctly points out that a "broader diffusion of data is not always desirable, either from a social welfare or from a competition perspective" due to privacy concerns; and that in addition to data interoperability, in some cases full protocol interoperability may be needed for competitors to be able to compete on an equal footing.

Second, in the B2C domain, EU institutions could decide to go beyond data access and interoperability obligations, and adopt policies aimed at returning control of their data to end users, or even treat data 'as labour' whenever possible, as advocated recently by the Report of the High Level Expert Group on the Impact of the Digital Transformation on EU Labour Markets.[121] This would lead to forms of remuneration from digital platforms to end users, which may take various forms, including the provision of free services, or a web tax along the lines currently considered by France, and which received a first political agreement in the G7 context in August 2019 in Biarritz, France. In that case, the tax would be based on the consideration that the digital platforms derive (some would say, extract) value from the end users, who provide data in exchange for being part of the platform: the main theoretical argument in favour of such a form of redistribution is the 'collective action problem' faced by end users, who are structurally unable to place a price on the data they provide, while these data, once aggregated, become extremely valuable to the platform. This form of positive externality could be seen as the market failure that a web tax, or any other form of redistribution, would seek to remedy. This approach, however, would not lead to the creation of more competition in the market, or possibly even the entry of European players in the B2C segment.

Third, and most importantly, the current wave of AI-enabled data analytics was spurred by one key factor: the explosion of digital data availability made possible by the first wave of the internet, which connected people across the globe. The availability of an end-to-end digital environment in which ever-growing computing capacity and enhanced broadband connectivity led to the 'zettabyte age', an extremely information-rich environment in which the availability of data in digital form roughly doubles every year: someone, or better something has to process all that information, and the use of AI has become inevitable to accompany this breathtaking development. In 2018, the amount of data created every day had reached 2.5 quintillion bytes, and the data created in the last two years amounts to more than 90% of the data ever created. While this is already mind-boggling, it is also still the beginning, and not necessarily the most important development in the use of data to ensure productivity, growth and prosperity. Given the current evolution of the internet 'of people', it is not surprising to find that the data and AI applications that have been entering the marketplace over the past years, starting from chatbots and recommendation engines to end with AI-enabled cameras for smartphones and personal fitness applications, are often unrelated to emerging existential challenges for our planet such as climate change. The data we need to tackle the climate challenge, and improve our productivity in factories, has not been created yet, and will be massively created in the future thanks to development such as the internet of things, 5G and edge computing. But for these types of data, which most often pertain to the B2B or G2C (government-to-citizens) domains, the there is no obvious leader around the world, and the processing of the information and related AI elaboration (in what is often called 'embedded AI') will take place more locally, and in a less standardised way compared to what happens in mass B2C markets.

In other, simpler words, the race to collect and process data has just started, and Europe has a chance to get it right. While the US and China are increasingly engaging in a digital arms race, the use of digital technologies for sustainable development suffers from a chronic lack of leadership, which only the EU can try to fill. Current initiatives such as the proposed creation of an Inter-Governmental Panel on Artificial Intelligence (modelled on the Inter-Governmental Panel on Climate Change), proposed by France and Canada within the G7, are meeting the resistance of the US and the silence of EU institutions, and may never be even seriously discussed. All this is occurring while the data related to climate and biodiversity are increasingly disastrous, and the widespread implementation data-hungry AI/IoT solutions appears as a necessary (albeit not sufficient) condition to bring the planet back towards a sustainable path (See Renda et al., forthcoming 2019). Rather than complaining about data that are stored in the US, EU institutions could instead grasp that much more data will now be created by connected things, and data can even be created by regulators simply through requiring regulated entities to report data on compliance, in what is often termed 'RegTech', or technology-enabled regulation and public services.

The adequate collection, processing and governance of data in support of Europe's sustainable development strategy, and in compliance with EU data protection standards, is one of the key challenges for Europe in the years to come, The reassuring news is that this future is not written yet, and not compromised yet: but it takes a massive commitment, a significant investment and a certain amount of industrial policy to bring it about in a sustainable way from an economic, social and environmental perspective.

10.3.5 New forms of governance for the single market

One corollary of Europe's 'difference' in digital technologies is that Europe has less to lose from moving from highly concentrated platform-to-consumer (P2C) markets towards more distributed governance forms. In fact, digital technologies today allow for forms of governance that were hardly feasible and cost-effective in the past. For example, the extreme redundancy of decentralised blockchain platforms such as Bitcoin is such that most existing applications have to sacrifice something in terms of speed of synchronisation, or in terms of scalability. But increasingly, the world of digital technology is making a broad variety of governance options available to policymakers.

More specifically, the economies of scale that characterise the analogue world are much less present in the digital space. This, in turn, means that markets that previously displayed oligopolistic structures, given the need for large-sized firms that would be able to invest in plants, factories and heavy infrastructure, can now work in a much more agile way. And in many sectors, even tangible assets such as lorries, medical equipment, servers, or drones are now being 'uberised', and require much less investment on the side of market players. If anything, economies of scale have now moved to data. This being the case, adopting interoperability obligations to enable more pluralistic market structures could also lead to configuring the single market in a much more fragmented way: as a common economic space in which public administrations share data between themselves and with businesses (through open APIs); in which citizens have control of their data and choice between a variety of different providers; and in which small competitors can thrive and provide local solutions to local problems, on equal conditions throughout the territory of the Union. This does not imply as such that distributed, or even decentralised forms of governance will always be the most efficient; in some cases, however, despite not being the most efficient, they may prove the most sustainable in the long run, and those less prone to creating inequality and allowing the ongoing distancing between value creation and value extraction in the digital economy.

10.4 Policy recommendations

The new von der Leyen Commission has promised to focus on digital technology, pursuing the work of the Juncker Commission in the period 2014-2019. There is a lot to be done, and quickly, to make sure Europe catches the new wave of technological developments, after admittedly having missed the first one. Below, we offer some policy recommendations on how to fully leverage the potential of digital technologies for Europe's competitiveness and sustainable development.

10.4.1 Build a new industrial policy on trusted data spaces

It is important that the EU rebalances the power of digital platforms in key sectors, by returning control of personal data to end users, and non-personal data to those market players that operate in the real economy, as close as possible to where value is created. Rather than the 'free flow' of data, what is most important is the controlled, managed and shared flow of data. And rather than data, trust should be the 'new oil': independently of how much data are used, the creation of trusted relationships through digital technology is the most important way for Europe to enhance its competitiveness and its vocation towards sustainability. Workers' data, when used to enhance the profitability of algorithms, should be adequately remunerated.

An important initiative, in this respect, would be to mobilise all public and private data resources to enable an unprecedented effort towards tackling the climate challenge through a smart use of data, AI and the internet of things. This, as always happens with data, requires human resources to collect and annotate data from various sources, and make them interoperable by placing them into a common 'data lake', which could then be used by researchers to devise new solutions to the worrying climate and biodiversity trends. Having a common, shared pool of data could also lead to launching open prizes and challenges to address key societal and environmental risks. All in all, this is a collective effort that requires the mobilisation of massive resources: something that private players alone would not be sufficiently incentivised to undertake absent a strong lead by government.

10.4.2 Invest in "embedded AI" for sustainable development

While the United States and China fight for digital supremacy in the B2C space, Europe has an opportunity to leverage its advanced technological base and a solid set of legal and ethical principles to support investment in solutions that integrate AI and the IoT, creating value that can be leveraged for sustainable development. Against this background, the European Commission has shown at times determination, at times elusiveness in its approach to SDGs. Although sustainable development is considered a fundamental and overarching objective of the EU, enshrined in Article 3 TEU, and despite the existence of an EU strategy since 2001 and a set of Sustainable Development Indicators since 2005, the salience of this strategy at the highest political level had never been particularly strong before the launch of Agenda 2030: indeed, the EU was heavily criticised for lacking ownership and governance (Gregersen et al., 2016). Over the past few years, the European Commission has shown, at least in theory, strong commitment towards the SDGs, in particular in a series of communications that outlined the future Agenda 2030, centred on SDGs. This patchwork of initiatives, still lacking full coordination, is reflected in the state of advancement of the EU towards SDGs. Recently, in a stocktaking exercise of progress achieved over the past five years, Eurostat found that progress was strongest for SDG 3 ('Good health and well-being'), SDG 4 ('Quality education') and SDG 7 ('Affordable and clean energy'); slow or inexistent for other SDGs, and even negative on SDG 10 ('Reduced inequalities'), due to the continued rise of income inequalities within member states.

Leveraging digital technologies to achieve sustainable development requires, *inter alia*, strong political will; specific, well-coordinated industrial policy measures (e.g. the strategic value chains approach adopted by the European Commission's DG GROW; but also the KICs, the Partnerships and the Missions launched by DG Research and Innovation; and the specific programmes such as "Digitising agriculture" launched by DG CONNECT); demand-side measures such as leveraging public procurement to create market opportunities for these technological solutions; and the use of taxation and regulatory incentives to steer market developments towards sustainable technological solutions. Such a complex mix of measures is something that the EU has proven to be capable of, but will require more coordination, implementation, monitoring and enforcement than in the past, and more agile forms of policymaking.

10.4.3 *Alternative visions for the single market*

As already explained, digital technologies make it possible to think about a more integrated single market, without always requiring the creation of large European champions. EU institutions should devote more attention to the study of alternative forms of governance, and evaluate them not only on the basis of economic efficiency (e.g. cost-cutting), but also in terms of their ability to trigger a sustainable, harmonious development of the European economy and society. In particular, the following actions appear essential during the life of the next Commission presided by Ursula von der Leyen.

First, as many sectors of the economy feature an ongoing process of 'servitisation', the need to complete the single market for services (notoriously less developed than that for goods) becomes more compelling every day. The servitisation of the economy is a well-known process that largely pre-dates the internet era; however, the internet economy has become almost an 'everything as a service' economy. Devices are given to mobile customers as a service bundled with subscriptions (and in exchange for customer loyalty); cloud services dominate the market in a large part of the application layer; previously downloaded 'to own' software is now accessed online; and even large supercomputers such as GPUs and TPUs are made available on a usage basis through the cloud. Moreover, the 'uberisation' of passenger transport, accommodation, child care, handyman jobs, IT work (e.g. Mechanical Turk, Upwork) and low-skilled jobs and many other markets has led to extreme situations in which humans, themselves, are offered 'as a service' (Prassl, 2018). Importantly, this leads to all imbalances of contractual power permeating relationships with no real safeguards offered by the legal system arising from contract law. One clear example is the application of product liability rules for cases in which software is provided as a service: since the scope of most product liability regimes does not include intangible goods, this means cases of inadequate services, careless advice, erroneous diagnostics and flawed information are as such not covered. A comparable situation exists in the field of product safety regulation, which so far has not been accompanied by a regulatory framework in the field of safety of services. In all these fields, the EU *acquis* appears far from complete, and will require more attention in the years to come.

Second, the transformation of the economic structure and business models made possible by the digital economy will lead in many circumstances to a convergence between the alternative modes of governance used in information systems (centralised, distributed, decentralised) and the conceptual models used in EU public policy to address problems such as subsidiarity, proportionality and resilience. In this respect, as already recalled, it will be possible to imagine a single market based on a network of interoperable administrations at the local level, which share data by joining a common, trusted data space, and offering APIs to businesses and academics willing to develop services, or perform research activities. In this way, a common, multi-level 'EU administrative space' would be offered 'as a platform' to businesses of all sizes, potentially eliminating, or mitigating, the competitive edge currently available to larger tech giants due to network effects and 'winner-takes-all' competition. This possible configuration, at least in some areas of the single market, would require that all member states deliver on the Tallinn declaration and take steps to make programmes like ISA2 mandatory (see above, Chapter 7).

10.4.4 Step up as a global leader of ethical and sustainable use of digital technologies

Europe must become a credible leader in setting a balanced approach to the regulation of the digital economy. Encouraging first steps were taken with the GDPR, and more recently with the Ethics Guidelines on Trustworthy AI adopted by the High-Level Expert Group on Artificial Intelligence, which were followed by policy and investment recommendations in June 2019. Much remains to be done, however, especially if one considers that this topic has been a nightmare for regulators when it comes to implementation and enforcement. The time is ripe to show how a safer, but still free and open internet can thrive thanks to adequate enforcement of principles-based regulation. At a time in which some countries already see the massive development of facial recognition (e.g. the US) and even forms of widespread social credit scoring (China), there is a clear need for strong leadership in urging the global community away from the weaponisation of cyberspace, as well as from a digital cold war.

The new legislature, with the European Commission led by a former Minister of Defence (in Germany), will need to pay close attention to preserving a constructive global dialogue, especially if oriented towards sustainable development, rather than focused on 'mutually assured hacking' (a new form of what used to be called 'mutually assured destruction' in the domain of nuclear weapons). Currently, countries seem to be increasingly exhibiting diverging visions of the internet economy and policy, as noted, among others, by O'Hara and Hall (2018), who identify as many as four internets, including a US "commercial" internet, an EU "bourgeois" internet, a Chinese "authoritarian internet", and a more vulnerability-exploiting internet (mostly in Russia, Iran and North Korea). These diverging views are also echoed in end users' preferences for specific policy priorities, such as protecting end-user privacy (Graf et al., 2016). These developments, coupled with the growing strategic importance of retaining control of internet infrastructure and the flow of data, ultimately led many countries to consider forms of 'data sovereignty' policies, as well as policies for 'strategic autonomy' as emerging priorities at the national and regional level (EPSC, 2019). Many countries are indeed discovering the enormous strategic importance of controlling the infrastructure, the data and the computing capacity related to the new technology stack: notable examples are the *querelle* over the possible ban of Huawei from the deployment of 5G networks in the United States and beyond; Europe's reported temptation to build its own European microprocessors and calls to launch an "Airbus for AI" as a form of industrial policy; and the European idea of building 'data spaces', which may evolve towards orchestrated ways to build European champions in key sectors such as automotive, healthcare, etc. Looming in this debate is also the growing competition between countries in securing advantage in new technologies such as quantum computing and cryptography (Gros et al., 2018); and the increased threat to national security represented by the expected boom in the internet of things over the next few years, which will expand the possible 'attack surface', thereby requiring enhanced control over data flows and ultimately, a likely deviation from internet openness principles.

Against this background, it is to be expected that Europe will be tempted by sovereignty-oriented policies in the years to come. And in some cases, it will become clear that infrastructure such as the internet of things and 5G should be given enhanced attention, as they significantly expand the attack surface, possibly requiring massive investment in strengthening the EU's cyber resilience and defence (Griffiths et al., 2019). But the real hidden treasure here is not strategic autonomy: there is indeed little merit in ring-fencing or even 'hard-forking' the internet. Rather, Europe's hidden treasure is its superior ability to reconcile technology with fairness, quality and sustainability (see Epilogue below), widely involving civil society in its governance decisions. Current steps are encouraging (think about the AI Alliance, an unprecedented forum for discussion that tops almost 4,000 participants), but a lot more needs to be done in the years to come to make EU institutions champions of trust at home, and leaders of peaceful, sustainable development on a global scale.

11. Epilogue:
Fairness, Quality, Sustainability and Trust as the Common Features of Europe's Hidden Treasures

In a world increasingly dominated by nationalism, protectionism, short-termism and deteriorating trust, Europe still has a choice, and a challenge. The choice is whether to do "more of the same, and better" by adapting to a global governance regime largely modelled on the experience of other blocs, and in particular the United States; or to nurture, deepen and expand a unique European way, politically, economically and socially, creating a distinct form of capitalism that can easily compete with financial capitalism and state capitalism. If successful, Europe would create a truly tripolar world and set an example for many countries to emulate, especially those that share with the Old Continent legal traditions and values (e.g. Latin American, and many African countries).

Europe can and should capitalise on its common deeper cultural and historical roots, longer history, and variety of experiences to learn from. But Europe also has a challenge: changing its governance to make the most of its invaluable wealth and political foundations and finding its post-Brexit identity by exploiting the aligned interests of continental European countries more fully.

Our analysis of the hidden treasures in ten different areas of policy should not be taken as exhaustive, but rather as a collection of 'low hanging fruits', some admittedly hanging lower than others. Other treasures wait to be discovered, and we have already started to identify future candidates: for example, vocational training, nearly free access to higher education, increasing labour market participation (from 60% in 2008 to 70% in 2018), universal health care coverage; and a better regulation agenda that is less slave to neoclassical economics. We believe that our recommendations, even if far-reaching, are actionable in policy terms during the legislature that has just started. They are the vanguard of several steps that should be taken to strengthen what is already strong. This is a cost-effective way to make progress, less subject to resistance on the part of vested interests: we call on EU institutions to start from Europe's strengths, rather that conceive of EU policies as always reacting to a (market) failure. This, in our humble opinion, should become a new *modus operandi* when crafting EU policies and strategies vis-à-vis European citizens and the global community. We also point at the need to work closely with the private sector, for example in putting the relationship between large companies and SMEs on a different footing in the interest of all and the economy at large.

Our recommendations also show a remarkable degree of alignment, which we had not anticipated when we started our research. Such alignment, in our *ex post* reflection, falls into a few different buckets. We explore them one by one below.

In the US and EU-27, fundamentally different views of the role of government prevail. Freedom to act and full ownership rights are important on both sides of the Atlantic; however, government regulation and taxation are seen in the US as attacks on these basic freedoms, while on the European continent regulation and taxation are forms of self-rule (*Selbstgesetzgebung*) enacted in order to protect economic freedom and, more generally, European citizens. In the US, this translates into perpetual antagonism between the state and its citizens.

Such a difference also reverberates in distributional policies on the two sides of the Atlantic. Back in 2003, Alesina and Angeletos synthesised the approach to government in the US and the EU with very clear words: "pre-tax inequality is higher in the United States than in continental Western European countries ... Nevertheless, redistributive policies are more extensive in Europe. The income tax structure is more progressive in Europe, and the overall size of government is about 50 per cent larger in Europe than in the United States". These differences are also a consequence of different approaches to the concepts of 'freedom' and 'equality' in the United States and in the EU. This appears to be more than a difference in implementation, and more than a constitutional divergence. As Eric

Foner (1998) explains in his history of American freedom, and as brilliantly echoed by Guido Calabresi (2016) in his analysis of equality in the US Constitution, the 14th amendment in the United States calls for a notion of equality that is substantive: as Calabresi recalls, citizens must "be willing to say, 'in my back yard,' 'raise my taxes,' 'on my back,' to achieve the substantive equality that the 14th amendment demands. Reneging on our 14th amendment promise of equality and avoiding paying the cost of achieving that equality ourselves: both of these are cursed in our Constitution". To the contrary, today's America seems to have embraced Nozick's "minimalist state", and ultimately a view of inequality-powered freedom that has little to do with the premises of the 14th Amendment. The Chicago School views of competition, and even more so Friedman's view of shareholder capitalism, which was analysed in Chapter 3, must be seen and approached in this context. And the revival of trickle-down economics, with the recent tax reform as a concrete example, confirms America's tendency towards a view of freedom 'from', rather than freedom 'of'.

These differences have profound consequences for many policy domains, for example securing fair competition and protecting privacy. In the US, competition rules are mostly for private players to settle private damages cases; whereas in the EU, they are largely entrusted to public authorities and enforced in the public interest (Renda et al., 2008). Provisions such as the "special responsibility of dominant players" and emphasis on the essential facility rule, among others, show how different EU antitrust is compared to the apparently similar rules applied on the other side of the Atlantic. Privacy rules in the US mostly refer to government interference with private life (e.g. the Fourth Amendment), whereas in the EU they also focus, and more prevalently, on the mishandling of personal data by private players. Tax rules are enforced in the name of mutual distrust between the IRS and the private sector in the US; in the EU, the search for fairness is frequently found to be in the general interest and the interest of the private sector.

This book has argued that there is no need for the EU to feel bound by elaborations and evolutions that pertain explicitly to the Anglo-Saxon world. Europe has managed to maintain its economic growth per capita on a par with the US despite the latter's many competitive advantages, ranging from one homogenous market for goods and services and one legal and fiscal system to deep capital markets and the most advanced universities in the world. In keeping up, Europe has also managed to remain more sustainable, less unequal, and on average a leading continent in terms of quality of life, as was recently recalled by EU leaders in their Sibiu Declaration. [122] Against this background, Brexit increasingly seems like a 'blessing in disguise', as Europe can now pursue well-established rules with new vigour, create new rules and build new institutions. This would provide remedies for some of the vexed problems that have emerged on the two sides of the Atlantic over the past decades. The analysis of the role and the merits of fairness and good faith in contract law, competition law, tax law and anti-corruption policies in Chapters 1, 6, 7 and 8 go exactly in that direction. Our discussions of the role of relationship banking and the emergence of the European Enterprise Model in Chapters 2 and 3 follow a similar pattern. Our view of innovation, outlined in Chapter 4, as a public-private endeavour, is very different from the perspective of Silicon Valley and Palo Alto as it is focused on legacy and emerging societal challenges. Innovation, in Europe, may be required to be 'fair' to society. Disruptive innovation is not necessarily good (as the verb disruptive suggests), unless it caters to the needs of society, and advances prosperity for all, not only the happy few.

All this demonstrates that Europe can build a different and appealing narrative. Not necessarily a brand new one: to some extent, our fairness- and sustainability-centred vision of Europe's hidden treasures can be traced back to the early days of economic theory, and to the renowned work of Adam Smith. Classical and neoclassical economics, including the Chicago School, largely referred to Smith's rather elusive "invisible hand" to build a theory of minimalistic state presence in the economy. In contrast, in Smith's *Theory of Moral Sentiments* the Scottish philosopher argued clearly and convincingly that justice, not efficiency, should be the basis for the distribution of rights in an economy. Justice, in Smith's words, is "the main pillar that upholds the immense fabric of human society". Europe's unique balance between freedom ('of', not 'from'), and justice explains its unique legal and economic tradition. Fairness, reasonableness, good faith, pre- and post-contractual obligations are time-tested principles and part of the heritage of continental Europe.

This book also shows that these principles are crucial for meeting the economic challenges of our time: insufficient investment, lack of socially relevant innovation, and slowing productivity growth. Chapters 2 and 3 show that the Shareholder Model of capitalism fails conspicuously on all three fronts. As things stand, only the EU-27 can be home to alternative enterprise models that make a positive difference. Focus on the creation of economic value, rather than short-term profit, unshackles innovation and investments. And the counter-argument, that well-functioning financial markets would price in long-term economic value is no longer convincing. Financial markets are guided by profit per share, are driven by algorithms that can only take the past into account and are therefore blind to trend breaks and are subject to biases in decision-making and herd behaviour. The causal link between corporate value and share price has gone, the rudder of financial capitalism is broken.

All this takes on new urgency as the global economy is appearing to run out of steam, the next recession is approaching rapidly, and central banks and governments have exhausted their ammunition for stimulating the economy (with the notable exception of Germany and some of its neighbours).

This book leads to two additional, essential findings related to technology and sustainability. On the one hand, Europe can harness the potential of digital technology 'for good', by setting ethical and policy standards through the sheer size of its single market, as well as through procurement, certification and trade policy. Europe's 'secret sauce' in digital technology can fill an existing gap in global governance, and help the 'Old Continent' find space for its approach to economic policy at the global level. This is crucially related to Europe's ability to treat technology as a means, not an end: in this respect, the recent ethical guidelines on artificial intelligence and the effective implementation of legislation such as the GDPR, rules on web taxation and platform-to-business practices will be essential in gauging Europe's ability to play a decisive role in this expanding space.

This also leads to a more general consideration on the broader, long-term picture. Looking at current trends such as the resurgence of nationalism in politics, deterioration in the rule of law (also in some European countries), new protectionist stances and tariff wars in trade, short-termism in social policy and recurring denials of climate change, the SDG agreement reached in September 2015 by 193 countries seems to belong to a very distant era. In the absence of any strong political will, the pursuit of the SDG agenda looks more dependent on technological breakthroughs and global private initiatives than on the alignment of governmental agendas in leading blocs. The contribution of the business community is greatly hampered by the focus on shareholder return, which discourages further investment. Stimulating investment, such as in replacing plant and equipment will not just increase productivity, but be key to the future of companies while reducing their environmental footprint, a key sustainability objective.

Only setting unequivocal standards will trigger such behaviour, and only Europe, today, can set these unequivocal standards. For now, with the exception of Scandinavian countries, all high-income countries are far from a trajectory that would lead them to achieve the 17 goals, and they struggle in particular with the four objectives related to sustainable consumption and production patterns, climate action, aquatic life and life on land. The EU has not shown enough ability to step up its efforts to date. Recently, in a stocktaking exercise of progress achieved over the past five years, Eurostat found slow progress in certain areas of sustainable development, and a worrying rise in inequality. It is now time to shift gear: the financial crisis is over, the Silicon Valley model is plateauing, and the world is witnessing the rise of less democratic, less open forces in both developed and developing countries, as well as in the private sector. The Old Continent can push back against these worrying trends. We believe Europe's hidden treasures offer an essential, compelling starting point to rethink Europe by retrieving its lost identity and strengthening its self-confidence.

Our recommendations are different from what is usual in EU circles. This flows for a large part from our methodology. We do not set targets for a limited number of key parameters, design policies to achieve those targets, evaluate progress and make policy adjustments. Rather, we take the world as it is – according to our analysis it is doing much better than *prima facie* evidence suggests –

and call for structural improvements. Hence the considerable differences in character and scope between our proposals. Still, we see three recurring themes.

The first is a strong emphasis on implementation and enforcement. The EU has a plethora of promising policies, well-thought-out regulations and high-quality legislation. However, in many instances implementation is below standard. This 'delivery phase' is the less glamourous, ill-funded and politically less convenient part of good government. And yet it is the area where Europe needs to improve the most. If the rule of law is important, we need to invest in our court system. If we believe in the common market it is about time that the European capital markets become operational. If we truly worry about corruption, we should make far more resources available for combatting it.

The second common denominator of our recommendations is the improvement of the position of SMEs. Their crucial contribution to innovation, economic development and employment is widely recognised, and many support programmes have been put in place. We point out that in the rough and tumble of day-to-day operations, SMEs are far more vulnerable than generally assumed, and the EU *acquis* is still insufficiently tailored to their specific needs. Our proposals thus seek to help SMEs (re)gain access to the courts, prevent abuses of power by their larger business partners, streamline the appeals process of the EPO and improve protection against corruption.

A third common denominator is an underlying emphasis on productivity, as a component of a long-term goal to improve living standards. The slowing down of productivity growth is a vexed problem and the diagnosis, let alone the solution, have escaped economists and politicians alike. In our view, this also happened because productivity was approached as a macroeconomic, not a microeconomic problem. As we show in Chapter 3, both the shareholder and the stakeholder model are deeply flawed and the responsibility for lower productivity growth should be laid at the doorstep of the boards and management of private companies and public institutions. Productivity growth is key to sustainable growth, as it requires focus on the prudent use of resources and on investment as each new generation of plant and equipment is far more efficient and more environmentally friendly then the previous one.

Moreover, our call for enabling fair, smart and flexible cooperation between large and small businesses is aimed at boosting productivity in the medium to long run, just as those for better access to capital, adopting a suitable enterprise model, and charting the way towards product, process and organisational innovation inspired by the pursuit of the common good. The same can of course be said for our proposals for the patent system, as well as those on competition and trade. We also believe that investment would be greatly facilitated by improvements in the tax system, as well as by a Europe free of corruption, which otherwise lowers productivity as a result of the mis-allocation of capital and human resources. And needless to say, we believe that digital technologies have the potential to massively improve productivity, but policymakers have to be wary of the sirens of 'automation at any cost'.

The final common denominator is that our proposals help to restore trust. Trust in the courts, trust in the banks, trust in large companies, trust between large and small companies, and overall trust in governments and EU institutions. The latter, after a worrying inflection, is now hitting new highs. And yet, the time is ripe for more agile, flexible institutions, able to deliver on policies that increasingly suffer from rapid obsolescence, and from pressure from other global superpowers aiming to outcompete each other. Our call to properly embed fairness in our institutions, in the economy and in work relationships is a necessary, albeit not sufficient, condition for trust to grow. No society and no economy can prosper on divisive policies, rising inequality and acrobatic economics. As the noise of post-truth geopolitics rises, and underlying patterns of development blur, Europe is increasingly forced to walk tall, rather than playing second fiddle, or dancing to someone else's drum. And as a starting point in the quest for this new course, there are a profusion of hidden treasures.

REFERENCES

AFME (2017). *The Shortage of Risk Capital for Europe's High Growth Businesses*. Published by AFME in conjunction with Accountancy Europe, BAE, BusinessEurope, Deutsche Börse Group, eban, European Investment Fund, Euronext, European Crowdfunding Network, FESE, Invest Europe, London Stock Exchange Group, Nasdaq.

Agarwal, S. and R. Hauswald (2010), "Distance and Private Information in Lending", The Review of Financial Studies, Volume 23, Issue 7, July 2010, Pages 2757–2788.

Agle, B. R., and R. K. Mitchell. 2008. "Introduction: Recent Research and New Questions." Introductory section of "Dialogue: Toward Superior Stakeholder Theory." Business Ethics Quarterly 18(2): 153–159.

Aguilera, R. and C. Williams (2009). 'Law and Finance': Inaccurate, Incomplete, and Important. Brigham Young University Law Review 6.

Akman, P. (2009), Searching for the Long-Lost Soul of Article 82EC, *Oxford Journal of Legal Studies*, Volume 29, Issue 2, Summer 2009, Pages 267–303.

Alesina, A., and G.-M. Angeletos (2005). "Fairness and Redistribution: US vs. Europe." American Economic Review 95: 913-35.

Alstadsæter, A., N. Johannesen and G. Zucman, (2018). Who owns the wealth in tax havens? Macro evidence and implications for global inequality. Journal of Public Economics 162, 89-100.

Anabtawi, I. (2006), Some Skepticism About Increasing Shareholder Power, 53 UCLA L. REV. 561, 579.

Anderson IV, R. (2016), The Long and Short of Corporate Governance, 23 Geo. Mason L. Rev. 19 (2015-2016).

Armour, J., S. F: Deakin and S. J. Konzelmann (2003), "Shareholder Primacy and the Trajectory of UK Corporate Governance". British Journal of Industrial Relations, Vol. 41, pp. 531-555, September 2003.

Arora, A., M. Ceccagnoli, and M. Cohen (2008). "R&D and the patent premium". International Journal of Industrial Organization. 26. 1153-1179. 10.1016/j.ijindorg.2007.11.004.

Ashford, N. A., C. Ayers, R.F. Stone (1985). "Using Regulation to Change the Market for Innovation," Harvard Environmental Law Review, Volume 9, Number 2, Summer 1985, pp. 419-466. Available at http://hdl.handle.net/1721.1/1555

Ashford, N. and A. Renda (2016), Aligning policies for low-carbon systemic innovation in Europe, Report for the European Climate Foundation's Institute for Industrial Innovation and Competitiveness (i24c), November 2016.

Ayadi, R., D.T. Llewellyn, R.H. Schmidt, E. Arbak and W.P. de Groen (2010), Investigating Diversity in the Banking Sector in Europe, CEPS Paperback, CEPS, Brussels (https://www.ceps.eu/publications/investigating-diversity-banking-sector-europe-keydevelopments-performance-and-role).

Ayadi, R., W.P. de Groen, I. Sassi, W. Mathlouthi, H. Rey and O. Aubry (2016), Banking Business Models Monitor 2015: Europe, Montreal: International Observatory on Financial Service Cooperatives (IOFSC) (http://financecoop

Backhaus J.G. (1998), "Efficient Statute Law", in The New Palgraves Dictionary of Economics and the Law, McMillan.

Balleisen, E.J., & Eisner, M.A. (2009). The Promise and Pitfalls of Co-Regulation: How Governments Can Draw on Private Governance for Public Purpose. In D. Moss and J. Cisternino (eds.), New perspectives on regulation, Cambridge, The Tobin Project, 2009.

Barker, R. M. and I. H-Y Chiu, "From Value Protection to Value Creation: Rethinking Corporate Governance Standards for Firm Innovation", 23 FORDHAM J. CORP. & FIN. L. 437 (2018).

Batsaikhan, U., Kalcik, R., & Schoenmaker, D. (2017). *Brexit and the European financial system: mapping markets, players and jobs.* Bruegel Policy Contribution Issue n°4.

Beck, T. and R. Levine (2002), Industry Growth and Capital Allocation: Does Having a Market- or Bank-based System Matter?, 64 J. FIN. ECON. 147, 161-64 (2002).

Beck, T. and R. Levine (2004), Legal Institutions and Financial Development, in Handbook of New Institutional Economics (Mary Shirley & Claude Ménard eds., 2004).

Beck, T., Demirgüç-Kunt, A. & Peria, M. S. M. (2011). *Bank financing for SMEs: Evidence across countries and bank ownership types.* Journal of Financial Services Research, 39(1-2), 35-54.

Begenau, Farboodi and Veldkamp (2018), Big data in finance and the growth of large firms, NBER Working Paper, 24550.

Behrens, V, P. Hünermund,; S. M. Leitner, G. Licht and B. Peters, State of Implementation and Direct Impact Assessment, Deliverable 4.2 of the I3U project, Ref. Ares(2018)14579 - 03/01/2018.

Bénézech, D. (2012). *The Open Innovation model: some issues regarding its internal consistency.* Journal of Innovation Economics & Management, 10(2), 145-165. doi:10.3917/jie.010.0145.

Bentham J. (1789), "An Introduction to the Principles of Morals and Legislation", London, T. Payne & son. Reissued, ed. J.H. Burns, H.L.A. Hart and F. Rosen, Oxford, Clarendon Press, 1996.

Berger and Udell (2000), *Small business and debt finance*, in Zoltan J. Acs and David B. Audretsch, eds.: Handbook of Entrepreneurship.

Berger, A. N. & Udell, G. F. (1998). The economics of small business finance: The roles of private equity and debt markets in the financial growth cycle. Journal of Banking & Finance, 22, 613-673.

Berger, A. N. & Udell, G. F. (2006). A more complete conceptual framework for SME finance. Journal of Banking & Finance, 30(11), 2945-2966.

Berggren, N., and H. Jordahl (2005), *Does Free Trade Really Reduce Growth? Further Testing Using the Economic Freedom Index.* Public Choice 122 (1–2): 99–114.

Berle jr., A. A. and G. C. Means (1933), The modern corporation and private Property 2-3.

Berndt, M. (2002), Global Differences in Corporate Governance Systems, in Ökonomische Analyse Des Rechts, Peter Behrens et al. eds.

Bertoni, Fabio, Massimo G. Colombo, and Annalisa Croce (2013). "Corporate Governance in High-Tech Firms." Oxford Handbook of Corporate Governance (2013): 365-388.

Bianchini, S., Krafft, J., Quatraro, F., & Ravix, J (2015). "Corporate Governance, Innovation and Firm Age: Insights and New Evidence". University of Turin, (Working Paper No. 201502).

Blair R.D. and D. D. Sokol (2012), The Rule of Reason and the Goals of Antitrust: An Economic Approach, 78 ANTITRUST L.J. 471.

Blanco, L. R. (2009), The Finance-Growth Link in Latin America (July 1, 2009). Southern Economic Journal, Vol. 76, No. 1.

Bolkestein, F. (2003) 'Corporate governance: does capitalism need fixing?', speech held at the US Bilderberg Meeting, Chantilly, 30 May 2002.

Bolton, P., X. Freixas, L. Gambacorta, P. E. Mistrulli (2016), "Relationship and Transaction Lending in a Crisis", The Review of Financial Studies, Volume 29, Issue 10, October 2016, Pages 2643–2676.

Boy, L. (2006), "Abuse of market power: controlling dominance or protecting competition?", in Hans Ullrich (ed.), The Evolution of European Competition Law: whose Regulation, which Competition? (Cheltenham and Northampton, MA, Edward Elgar, 2006), p. 220.

Brandt, F. and K. Georgiou (2016), "Shareholders vs Stakeholders Capitalism". Comparative Corporate Governance and Financial Regulation. Paper 10.

Brookings Institution (2018), Global Metro Monitor 2018, available online at https://www.brookings.edu/research/global-metro-monitor-2018/.

Brunswicker, S. (2012), "Open Innovation Sourcing in Small and Medium-sized Enterprises (SMEs): Choice or Curse?". Academy of Management Proceedings, 2012:1.

Brynjolfsson, E., D. Rock and C. Syverson, (2017), Artificial Intelligence and the Modern Productivity Paradox: A Clash of Expectations and Statistics, No 24001, NBER Working Papers, National Bureau of Economic Research, Inc.

Buchak, Matvos, Piskorski and Seru (2017), Fintech, regulatory arbitrage, and the rise of shadow banks, NBER Working Paper, 23288.

Byrnes, IV, W. H. (2017), Background and Current Status of FATCA and CRS (Sept. 2017 edition) (September 29, 2017). William Byrnes, Guide to FATCA and CRS Compliance, Lexis (Sept. 2017); Texas A&M University School of Law Legal Studies Research Paper No. 17-75.

Calabresi G. (2016), "Thoughts on Equality in the American Constitution", Lecture at Columbia University, at https://www.law.columbia.edu/sites/default/files/micros ites/law-theory-workshop/files/GCalabresi.pdf.

Calabresi, G. (2017), *The Future of Law and Economics. Essays in Reform and Recollection*; Yale University Press.

Campbell, J. L. (2007). "Why Would Corporations Behave in Socially Responsible Ways? An Institutional Theory of Corporate Social Responsibility." Academy of Management Review 32(3): 946–967.

Campbell, R. A. (2016), "Impact Analysis of The Leahy-Smith America Invents Act". Senior Projects. Paper 4. http://scholarworks.gvsu.edu/lib_seniorprojects/4

Carbonara, E., F. Parisi, and G. Von Wangenheim (2015), "Rent-Seeking and Litigation: The Hidden Virtues of Limited Fee Shifting", REVIEW OF LAW & ECONOMICS, 2015, 11, pp. 113 – 148

Casi, E., C. Spengel and B. Stage (2019), Cross-Border Tax Evasion after the Common Reporting Standard: Game Over? (July 20, 2019). ZEW - Centre for European Economic Research Discussion Paper No. 18-036.

Cassis, Y, A. Colli and H. Schröter (2016), The Performance of European Business in the Twentieth Century, Oxford University Press.

Castro, R. J. (2011), Castro, R.J. (2010), *Ex Post Liability Rules in Modern Patent Law*, Intersentia European Law and Economics Series.

Cheffins, B. R. (2001). "Does Law Matter? The Separation of Ownership and Control in the United Kingdom." Journal of Legal Studies 30.

Chen et al. (2016), *Global economic impacts associated with artificial intelligence*, Analysis Group, February 2016;

Chen, Q. (2015), "The Effect of Patent Laws on Economic Growth: Evidence from Cross-Country Panels during 1600-1913", Intellectual Property Rights 3: 145.

Chesbrough, H. (2003), *Open Innovation: The New Imperative for Creating and Profiting from Technology*, Harvard Business Press, 2003.

Chien, Colleen V., Comparative Patent Quality (September 1, 2016). 50 Arizona State Law Journal 71 (2018); Santa Clara Univ. Legal Studies Research Paper, No. 2016-13.

Chirico, F. (2010) "The Economic Function of Good Faith in European Contract Law", in Pierre Larouche, Filomena Chirico, (eds.), Economic Analysis of the DCFR: The work of the Economic Impact Group within CoPECL network of Excellence, Sellier.

Coase R. H. (1960), "The Problem of Social Cost", Journal of Law and Economics, 1.

Coase, R. H. (1937) "The Nature of the Firm," Economica 4, no. 16: 386–405.

Coffee, J. C. (2000). "The Rise of Dispersed Ownership: The Role of Law in the Separation of Ownership and Control." Columbia Law and Economics Working Paper 182: 1- 95.

Conac, P.-H. (2015): "The Societas Unius Personae (SUP): A "Passport" for Job Creation and Growth", European Company and Financial Law Review 12, pp. 139-176.

Cools, S. (2005), "The Real Difference in Corporate Law between the United States and Continental Europe: Distribution of Powers". Harvard Law School John M. Olin Center for Law, Economics and Business Discussion Paper Series. 490. Delaware Journal of Corporate Law Vol. 30, 698-733.

Cordero-Moss, G. (2007) "International Contracts between Common Law and Civil Law: Is Non-state Law to Be Preferred? The Difficulty of Interpreting Legal Standards

Such as Good Faith," Global Jurist: Vol. 7: Iss. 1 (Advances), Article 3.

Cordero-Moss, G. (2014), International Commercial Contracts, Cambridge Univ. Press Diniz, M. H. (2010), Código Civil Anotado, Ed. Saraiva.

Cornelius, K. B. (2018). Standard form contracts and a smart contract future. Internet Policy Review, 7(2). DOI: 10.14763/2018.2.790.

Corry, M- and G. Mather (2012), *Taxing Savings Sensibly. Is the EU Savings Tax Directive Overtaken by Events?*, European Policy Forum, at https://www.hossli.com/wp-content/uploads/2012/12/Taxing-Savings-Sensibly1.pdf

Cortinovis, N., Xiao, J., Boschma, R., and Van Oort, F. (2016), Quality of government and social capital as drivers of regional diversification in Europe. PEEG Series, 16.10.

Crane, D. A. (2009), "Chicago, Post-Chicago, and Neo-Chicago." Review of How Chicago Overshot the Mark: The Effect of Conservative Economic Analysis on US Antitrust, by R. Pitofsky, editor. U. Chi. L. Rev. 76, no. 4 (2009): 1911-33.

Crémer, J., Y-A de Montjoye, H. Schweitzer (2019), *Competition Policy for the Digital Era*, Report for the European Commission, DG Competition, At https://ec.europa.eu/competition/publications/reports/kd0419345enn.pdf.

CSES and Panteia (2014), *Evaluation of Market Practices and Policies on SME Rating*. Final report for the European Commission DG GROW, Ref. Ares(2014)1101684, 08/04/2014.

Cumberbatch, J. (1992), *In Freedom's Cause: The Contract to Negotiate*, Oxford Journal of Legal Studies, Volume 12, Issue 4, 1 December 1992, Pages 586-589, https://doi.org/10.1093/ojls/12.4.586

Czarnitzki, D., P. Hünermund, and N. Moshgbar (2018), Public Procurement as Policy Instrument for Innovation, ZEW Discussion Paper No. 18-001.

D. Acemoglu, K. Bimpikis, A. Ozdaglar (2011), "Experimentation, Patents, and Innovation" *American Economic Journal: Microeconomics*, vol. 3, no. 1, pp. 37-77.

Dahlberg, L. and F. Wiklund (2018), ESG INVESTING IN NORDIC COUNTRIES. An analysis of the Shareholder view of creating value, Umeå University School of Business, Economics and Statistics. https://umu.diva-portal.org/smash/get/diva2:1229424/FULLTEXT01.pdf

Davignon Group (1997) Report of the High Level Group of Experts on 'European Systems of Worker's Involvement', Brussels: European Commission.

Davis, I. (2019), Resurrecting Magnuson-Moss Rulemaking: The FTC at a Data Security Crossroads (February 20, 2019). Emory Law Journal, Forthcoming. SSRN: https://ssrn.com/abstract=3363925.

de Larosière Group (2009), Final Report of the High Level Group on Financial Supervision in the EU, https://ec.europa.eu/info/system/files/de_larosiere_report_en.pdf.

De Streel, A. (2018), Online Intermediation Platforms and Fairness: An assessment of the recent Commission Proposal, Université de Namur, CRIDS, CERRE, http://www.crid.be/pdf/public/8297.pdf.

Deffains B. and Kirat T. eds (2001), "Law and Economics in Civil Law Countries", Elsevier.

Deffains, Bruno. (2011). Efficiency of Civil Law.

Derbel, H, R. Abdelkafi and A. Chikir (2011), The Effects of Economic Freedom Components on Economic Growth: An Analysis with A Threshold Model, Journal of Politics and Law Vol. 4, No. 2.

Dougherty, S. and A. Renda (2017). Pro-Productivity Institutions: Learning from National Experience, International Productivity Monitor 2017, vol. 32, 196-217, OECD.

Draca, M. (2014), *Institutional Corruption? The revolving door in American and British politics*, SMF-CAGE Global Perspectives Series: Paper 1.

Drahos, P. (2010), *The Global Governance of Knowledge: Patent Offices and Their Clients*, Cambridge, Cambridge University Press.

Edlin, A. S. (2002), Stopping Above-Cost Predatory Pricing, 111 YALE L.J. 941.

Edmans, A. (2014). "Blockholders and Corporate Governance," Annual Review of Financial Economics, Annual Reviews, vol. 6(1), pages 23-50, December.

Eidenmueller, H. (2018), Collateral Damage: Brexit's Negative Effects on Regulatory Competition and Legal Innovation in Private Law, ECGI Law Working Paper 403/2018.

Elhauge, E. (2003), Why Above-Cost Price Cuts to Drive Out Entrants Are Not Predatory — and the Implications for Defining Costs and Market Power, 112 YALE L.J. 681 (2003).

EPRS (2017), Corruption in the European Union Prevalence of corruption, and anti-corruption efforts in selected EU member states.

Epstein, L. Landes and Posner (2017), When it comes to business, the right and left sides of the court agree, Washington University Journal of Law & Public Policy 54:33-55.

Escobar Ribas, A. (2017), "And Here Remain with Your Uncertainty: the Consequences of Brexit for Business Law*, Working Paper IE Law School, AJ8-239, 27 July 2017.

Esho, E. and G. Verhoef (2018), *The Funding Gap and the Financing of Small and Medium Businesses: An Integrated Literature Review and an Agenda*, MPRA Paper No. 90153.

European Central Bank (2018), Survey on the Access to Finance of Enterprises in the euro area October 2017 to March 2018.

European Commission (2003) Modernising Company Law and Enhancing Corporate Governance in the European Union – A plan to move forward, EU Com (2003) 284 (21.5.2003), http://ec.europa.eu/internal_market/company/modern/index_en.htm.

European Commission (2014), Report from the Commission to the Council and the European Parliament, EU anti-corruption report, European Union.

European Commission (2016), Communication from the Commission to the European Parliament, the Council, the European Economic and Social Committee and the Committee of the Regions, Next steps for a sustainable European future. European action for sustainability

{SWD(2016) 390 final}, COM(2016) 739 final, Strasbourg, 22.11.2016.

European Commission (2019), Reflection paper: Towards a Sustainable Europe by 2030. COM(2019)22 of 30 January 2019.

European Commission, (2018), EU Justice Scoreboard 2018, Communication from the Commission to the European Parliament, the Council, the European Central Bank, the European Economic and Social Committee and the Committee of the Regions, COM(2018) 364 final.

European Economic and Social Committee (EESC) (2008) Employee participation as an aspect of good business management in Europe, SOC/305 (11.4.2008), Brussels.

European Investment Bank (2018), Retooling Europe's Economy, EIB Investment Report 2018/2019.

European IPR Helpdesk (2015). Fact Sheet. Intellectual Property management in open innovation, October 2015

European patent Office (2017), Patents, trade and foreign direct investment in the European Union November 2017.

European Patent Office (2019), Annual Report of the Board of Appeals.

European Patent Office and the European Union Intellectual Property Office (2019), High-growth firms and intellectual property rights IPR profile of high-potential SMEs in Europe, May 2019.

European Political Strategy Centre (EPSC), *Rethinking Strategic Autonomy in the Digital Age*, EPSC Strategic Notes, Issue 30, July 2019.

European Trade Union Confederation (2004) ETUC press release from 19/10/2004 on the first Corporate Governance Conference of the European Commission held in Den Haag, Brussels.

European Trade Union Confederation (2006) Corporate Governance at European level. Resolution adopted by the ETUC Executive Committee in their meeting held in Brussels on 14-15 March 2006, Brussels.

Evan, W. M. and R. E: Freeman (1983), "A stakeholder theory of the Modern Corporation: Kantian Capitalism", in T. Beauchamp

& N. Bowie (Eds), Ethical theory and Business, Englewood Cliffs, Prentice Hall, New Jersey, pp. 75-93.

Ezrachi, D. (2018), EU Competition Law Goals and the Digital Economy, Discussion Paper for BEUC; https://www.beuc.eu/publications/beuc-x-2018-071_goals_of_eu_competition_law_and_digital_economy.pdf.

Fabre-Magnan M. (1992), "De l'obligation d'information dans les contrats: essai d'une théorie", Librairie Générale de Droit et de Jurisprudence, Paris.

Fahlenbrach, R. & Stulz, R. (2011). Bank CEO incentives and the credit crisis. Journal of Financial Economics, 99.

Faure M. (2000), "Economic Analysis of French Civil Liability Law", in Deffains and Kirat eds (2000), "Law and Economics in Civil Law Countries", Elsevier.

Fenwick, M. and E.P.M. Vermeulen (2018), Technology and Corporate Governance: Blockchain, Crypto, and Artificial Intelligence, ECGI Working Paper Series in law, Working Paper N° 424/2018.

Foner, E. (1998), *The Story of American Freedom,* W. W. Norton.

Foster, S. and D. Bonilla (2011), The Social Function of Property: A Comparative Perspective. Fordham Law Review, Vol 80, p 1003.

Fox, E. (2003), "We Protect Competition, You Protect Competitors", 26 World Competition 149.

Freeman, R. E, and W. M. Evan. (1990). "Corporate Governance: A Stakeholder Approach." Journal of Behavioral Economics 19(4): 337–359. doi: http://dx.doi.org/10.1016/0090-5720(90)90022-Y

Freeman, R. E. (1984). *Strategic Management: A Stakeholder Approach.* Boston: Pitman Publishing Inc.

Freeman, R. E. (1994). "The Politics of Stakeholder Theory: Some Future Directions." Business Ethics Quarterly 4(4): 409–421.

Freeman, R. E. (2008). "Ending the So-called 'Friedman-Freeman' Debate." Section II of "Dialogue: Towards Superior Stakeholder Theory." Business Ethics Quarterly 18(2): 153–190.

Freeman, R. E., and R. A. Phillips (2002). "Stakeholder Theory: A Libertarian Defense." Business Ethics Quarterly 12(3): 331-349.

Freeman, R. E., J. Harrison, A. Wicks, B. Parmar, and S. de Colle (2010). Stakeholder Theory: State of the Art. Cambridge: Cambridge University Press. doi: http://dx.doi.org/10.1017/CBO9780511815768.

Freeman, R. E., J. Harrison, and A. Wicks (2007). *Managing for Stakeholders: Survival, Reputation, and Success*. New Haven and London: Yale University Press.

Freeman, R.E and Evan, W.M. (1990). "Corporate Governance: A stakeholder Interpretation", Journal of Behaviour Economics, 19: 337-59.

Freire, P. V. (2016), Good Faith in Contractual Law: a "Law and Economics" Perspective, RJLB, Ano 2, n° 4, 1381-1393.

Friedman, A. and Miles, S. (2006), Stakeholders: Theory and Practice, Oxford University Press, Oxford.

Friedman, M. (1962), *Capitalism and Freedom,* University of Chicago Press.

Friedman, M. (1970), "The Social Responsibility of Business is to Increase Profits," New York Times Magazine, September 13, 1970.

Furman J. And R. C. Seamans (2019), "AI and the Economy". Innovation Policy and the Economy 19:161-191

Garoupa and Liguerre (2014), https://www.bu.edu/ilj/files/2014/05/GaroupaLiguerre-finalpdf.pdf

Garoupa and Morris (2012), https://illinoislawreview.org/wp-content/ilr-content/articles/2012/5/Garoupa.pdf

Garoupa, N., C. Gómez Ligüerre and Lela Mélon (2016) Legal Origins and the Efficiency Dilemma, Routledge, London.

Gelter, M. (2017), *EU Company Law Harmonization between Convergence and Varieties of Capitalism*, ECGI Working Paper Series in law, Working Paper N° 355/2017 https://ecgi.global/sites/default/files/working_papers/documents/3552017.pdf

Gerber, D (1998) Law and Competition in Twentieth Century Europe. Oxford: Oxford University Press.

Gessel, B. (2017), Mixing Legal Systems in Europe; the Role of Common Law Transplants (Polish Law Example), European Review of Private Law 4-2017 [789–812]

Ginsburg, Douglas H. and Wright, Joshua D., Antitrust Courts: Specialists Versus Generalists (July 3, 2013). Fordham International Law Journal, Vol. 36, No. 4, pp. 788-811, May 2013; George Mason Law & Economics Research Paper No. 13-42.

Glick, M. (2018), "The Unsound Theory Behind the Consumer (and Total) Welfare Goal in Antitrust," 63 ANTITRUST BULL. 455 (2018).

Glick, M. (2018), American Gothic: How Chicago Economics Distorts "Consumer Welfare" in Antitrust, INET Working Paper No. 99, July 2019.

Graf, M., J. P. Hlavka, and B. L. Triezenberg (2016), A Change is in the Air: Emerging Challenges for the Cloud Computing Industry. Santa Monica, CA: RAND Corporation, 2016. https://www.rand.org/pubs/working_papers/WR1144.html.

Graff, M. (2008). "Law and Finance: Common-law and Civil-law Countries Compared: An Empirical Critique", Economica New Series, Vol. 75, No. 297 (Feb., 2008), pp. 60-83.

Granieri, M and A. Renda (2012). Innovation Policy in the European Union: towards Horizon2020, Springer Publishers, April 2012.

Gregersen, C., J. Mackie and C. Torres (2016). Implementation of the 2030 Agenda in the European Union. ECDPM Discussion Paper No. 197. Maastricht: European Centre for Development Policy Management (ECDPM).

Gries, T., M. Kraft and D. Meierrieks, (2009), "Linkages Between Financial Deepening, Trade Openness, and Economic Development: Causality Evidence from Sub-Saharan Africa", World Development, Volume 37, Issue 12, 2009, Pages 1849-1860.

Griffiths, M., L. Pupillo, S. Blockmans and A. Renda (2019), Strengthening the EU's Cyber Defense Capabilities, Report of a CEPS Task Force. At https://www.ceps.eu/wp-content/uploads/2018/11/CEPS_TFR%20on%20Cyber%20Defence_1.pdf

Gros, D., C. Alcidi, M. Busse, M. Elkerbout, N. Laurentsyeva, A. Renda (2018), Global Trends to 2035, Study for the European Parliamentary Research Service, Global Trends Unit PE 627.126 - November 2018.

Grossman, N. (2010), Turning a Short-Term Fling into a Long-Term Commitment: Board Duties in A New Era, 43 U. MICH. J.L. REFORM 905, 923-31 (2010).

Group of States Against Corruption (2017), Anti-corruption trends, challenges and good practices in Europe & the United States of America, Council of Europe.

Guinea, O. and F. Erixon (2019), Standing up for Competition: Market Concentration, Regulation, and Europe's Quest for a New Industrial Policy, ECIPE Occasional Paper n. 01/2019.

Gupta et al. (2016), Corruption: Costs and Mitigating Strategies, IMF Staff Discussion Note http://www.imf.org/external/pubs/ft/sdn/2016/sdn1605.pdf.

Gutierrez Gallardo, G. and T. Philippon (2017), Declining Competition and Investment in the U.S (July 2017). NBER Working Paper No. w23583.

Gwartney, James D., Randall G. Holcombe, and Robert A. Lawson. 2004. Economic Freedom, Institutional Quality, and Cross-Country Differences in Income and Growth. Cato Journal 24 (3): 205–233.

Hadjemmanuil, C. (2018), *The Private Law Framework for Financial Transactions Post-Brexit: A Shift from English to Continental European Governing Law and Jurisdiction?* At https://ebi-europa.eu/wp-content/uploads/2018/01/The-Private-Law-Framework-for-Financial-Transactions-Post-Brexi.pdf

Haiss, P., H. Juvan and B. Mahlberg (2016), "The Impact of Financial Crises on the Finance–Growth Relationship: A European Perspective", Economic Notes, 2016, vol. 45, issue 3, 423-444.

Hakenes, H., I. Hasan, P. Molyneux, and R. Xie (2014). Small Banks and Local Economic Development. Review of Finance, 19(2), 653-683.

Hamilton, D. S. and J. Pelkmans (2015), *Rule-makers or rule-takers? Exploring the Transatlantic Trade and Investment Partnership*, Rowman & Littlefield, London.

Han, X. H. Khan, and J. Zhuang (2014), Do governance indicators explain development performance? A cross-country analysis. ADB Economics Working Paper Series n. 417, November 2014.

Han, X., Khan, H. A., & Zhuang, J. (2014). *Do Governance Indicators Explain Development Performance? A Cross-Country Analysis.* Asian Development Bank Economics Working Paper Series, (417).

Hanlon, M., E. L. Maydew, J. R. Thornock (2015). Taking the long way home: U.S. tax evasion and offshore investments in U.S. equity and debt markets. The Journal of Finance 70, 257-287.

Hanlon, M., Maydew, E. L., & Thornock, J. R. (2015). Taking the Long Way Home: US Tax Evasion and Offshore Investments in US Equity and Debt Markets. The Journal of Finance, 70.: 257-287.

Harberger, A. (1998), A Vision of the Growth Process, in: American Economic Review, Vol. 88, No. 1, 1998, pp. 1-32.

Hassan, I., Jackowicz, K., Kowalewski, O., & Kozlowski, L. (2017). Do local banking structures matter for SME financing and performance? New evidence from an emerging economy? Journal of Banking & Finance, 79, 142-158.

Hatzis A. (2000), "The Anti-Theoretical Nature of Civil Law Contract Scholarship and the Need for an Economic Theory", Working Paper.

Hazen, T. L. (1991), The Short-Term/Long-Term Dichotomy and Investment Theory: Implications for Securities Market Regulation and for Corporate Law, 70 N.C. L. REV. 137, 140 (1991).

Heremans, D. and K. Bosquet (2011). "The Future of Law and Finance after the Financial Crisis: New Perspectives on Regulation and Corporate Governance for Banks". 5 University of Illinois Law Review 1551.

Hernandez-Canovas, G. & Martinez-Solano, P. (2010). Relationship lending and SME financing in the continental European bank-based system. Small Business Economics, 34, 465-482.

High-Level Expert Group on Artificial Intelligence (AI HLEG) of the European Commission (2019a), *Ethics Guidelines for*

Trustworthy AI, at https://ec.europa.eu/digital-single-market/en/news/ethics-guidelines-trustworthy-ai

High-Level Expert Group on Artificial Intelligence (AI HLEG) of the European Commission (2019b), *Policy and investment recommendations for trustworthy Artificial Intelligenc*, at https://ec.europa.eu/digital-single-market/en/news/policy-and-investment-recommendations-trustworthy-artificial-intelligence.

Horn L. (2012) Company Law in the European Union – From Industrial to Shareholder Democracy?. In: Regulating Corporate Governance in the EU. International Political Economy Series. Palgrave Macmillan, London

Horn., L. (2011), *Regulating Corporate Governance in the EU: Towards a Marketization of Corporate Control*, Palgrave Macmillan.

Hornuf, L., Mohamed, A., and Schwienbacher, A. (2019) The Economic Impact of Forming a European Company. JCMS: Journal of Common Market Studies, 57: 659– 674. https://doi.org/10.1111/jcms.12839.

Hovenkamp, H. J. (2009), Antitrust Policy After Chicago (May 1, 2009). U Iowa Legal Studies Research Paper No. 09-21; Michigan Law Review, Vol. 84, p. 214, 1985.

Hovenkamp, H. J., "Is Antitrust's Consumer Welfare Principle Imperiled?" (2019). Faculty Scholarship at Penn Law. 1985. https://scholarship.law.upenn.edu/faculty_scholarship/1985

IRGC. (2017). *Transatlantic patterns of risk regulation: Implications for international trade and cooperation*. Report. Lausanne: EPFL International Risk Governance Center.

Jay B. Barney, "Shareholders, Stakeholders, and Strategic Factor Markets," in Performance and Progress: Essays on Capitalism, Business, and Society, ed. Subramanian Rangan (Oxford: Oxford University Press, 2015)

Jensen, M. (2002), "Value maximization, stakeholder theory, and the corporate objective function", Business Ethics Quarterly, Vol. 12 No. 2, pp. 235-56.

Jensen, M. C. and W. H. Meckling (1976), "Theory of the Firm: Managerial Behavior, Agency Costs, and Ownership Structure," Journal of Financial Economics 3, no. 4: 305-360.

Jhering, R.v. (1861), *Culpa in contrahendo oder Schadensersatz bei nichtigen oder nicht zur Perfektion gelangten Vertragen*, in: Jherings Jahrbücher, Bd. 4. 1861.

Kahan, M. and E. B. Rock (2007), Hedge Funds in Corporate Governance and Corporate Control, 155 U. PA. L. REV. 1021, 1083.

Kalff, D. (2008), *An UnAmerican Business: The Rise of the New European Enterprise*, Kogan Page; Reprint edition (February 1, 2008).

Kalff, D. (2017), *The European Enterprise. Value Creation for Society. At* https://www.donaldkalff.eu/site/wp-content/uploads/2017/12/17-10-05-European-Enterprises-scherm-spreads.pdf.

Karmel, R. (2004). Should a Duty to the Corporation Be Imposed on Institutional Shareholders? The Business Lawyer, 60(1), 1-21.

Kelsen H. (1979), "Allgemeine Theorie der Normen", Manzsche Verlags-und Universitätsbuchhandlung, Vienna.

Kern, C. A. (2012), English as a Court Language in Continental Courts, Erasmus Law Review, Volume 5, Issue 3 (2012).

Kessler, F. and E. Fine (1964), "Culpa in Contrahendo, Bargaining in Good Faith, and Freedom of Contract: A Comparative Study". Faculty Scholarship Series. Paper 2724.

Key, S. (1999), "Toward a new theory of the firm: a critique of stakeholder "theory"", Management Decision, Vol. 37 No. 4, pp. 317-328.

Khan, L. (2016), Amazon's Antitrust Paradox, 126 Yale L.J. (2016).

Khan, L. (2018), "The New Brandeis Movement: America's Antimonopoly Debate," 9 J. OF EURO. COMP. LAW 131, 132 (2018)

Konnola, T., J. Leceta, A. Renda and F. Simonelli (2016), Unleashing Innovation and Entrepreneurship in Europe: People, Places and Policies, Report of a CEPS Task Force, to be published by CEPS in May 2016.

La Porta, Lopez-de-Silanes, Shleifer and Vishny (1997), "Law and Finance", Journal of Political Economy, 106, p. 1131-1150.

La Porta, R. et al. (1997), Legal Determinants of External Finance, 52 J. FIN. 1131

La Porta, R. et al. (2000), Agency Problems and Dividend Policies Around the World, 55 J. FIN. 1, 27.

La Porta, R. et al. (2000), Investor Protection and Corporate Governance, 58 J. FIN. ECON. 3, 13-17

La Porta, R. et al. (2002), Investor Protection and Corporate Valuation, 57 J. FIN. 1147, 1166-69 (2002).

La Porta, R., F. Lopez-de-Silanes, and A. Shleifer (2008). The economic consequences of legal origins. Journal of Economic Literature 46, 285–332.

La Porta, R., López de Silanes, F., Shleifer, A., Vishny, R., 1999. The quality of government. Journal of Law, Economics & Organization 15, 222-279.

Laeven, L. and R. Levine (2009), Bank governance, regulation and risk taking. Journal of Financial Economics 93, 259-75.

Larouche, P. and Schinkel, M.P. (2014) "Continental Drift in the Treatment of Dominant Firms: Article 102 TFEU in Contrast to § 2 Sherman Act", in D. Sokol and R. Blair, eds., Oxford Handbook of International Antitrust Economics – Vol. 2, Oxford: Oxford University Press, 153-187.

Laszlo, C. (2003) The Sustainable Company: How to Create Lasting Value Through Social and Environmental Performance, Washington, D.C.: Island Press.

Lazonick, W. and M. O'Sullivan (2000), "Maximizing Shareholder Value: A New Ideology for Corporate Governance," Economy and Society, 29, 1: 13-35.

Lazonick, W. and M. O'Sullivan (2000), Corporate Governance, Innovation and Economic Performance in the EU – CGEP, Final report Project SOE1-CT98-1114 Funded under the Targeted Socio-Economic Research Programme (TSER) Directorate-General for Research, European Commission.

Lévêque, F. and Y. Ménière (2006), *Patents and Innovation: Friends or Foes?*, Cerna, Centre d'économie industrielle Ecole Nationale Supérieure des Mines de Paris.

Levine, R. (2003), Bank-Based or Market-Based Financial Systems: Which is Better?, 11 J. FIN. INTERMED 398.

Levine, R. (2005). "Finance and growth: Theory and evidence". In Aghion, P., and Durlauf, S., (Eds.), Handbook of Economic Growth. Amsterdam: North-Holland Elsevier Publishers.

Leydesdorff, L., Etzkowitz, H., & Kushnir, D. (2016). Globalization and growth of US university patenting (2009–2014). Industry and Higher Education, 30(4), 257–266.

Licht, A. N. et al. (2004), Culture, Law, and Corporate Governance (2004), at http://ssrn.com/abstract=508402

Luetjens, J. and P. 't Hart (2018), Governing by Looking Back: Learning from Successes and Failures, An ANZSOG Research Paper for the Australian Public Service Review Panel, September 15, 2018.

Mackaay, E. (2009), "The Economics of Civil Law Contract and Good Faith" https://papyrus.bib.umontreal.ca/xmlui/bitstream/handle/1866/3016/Mackaay_Trebilcock Symposium%20_3_.pdf

Mackaay, E. (2013), Law and Economics for Civil Law Systems, Edward Elgar.

Mackaay, E. and V. Leblanc (2003), "The Law and Economics of Good Faith in the Civil Law of Contract", https://papyrus.bib.umontreal.ca/xmlui/bitstream/handle/1866/125/Article%20papyrus.pdf

Marcus Corry and Graham Mather (2012), Taxing Savings Sensibly, Is the EU Savings Tax Directive Overtaken by Events? European Policy Forum.

Mattei U. (1997), "Comparative Law and Economics", The University of Michigan Press.

Mayer, C. (2013), Firm Commitment: Why the Corporation Is Failing Us and How to Restore Trust in It (Oxford: Oxford University Press, 2013).

Mazzucato, M. (2018), *The Value of Everything*, Penguin Books.

McChesney, F.S., (1977). "On the Procedural Superiority of a Civil Law System: A Comment," Kyklos, Wiley Blackwell, Vol. 30(3), pages 507-510.

Mcwilliams, A. and D. Siegel (2001). "Corporate Social Responsibility: A Theory of the Firm Perspective". The Academy of Management Review. 26. 117-127.

Meiselles, M. and Graute, M. (2017) 'The Societas Europaea (SE) – Time to Start Over? Capturing the Zeitgeist of the 21st Century' European Business Law Review, Vo. 28 Issue 5, pp. 667–688

Melamed, D. and N. Petit (2018), The Misguided Assault on the Consumer Welfare Standard in the Age of Platform Markets. Available at SSRN: https://ssrn.com/abstract=3248140.

Menezes Leitão, L. (2000), "Negociações e Responsabilidade Pré-Contratual nos Contratos Internacionais", ROA, 60 Menezes Cordeiro, A, (2012), Tratado de Direito Civil I, Almedina.

Merges, Robert P., As Many as Six Impossible Patents Before Breakfast: Property Rights for Business Concepts and Patent System Reform. Berkeley Technology Law Journal, Vol. 14, Pp. 577-615, 1999.

Michelman F. (1980), "Constitutions, Statutes and the Theory of Efficient Adjudication", Journal of Legal Studies, 9, p. 431-461.

Miles, S. (2011), "Stakeholder definitions: profusion and confusion", Proceedings of the EIASM 1st Interdisciplinary Conference on Stakeholder, Resources and Value Creation, IESE Business School, University of Navarra, Barcelona.

Miles, S. (2012), "Stakeholder: essentially contested or just confused?", Journal of Business Ethics, Vol. 108 No. 3, pp. 285-298.

Milhaupt, C. J. and K. Pistor (2008), *Law and Capitalism: What Corporate Crises Reveal about Legal Systems and Economic Development around the World*. University of Chicago Press, 2008; Columbia Law and Economics Working Paper No. 313.

Muir Watt H. (2000) "Les forces de résistance à l'analyse économique du droit dans le droit civil", working paper.

Musacchio, A. and J. D. Turner (2013) "Does the law and finance hypothesis pass the test of history?", Business History, 55:4, 524-542.

Naceur, S. B., R. Blotevogel, M. Fischer and H. Shi (2017), "Financial Development and Source of Growth: New Evidence", IMF Working Paper WP/17/143.

Nerudova, D. (2007). Tax and legal aspects of Societas Cooperativa Europaea. Acta Universitatis Agriculturae et Silviculturae Mendelianae Brunensis. 55. 107-114. 10.11118/actaun200755060107.

Noked, N. (2018). Tax Evasion and Incomplete Tax Transparency. Laws. 7. 31. 10.3390/laws7030031.

North, D. (1990), Institutions, Institutional Change, and Economic Performance. Cambridge: Cambridge University Press.

O'Hara, K and W. Hall (2018), Four Internets: The Geopolitics of Digital Governance, CIGI Paper No. 206

OECD (2015), "Data-Driven Innovation: Big Data for Growth and Well-Being", Paris, DOI: http://dx.doi.org/10.1787/9789264229358-en.

OECD (2015), "OECD Innovation Strategy 2015: An Agenda for Policy Action", Paris (www.oecd.org/sti/OECD-Innovation-Strategy-2015-CMIN2015-7.pdf).

Olson, M. (1990), *The Logic of Collective Action in Soviet-type Societies*, in Journal of Soviet Nationalities, 1 (2).

Ost F. (1985), " ", in Ost and Van de Kerchove, "Fonction de juger er pouvoir judiciaire: transformation et déplacement", Bruylant, Brussels.

Pargendler (2018) https://cpb-us-w2.wpmucdn.com/ campuspress.yale.edu/dist/8/1581/files/2018/02/143_The -Role-of-the-State-in-Contract-Law-2416e28.pdf

Parisi, F. (2004), Positive, Normative and Functional Schools in Law and Economics. European Journal of Law and Economics, Vol. 18, No. 3, pp. 259-272, December 2004; George Mason Law & Economics Research Paper No. 04-22.

Parisi, F., B. Luppi and A. Guerra (2016), *Gordon Tullock and the Virginia School of Law and Economics*. In: Constitutional Political Economy, 23.04.2016.

Patel, K and H. Schweitzer (eds.) (2013), Historical Foundations of EU Competition Law, Oxford University Press, 2013.

Paun, C.V.; Musetescu, R.C.; Topan, V.M.; Danuletiu, D.C. The Impact of Financial Sector Development and Sophistication on Sustainable Economic Growth. Sustainability 2019, 11, 1713.

Pelkmans J. and P. Brenton P. (1999) Bilateral Trade Agreements with the EU: Driving Forces and Effects. In: Memedovic O., Kuyvenhoven A., Molle W.T.M. (eds) Multilateralism and Regionalism in the Post-Uruguay Round Era. Springer, Boston, MA.

Pelkmans, J. (2019), The Single Market: Workshporse for EU prosperity, in Blockmans (Ed), *What comes after the Last Chance Commission?*, CEPS, Brussels.

Pelkmans, J. and A. Renda (2011), Single eComms market? No such thing. Communications & Strategies, 2nd quarter 2011.

Pelkmans, J. and A. Renda (2014), Does EU Regulation Hinder or Stimulate Innovation? (November 19, 2014). CEPS Special Report No. 96. Available at SSRN: http://ssrn.com/abstract=2528409 (with Jacques Pelkmans).

Pelkmans, J. and W. Hu (2018), China-EU Leadership in Globalisation: Ambition and capacity, CEPS Policy Insights 2017/18.

Pelkmans, J., W. Hu, F. Mustilli, M. Di Salvo, J.F. Francois, E. Bekkers (2018), *Anabtawi, I. (2006), Some Skepticism About Increasing Shareholder Power, 53 UCLA L. REV. 561, 579.*

Perez, C. (2002) Technological Revolutions and Financial Capital: The Dynamics of Bubbles and Golden Ages, Cheltenham 2002, Edward Elgar.

Perez, C. (2002). Technological Revolutions and Financial Capital – The Dynamics of Bubbles and Golden Ages. Cheltenham, UK: Edward Elgar.

Petersen, M.A., and R.G. Rajan (2002), Does Distance Still Matter? The Information Revolution in Small Business Lending, *The Journal of Finance*, Vol. 57, No. 6.

Petersen, T. (2016), GED Explains: Why More Foreign Trade Means More Growth, at https://ged-project.de/videos/international-trade/why-more-foreign-trade-means-more-growth/

Petit, N. (2014), Price Squeezes with Positive Margins in EU Competition Law: Economic and Legal Anatomy of a Zombie (May 7, 2014). Available at SSRN: https://ssrn.com/abstract=2506521 or http://dx.doi.org/10.2139/ssrn.2506521

Philippe, D. (2018), "The Best Efforts Clauses: Analysis of Anglo-Saxon Jurisprudence and Interpretation of the Civil Law Clauses", Text of an address presented on March 9, 2010 in the framework of a symposium of the firm Philippe & Partners on the drafting of international contracts, at the *Maison de l'Avocat* in Brussels, available online at https://www.ibj.be/img/user/files/pdf-fr/besteffortclausules.PDF.

Phillips, R. A. (1997). "Stakeholder Theory and a Principle of Fairness." Business Ethics Quarterly 7(1): 51–66.

Phillips, R. A. (2013), Stakeholder Theory and Organizational Ethics, Berrett-Koehler publishers.

Phillips, R.A., R. Freeman and A. Wicks (2005). "What Stakeholder Theory Is Not". Business Ethics Quarterly. 13. 10.2307/3857968.

Picker, C. B. (2008), *International Law's Mixed Heritage: A Common/Civil Law Jurisdiction*, 41 Vanderbilt Transnat'l L. Rev. 1083-1138 (2008).

Picker, C.B. (2008), "International Law's Mixed Heritage: A Common/Civil Law Jurisdiction". Vanderbilt Journal of Transnational Law, Vol. 41, 2008.

Porter M. and C. van der Linden (1995). "Green and Competitive: Ending the Stalemate" Harvard Business Review. September/October 1995, 73:120-134. See also Porter, M. and van den Linden, C. (1995) Towards a New Conceptualization of the Environment-Competitiveness Relationship. Journal of Economic Perspectives 9(4), 97-118.

Posner R.A. (1972), "Economic Analysis of Law", Boston: Little, Brown.

Prassl, J. (2018), *Humans as a Service: The Promise and Perils of Work in the Gig Economy*, Oxford University Press.

Prochniak, M. and K. Wasiak (2017), "The impact of the financial system on economic growth in the context of the global crisis: empirical evidence for the EU and OECD countries", Empirica 44: 295.

Rajan and Zingales (1998), "Financial Dependence and Growth", American Economic Review, 88, p. 559-586.

Rand Europe (2016), The Cost of Non-Europe in the area of Organised Crime and Corruption, Annex II - Corruption, EPRS.

Raworth, K. (2018), *Doughnut Economics*, Chelsea Green Publishing.

Renda, A. (2010), Competition-regulation interface in telecommunications: What's left of the essential facility doctrine. Telecommunications Policy. 34. 23-35.

Renda, A. (2011). Law and Economics in the RIA world, Intersentia Series in European Law and Economics, July 2011.

Renda, A. (2012). Competition, neutrality and diversity in the cloud, Communications & Strategies, Vol. 85, Issue 1, pages 20-35, 2012.

Renda, A. (2015), Cloud Privacy law in the United States and the European Union, chapter in the book "Regulating the Cloud: Policy for Computing Infrastructure", edited by Cristopher S. Yoo and Jean-Francois Blanchette, MIT Press, August 2015.

Renda, A. (2015), Europe and innovation: is 2020 on the Horizon?, Intereconomics, January 2015.

Renda, A. (2015), Regulatory Impact Assessment and Regulatory Policy: Progress Report and Policy Recommendations, in OECD (2015), Regulatory Policy in Perspective: A Reader's Companion to the OECD Regulatory Policy Outlook 2015, OECD Publishing, Paris. DOI: http://dx.doi.org/10.1787/9789264241800-en

Renda, A. (2016), Private Antitrust Damages Actions in the EU: Chronicle of an Attempted Golpe, Chapter 13 in Micklitz, H. and A. Wechsler (forthcoming September 2015), "The Transformation of Enforcement: European Economic Law in a Global Perspective", Hart Publishing.

Renda, A. (2016), Regulation and R&I policies. Comparing approaches in Europe and the U.S. Special Report for the

European Commission, Directorate General for Research and Innovation, forthcoming April 2016.

Renda, A. (2017), How can Sustainable Development Goals be 'mainstreamed' in the EU's Better Regulation Agenda?, CEPS Policy Insights No 2017/12, March 2017.

Renda, A. (2017), Will the DSM Strategy Spur Innovation?, Intereconomics, Volume 52, Number 4, pages 197-201.

Renda, A. (2018), Cost-benefit analysis – Limits and Opportunities, chapter in the book edited by Garben, S. and I. Govaere (2018), "The EU Better Regulation Agenda: Critical Reflections on the Past, Present and Future", Hart Publishing.

Renda, A. (2018), The Trolley Problem and Self-Driving Cars: A Crime-Scene Investigation into the Ethics of Algorithms, CEPS Policy paper and College of Europe Working Paper, Economics Department.

Renda, A. (2019), Artificial Intelligence: Ethics, Governance and Policy Challenges. CEPS Monograph.

Renda, A. (2019), Helping the EU Win the Trust Game, CEPS Commentary, at https://www.ceps.eu/helping-the-eu-win-the-trust-game/

Renda, A. and C. S. Yoo (2015), Telecommunications and Internet Services: The digital side of the TTIP, in Rule-Makers or Rule-Takers? Exploring the Transatlantic Trade and Investment Partnership, Edited by Jacques Pelkmans and Daniel S. Hamilton, Rowman & Littlefield.

Renda, A. and F. Simonelli (2019), Study supporting the interim evaluation of the innovation principle, Study for the European Commission, DG Research and Innovation.

Renda, A. et al. (2014), Study on the Legal Framework Covering Business-To-Business Unfair Trading Practices in the Retail Supply Chain, study for the European Commission, DG MARKT.

Renda, A., N. Reynolds, M. Laurer, G. Cohen (2019, forthcoming), FoodTech for the Earth. Leveraging Digital Technology to Achieve a Sustainable AgriFood Chain, forthcoming report for the Barilla Centre for Food and Nutrition.

Renda, A., R. J. Castro, N. Es-Sadki, M. Granieri, F. Simonelli, A. Zarra (2019, forthcoming), Technology Transfer Agreements in Europe (PP-02821-2015), Submitted to the European Commission, DG Research and Innovation.

Renda, A., R. Van Den Bergh, R. Pardolesi, A. Riley, J. Peysner, B. Rodger, S. Keske, E. Camilli, P. Caprile (2008). *Making antitrust damages actions in the EU more effective*. Study in support of the impact assessment of the EC White Paper on antitrust damages actions).

Ripert G. (1951), "Aspects juridiques du capitalisme moderne", Librairie Générale de Droit et de Jurisprudence, Paris.

Rodriguez-Pose, A., R. Boschma, L. Tsipouri, A. Bonaccorsi (2017), The Diffusion Deficit and Economic Convergence, in Soete et al. (2017), Europe's Future: Reflections of the Research, Innovation and Science Policy Experts (RISE) High Level Group, March 2017.

Roe, M. and J. Siegel. (2009) "Finance and Politics: A Review Essay Based on Kenneth Dam's Analysis of Legal Traditions in The Law–Growth Nexus", Journal of Economic Literature, 47(3): 781-800.

Rönnegard, David and N. C. Smith (2018) "Shareholder Primacy vs. Stakeholder Theory: The Law as Constraint and Potential Enabler of Stakeholder Concerns" (April 20, 2018). INSEAD Working Paper No. 2018/15/ATL/Social Innovation Centre.

Roth, G. H. and P. Kindler (2013). *The Spirit of Corporate Law*, Munich: C.H. Beck.

Rubin, P. H. (1977), 'Why is the Common Law Efficient?', The Journal of Legal Studies, 6(1): 51–63.

Rubin, P. H. (1982), 'Common Law and Statute Law', The Journal of Legal Studies, 11(2): 205–223.

Salter, M. S. (2019), Rehabilitating Corporate Purpose How the Evolution of Corporate Purpose Has Contributed to a Widening Breach Between Capitalism and Justice ... and What to Do about It. Edmund J. Safra Center for Ethics Harvard University, Working Paper 19-104.

Satel, G. (2018), "Why Some of the Most Groundbreaking Technologies Are a Bad Fit for the Silicon Valley Funding

Model, Harvard Business Review", at https://hbr.org/2018/04/why-some-of-the-most-groundbreaking-technologies-are-a-bad-fit-for-the-silicon-valley-funding-model.

Schäfer, H. and C. Ott (2004), The Economic Analysis of Civil Law, Edward Elgar, p. 385.

Schilling, M. A. (2018). Potential Sources of Value from Mergers and Their Indicators. The Antitrust Bulletin, 63(2), 183–197.

Schnyder, G., M. Siems and R. Aguilera (2018), "Twenty Years of 'Law and Finance': Time to Take Law Seriously", Centre for Business Research, University of Cambridge Working Paper No. 501.

Schröter, H. (2007). Economic Culture and its Transfer: Americanization and European Enterprise, 1900-2005. Revue économique, vol. 58, (1), 215-229. doi:10.3917/reco.581.0215.

Shapiro, C. (2001) Navigating the Patent Thicket Cross Licenses, Patent Pools, and Standard Setting. Innovation Policy and the Economy, 1, 119-150.

Shavell, S. (1987), "Economic Analysis of Accident Law", Harvard University Press, Cambridge M.A.

Simonelli, F. (2016). Is Horizon 2020 really more SME-friendly? A look at the figures. CEPS Commentary, 17 February 2016.

Smith, A. (1790). *Theory of Moral Sentiments, or An Essay towards An Analysis of the Principles by which Men naturally judge concerning the Conduct and Character, first of their Neighbours, and afterwards of themselves, to which is added a Dissertation on the Origin of Languages.* II (Sixth ed.). London.

Social Development Agency (SDA) (ed.) (2006) Paths to progress. Mapping innovation on information, consultation and participation for employee involvement in corporate governance, Brussels: SDA.

Soete, L. & Foray, Dominique & Licht, Geog & Llerena, Patrick & Martinez Ros, Ester & Mazzucato, Mariana & Renda, Andrea & Serger, Sylvia & Weresa, Marzenna. (2017). *Towards a Mission-Oriented Research and Innovation Policy in the European Union;* An ESIR Memorandum. 10.2777/715942.

Soete, L. & Foray, Dominique & Licht, Geog & Llerena, Patrick & Martinez Ros, Ester & Mazzucato, Mariana & Renda, Andrea

& Serger, Sylvia & Weresa, Marzenna. (2018), Implementing EU Missions – EU Study, Second ESIR Memorandum, at https://ec.europa.eu/info/sites/info/files/ki0618012enn.pdf

Soete, L. et. al. (2017), Europe's future: Open innovation, open science, open to the world: reflections of the Research, Innovation and Science Policy Experts (RISE) High Level Group.

Spamann, H. (2010). "The Antidirector Rights Index Revisited." Review of Financial Studies, 23, pp. 467-486.

Special Eurobarometer 470 (2017), Corruption, European Union.

Spencer, D. A. (2019), Economics and 'bad' management: the limits to performativity, *Cambridge Journal of Economics*, BEZ033, 4 July 2019, https://doi.org/10.1093/cje/bez033

Stein (2002), Information production and capital allocation: Decentralized versus hierarchical firms, Journal of Finance 57, 1891-1921.

Steinbaum, M. and M. E. Stucke (2018), "The Effective Competition Standard: A New Standard for Antitrust". University of Chicago Law Review, Forthcoming; University of Tennessee Legal Studies Research Paper No. 367.

Sternberg, E. (2004). Corporate Governance: Accountability in the marketplace, 2nd Edition, The Institute of Economic Affairs, London, UK.

Stiglitz, G. (2017), *Rewriting the Rules of the American Economy: An Agenda for Growth and Shared Prosperity*, WW Norton.

Stiglitz, G. (2018), *Rewriting the Rules of the European Economy*, Report for the Foundation of European Progressive Studies.

Stout, L. (2012), *The Shareholder Value Myth: How Putting Shareholders First Harms Investors, Corporations, and the Public*, Berrett-Koehler Publishers; 1 edition (May 7, 2012).

Stout, L. A. (2012), The Shareholder Value Myth, San Francisco: Berrett-Koehler.

Teichmann, C. and A. Fröhlich (2014): "Societas Unius Personae (SUP). Facilitating Cross-Border Establishment", Maastricht Journal of European and Comparative Law 21, pp. 536-543.

Tetley, W. (2000), *Mixed Jurisdictions: Common Law vs. Civil Law (Codified and Uncodified)*, 60 LA L. REV. 618-738.

Timmermans, F. (2017), *Letter to Claude Moraes, MEP, Chair of the Committee on Civil Liberties, Justice and Home Affairs (LIBE), European Parliament*, ARES(2017)455202, 25 Jan. 2017, Brussels.

Tomberlin, J. (2018), "*Don't Elect Me*": *Sheriffs and the Need for Reform in County Law Enforcement*, Virginia Law Review, Vol. 104(1), pp. 113-157.

Tomorrow's Silk Road: Assessing an EU-China Free Trade Agreement, CEPS Paperback.

Tørsløv T. R., L. S. Wier and G. Zucman (2018), The missing profits of nations, National Bureau of Economic Research, Working Paper No 24701.

Transparency International (2015), Exporting Corruption. Progress Report 2015: Assessing Enforcement of the OECD Convention on Combatting Foreign Bribery, available online at: https://www.transparency.org/whatwedo/publication/exporting_corruption_progress_report_2015_assessing_enforcement_of_the_oecd.

Transparency International (2017), Corruption Perceptions Index 2017: Global Scores.

Transparency International (2017), G20 Leaders or Laggards? Reviewing G20 Promises on Ending Anonymous Companies, available online at: https://www.transparency.org/whatwedo/publication/g20_leaders_or_laggards

Tullock, G. (1988). Defending the Napoleonic Code over the Common Law, in Stuart S. Nagel (ed.), Research in Law and Policy Studies, 2, 2-27.

Tullock, G. (1997). The Case Against the Common law. The Blackstone Commentaries, Fairfax: Locke Institute.

Tunc A. (1989), "La responsabilité civile", Economica, Paris.

Ullrich, H. (2005), Anti-Unfair Competition Law and Anti-Trust Law: A Continental Conundrum? (February 2005). EUI Law Working Paper No. 2005/01.

Uzzi (2000), Getting the best deal: The governance benefits of social networks in business lending, Working paper, Northwestern University.

Vagts, D. (2002), Comparative Company Law — The New Wave, in Festschriftfür Jean Nicolas Druey, Rainer J. Schweizer et al. eds.

Van Ark B., de Vries K., Jäger K. (2018), Is Europe's Productivity Glass Half Full or Half Empty?, Intereconomics, April 2018.

Van den Bergh R. (1988), "Le droit civil face à l'analyse économique du droit", Revue Internationale de Droit Economique, p. 249.

van Pottelsberghe de la Potterie, B. (2011), The Quality Factor in Patent Systems, 20 Indus. & Corp. Change 1755, 1776-77 (2011).

Veugelers, Reinhilde, (2017), "Remaking Europe: the new manufacturing as an engine for growth", Bruegel, Brussels.

Vogel, D. (2012), The Politics of Precaution: Regulating Health, Safety, and Environmental Risks in Europe and the United States, Princeton University Press.

Vogenauer, S. (2013), Regulatory Competition Through Choice of Contract Law and Choice of Forum in Europe: Theory and Evidence (February 4, 2013). (2013) 21 European Review of Private Law 13-78; Horst Eidenmüller (ed), Regulatory Competition in Contract Law and Dispute Resolution (Oxford/Munich, Hart and C.H. Beck); Oxford Legal Studies Research Paper No. 9/2013. Available at SSRN: https://ssrn.com/abstract=2211557

Wadlow, Christopher (2007) *The case for reclaiming European unfair competition law from Europe's consumer lawyers.* In: The Regulation of Unfair Commercial Practices under EC Directive 2005/29—New Rules and New Techniques. Studies of the Oxford Institute of European and Comparative Law (4). Hart Publishing, Oxford, pp. 175-189.

Werden, G. J. (2014), Antitrust's Rule of Reason: Only Competition Matters, 79 ANTITRUST L.J. 713, 718-21 (2014).

Werlauff, E. (2003). The SE Company: A New Common European Company from 8 October 2004. *European Business Law Review*, 14(1), 85.

West, D. (2011), The Purpose of the Corporation in Business and Law School Curricula, Brookings, at https://www.brookings.edu/wp-content/uploads/2016/06/0719_corporation_west.pdf.

Westman, H. U. (2015), Crisis Performance of European Banks – Does Management Ownership Matter? (January 23, 2015). Bank of Finland Research Discussion Paper No. 28/2014.

Wiener, J. B., M. D. Rogers, J. K. Hammitt, P. H. Sand (2011), *The Reality of Precaution – Comparing Risk Regulation in the United States and Europe*, RFF Press, 2011

Williams, C. A. and J. M. Conley (2005) "An Emerging Third Way - The Erosion of the Anglo-American Shareholder Value Construct," Cornell International Law Journal: Vol. 38: Iss. 2, Article 5. http://scholarship.law.cornell.edu/cilj/vol38/iss2/5

Williamson, O. E. (1979), "Transaction-Cost Economics: The Governance of Contractual Relations", Journal of Law and Economics, Vol. 22, No. 2 (Oct., 1979), pp. 233-261

Williamson, O. E. (1985), The Economic Institutions of Capitalism, New York, Free Press, p. 47.

Zucman, G. (2013). The missing wealth of nations: Are Europe and the U.S net debtors or net creditors? The Quarterly Journal of Economics 128, 1321-1364.

Zywicki, T. J. (2008). Spontaneous Order and the Common Law: Gordon Tullock's Critique, 135 PUB. CHOICE 35.

DESCRIPTION OF THE RESEARCH TEAM

Main Authors

Donald Kalff

After receiving his PhD from the Wharton School of the University of Pennsylvania, Donald Kalff spent most of his professional life as a manager at Royal Dutch Shell and as a member of the Executive Board of KLM, Royal Dutch Airlines. During the last 15 years, he co-founded AIMM Therapeutics, a biotech company that generates antibodies against infectious diseases and cancer with unique proprietary technologies and he also  founded MondialDx, a company which markets and develops diagnostic tests for tropical diseases. Moreover, he participates in two companies that develop more effective formulas for medicines for skin diseases and women's health in the tropics. He has also invested in two companies in the field of cyber security. Donald Kalff is the author of two books and numerous articles on the governance and management of large enterprises and on the competitiveness of Europe. His latest book, *The European Enterprise, value creation for society*, will appear in 2019. He is a member of the board of the Dutch chapter of Transparency International, the largest anti-corruption network in the world.

Andrea Renda

Senior Research Fellow and Head of Global Governance, Regulation, Innovation and the Digital Economy at CEPS. He currently holds the Chair in Digital innovation at the College of Europe in Bruges (Belgium). He is a non-resident fellow at the Kenan Institute for Ethics at Duke University, and a Fellow of the World Academy of Arts and  Science. His current research interests include regulation and policy evaluation, regulatory governance, private regulation, innovation

and competition policies, internet policy, cybersecurity and artificial intelligence. Andrea provided academic advice to several institutions, including the European Commission, the European Parliament, the OECD, the World Bank, the Inter-American Development Bank and several national governments around the world. Andrea Renda earned a BA *cum laude* in Economics from LUISS Guido Carli University, Rome, in 1995 (Dissertation awarded a special distinction) and is European Master of Law and Economics (LL.M., with distinction, University of Hamburg, 1996). He holds a Ph.D. degree in Law and Economics awarded by the Erasmus University of Rotterdam. He is *i.a.* a member of the High-Level Expert Group on Artificial Intelligence set up by the European Commission in 2018.

Contributors

Willem Pieter de Groen (Chapter 2). Willem Pieter de Groen is a Research Fellow & Heading the Financial Markets and Institutions Unit at the CEPS and an associate researcher at the International Research Centre on Cooperative Finance (IRCCF) of HEC Montréal. He has since joining CEPS in 2009 (co)-authored studies and coordinated projects on EU and Near East financial institutions regulation,  diversity in bank ownership and business models, retail financial services and financial instruments. Moreover, he also works on small and medium-sized enterprises obstacles to growth and access to finance as well as collaborative economy and taxation. Willem Pieter has further extensive experience in gathering and analysing data, e.g. product prices, executive compensation, financial performance, bank structures, online platforms and offshore entities. In addition, Willem Pieter has worked extensively with the European Commission Better regulation guidelines and toolbox and designed and conducted surveys/interviews for various projects commissioned by EU institutions. Willem Pieter holds a bachelor in Economics from Utrecht University, and a Master in Finance from VU University in the Netherlands. Moreover, he is enrolled in a PhD programme of Tilburg University.

Karel Lannoo (Chapters 3 and 7). Karel is Senior Research Fellow in the Financial Markets and Institutions Unit and CEO of CEPS since 2000. He directs the European Capital Markets Institute (ECMI) and the European Credit Research Institute (ECRI), which are both operated by CEPS. Independent director of BME (Bolsas y Mercados Espanoles), the listed company that manages the Spanish securities markets (since 2006); Member of the Euribor Steering  Committee, European Money Markets Institute (EMMI) (2013 – 2017); member of advisory councils of charities and foundations. Karel holds a baccalaureate in philosophy (1984) and a MA in modern history (1985) from the University of Leuven, Belgium and obtained a postgraduate in European studies (Centre d'Etudes Européennes, CEE) from the University of Nancy, France (1986). Before joining CEPS, he worked for STUC (students' cultural centre in Leuven), did a stage at the European Commission (spokesperson's service), was employed by an Italian agri-food company (Ferruzzi) and a professional association, and was also active as a free-lance journalist.

Felice Simonelli (Chapter 8). Head of Policy Evaluation at CEPS. He is also Associate Researcher at the Research Centre in Industrial Organization and Finance of LUISS "Guido Carli" University (Rome). Expert in better regulation, innovation and digital economy with over eight years of professional experience. Felice provided research and consulting services to various  public institutions, trade associations, and private companies. He managed several impact assessments and evaluation assignments for the European Commission and the European Parliament. Felice holds a Ph.D. in Law and Economics from LUISS University, an LL.M. cum laude in Law and Economics from the Erasmus University of Rotterdam and from Ghent University, a M.Sc. cum laude in Law and Economics and a Bachelor cum laude in Economics and Business from LUISS University.

Nadina Iacob (Chapter 8). Nadina is a Research Assistant within the Global Governance, Regulation, Innovation, and Digital Economy unit (GRID) at CEPS. Her work mainly focuses on EU policy evaluation, including contributions to studies on corruption and renewable energy. Prior to joining CEPS, she earned a Master of Public Policy degree from the Hertie School of  Governance in Berlin, where she focused on quantitative methods for policy analysis, EU governance, and economic policies. Nadina has worked for a variety of organisations: researching the state of the art in entrepreneurial ecosystems as a research analyst at the Berlin-based NGO enpact; tracking budgetary and financial legislative developments as an intern in the Parliament of Romania; and gaining insights into EU legislative procedures as a trainee at the European Parliament Information Office, Bucharest.

Jacques Pelkmans (Chapter 9). Jacques studied economics at Tilburg University, International Relations at Johns Hopkins and gained his Ph. D. in economics from Tilburg. Previously, he was a professor of economics at the European University Institute in Florence, at the European Institute of Public Administration in Maastricht and at Maastricht University. Jacques held the Jan Tinbergen Chair at the College of Europe in  Bruges. He has also been an advisor to several Asian and European governments, as well as the OECD, the European Commission (was a member of the Cecchini group), ASEAN and UNIDO. He has authored several studies for the European Parliament and for the European Commission and published extensively on EU economic integration, ASEAN economic integration, world trade, regulation and technical standards. Since 1990 Jacques has been Senior Fellow at CEPS, specialising in EU trade and investment policy, the EU single market and the economics and political economy of EU regulation.

NOTES

1 See *i.a.*, Moedas, C. (2016), Presentation of the report 'Science, Research and Innovation Performance of the EU 2016' 10 March 2016, Lisbon Council. And the so-called "Lamy Report" (2017), "LAB-FAB-APP. Investing in the European future we want". Report of the independent High Level Group on maximising the impact of EU Research & Innovation Programmes, which argues that Europe does not feature breakthrough innovation due to "a range of factors, including lack of venture capital, a deep rooted aversion to risk and an inability to exploit the scale that an economy of half a billion people represents" (page 12).

2 For example, one of the candidates in a recent political debate ahead of the election s, Guy Verhofstadt, argued that "The best way to tackle Facebook is to have a European Facebook". See https://sciencebusiness.net/news/bolder-action-climate-change-and-curbs-us-internet-giants-dominate-eu-election-debate.

3 Indeed, our search for hidden treasures was motivated by the realisation that European companies must have some source of competitive advantage that compensates for these structural American strengths.

4 See the EU Justice Scoreboard 2018, Communication from the Commission to the European Parliament, the Council, the European Central Bank, the European Economic and Social Committee and the Committee of the Regions, COM(2018) 364 final.

5 Common law has been very influential also in civil law countries, the most vivid example being antitrust law. For an analysis of common law transplants in a former communist country (Poland), see e.g. Gessel (2017).

6 One of the potential negative consequences of Brexit is the possible reduction of regulatory competition and consequently, of regulatory innovation in Europe. See Eidenmueller (2018).

7 But see *contra*, McChesney (1977).

8 Unlike in many other legal systems around the world, English common law does not recognise a general contractual duty to act in good faith either when negotiating or when performing contracts.

9 Parties would need to compensate negative interest.

[10] In US law, good faith was incorporated, in the 1950s, into the Uniform Commercial Code (Section 1-304), and codified as Section 205 of the Restatement (second) of Contracts (1981). Most US jurisdictions apply only the notion of breach of contract, that gives rise to ordinary contractual damages; hence, they do not recognise the existence of a general duty of good faith which, in case of violation, would give rise to tort liability (compensatory damages and punitive damages).

[11] Another set of objections stresses the moral dimension inherent to the notion of good faith and therefore rejects it, in order to avoid a "moralisation of civil law".

[12] As Observed by Deffains (2003): the obligation to facilitate the other party's contractual performance or the obligation to ensure that in carrying out one's contractual promises, one's performance is useful, appear in French law as participating in the concrete realisation of the apparently moral precepts of good faith and loyalty that guide contract law. The famous adage, "to promise to do something is to promise to do something useful", credited to Pothier (one of the French Civil Code's 'founding fathers'), illustrates the same ideas: if a party is under the obligation "to fulfil his promise in the most useful way for his partner, failing a contract that has spelt out the complete details of its performance" or if he must "endeavour to quash selfish, personal considerations in order to facilitate the successful undertaking of his creditor", he is obeying one and the same legal rule, the rule of loyalty embodied in Article 1134 of the Civil Code. In the same way, the duty to cooperate, that is to say the obligation for the debtor to perform his task in such a way as to 'maximise utility' is directly linked to the duty of loyal contractual performance. Logically, duties to inform can also be seen as related to loyalty.

[13] Garoupa and Morris (2012) list six important factors identified from the nineteenth century codification debate and their review of the efficiency literature for legal systems' ability to generate economic growth: (1) the costs of identifying and applying efficient rules, (2) the system's ability to restrain rent-seeking in rule formulation and application, (3) the cost of adapting rules to changing circumstances, (4) the transaction costs to parties needing to learn the law, (5) the ease of contracting around rules, and (6) the costs of transitions between systems.

[14] See also Parisi et al. (2016).

15 See http://europa.eu/rapid/press-release_MEMO-13-530_en.htm and the Recommendation on Collective Redress, paras. 21-24.

16 In the Netherlands, the Rotterdam District Courts allows use of English since January 2016 in cases involving maritime, transport law and international sales of goods. The Netherlands is setting up a specialised court, the Netherlands Commercial Court (NCC), to be opened in 2017/2018. In Germany, the District Courts of Aachen, Bonn and Cologne have started a pilot project where hearings can be conducted, and documentary evidence can be presented in English without interpretation. And in France since 2010, the International Courtroom of the Paris Commercial Court has been accepting hearings and processing of case documents in English, German and Spanish, while the final decisions have to be delivered in French. However, a proposal was made recently to create a specialised chamber within the Court of Appeal in Paris to deal with international trade and financial market disputes, applying common law where needed. See Batsaikhan, Kalcik and Schoenmaker (2017).

17 https://www.iptalks.eu/key-issues/sme-manifesto/

18 European Commission (2015), *Action Plan on Building a Capital Markets Union*, https://eur-lex.europa.eu/legal-content/EN/TXT/PDF/?uri=CELEX:52015DC0468&from=EN.

19 https://www.weforum.org/agenda/2018/04/patient-capital/

20 A recent report by the New Economics Foundation (2018) confirms the view that stakeholder banks can deliver broader social and economic value. They fulfil a social mission and have a strong positive impact on local economic development. In general, they deliver more stable returns and lending than commercial banks and performed well during the financial crisis.

21 International Financial Reporting Standards, usually called IFRS, are standards issued by the IFRS Foundation and the International Accounting Standards Board (IASB) to provide a common global language for business affairs so that company accounts are understandable and comparable across international boundaries.

22 See Wall Street Journal, January 29, 2019, *More US Companies Separating Chief Executive and Chairman Roles*, at https://www.wsj.com/articles/more-u-s-companies-separating-chief-executive-and-chairman-roles-11548288502.

²³ See Renda, A. (2019), Helping the EU Win the Trust Game, CEPS Commentary, at https://www.ceps.eu/helping-the-eu-win-the-trust-game/

²⁴ Among others, Westman (2015) observes that failures in bank corporate governance have been seen as a contributing factor to excessive risk-taking pre-crisis with devastating implications as risks realised during the financial crisis, and empirically finds a positive impact of management ownership in small diversified banks and non-traditional banks. Her final sample included 95 listed and 105 unlisted banks from 35 European countries, more than two thirds of which headquartered in a western European country. She finds support for the finding of Fahlenbrach and Stulz (2011) that aligning shareholder and management interests by means of shareholdings induced managers to take on too much risk.

²⁵ COM (2008) 396/3 of 25 June 2008.

²⁶ See, for an even more critical account, Martin Parker, Why we should bulldoze the business school, The Guardian, 27 April 2018, at https://www.theguardian.com/news/2018/apr/27/bulldoze-the-business-school

²⁷ See IESE Cities in Motion Index at https://media.iese.edu/research/pdfs/ST-0509-E.pdf.

²⁸ The European Commission in its contribution to the informal meeting of ministers of innovation in Sofia observes that "Europe is experiencing an innovation deficit. This is not down to a lack of ideas or initial start-ups: the problem is rather a lack of scale-up and diffusion, with innovations not always being translated into new market and growth opportunities". See Communication from the Commission to the European Parliament, the European Council, the Council, the European Economic and Social Committee and the Committee of the Regions. A renewed European Agenda for Research and Innovation - Europe's chance to shape its future. The European Commission's contribution to the Informal EU Leaders' meeting on innovation in Sofia on 16 May 2018, COM/2018/306 final.

²⁹ Examples include the US standards on particulate matter (PM2.5), which are far more stringent than in Europe, and are also more strictly enforced. More generally, the authors have expanded the number and diversity of qualitative case studies to risk connected to food safety (genetically modified foods, beef hormones, mad cow disease), air pollution, climate change, nuclear power, tobacco,

chemicals, marine and terrestrial biodiversity, medical safety, terrorism and precaution embodied in risk information disclosure and risk assessment systems. In addition to detailed case studies, they also presented a broad quantitative analysis of specific precaution based on a sample of 100 risks drawn from a dataset of nearly 3,000 risks from the 1970s up to 2004 in both the United States and the EU. The results suggest that the degree of precaution exhibited in European and American risk regulation is very similar: averaging across the 100 risks sample over a 35 year period, there are 36 risks that show greater US precaution and 31 risks that show greater EU precaution. In the quantitative analysis the authors find no difference between the relative levels of precaution.

30 https://www.bcg.com/en-be/publications/2018/how-diverse-leadership-teams-boost-innovation.aspx

31 https://www.bertelsmann-stiftung.de/fileadmin/files/Projekte/ Vielfalt_Leben/ ExecSummary_LW_The_ Diversity_Factor_2018.pdf

32 Political guidelines for the next European Commission, Jean-Claude Juncker, Candidate for President of the European Commission, 22 October 2014. "I want to promote a new European policy on legal migration. Such a policy could help us to address shortages of specific skills and attract talent to better cope with the demographic challenges of the European Union. I want Europe to become at least as attractive as the favourite migration destinations such as Australia, Canada and the USA. As a first step, I intend to review the 'Blue Card' legislation and its unsatisfactory state of implementation. I also believe that we need to deal more robustly with irregular migration, notably through better cooperation with third countries, including on readmission."

33 At companies like Facebook, not only is the median salary of an engineer $240,000, but Facebook's stock has also increased 268% over the past five years. Therefore, the risk-reward equation for an employee with a hefty salary and competitive stock options to leave a large company to go to a start-up is a much, much harder calculation than it has been historically in the Valley.

34 See European Commission Staff Working Document, "Better regulations for innovation-driven investment at EU level", SWD (2015) 298 final, 15 December 2015.

35 See e.g. https://bankwatch.org/wp-content/uploads/2017/11/same-thing-EFSI.pdf

[36] See https://rio.jrc.ec.europa.eu/en/library/supply-and-demand-side-innovation-policies.

[37] See the European Commission's Interim evaluation report on the Horizon 2020 programme, available online at https://ec.europa.eu/research/evaluations/pdf/book_interim_evaluation_horizon_2020.pdf#view=fit&pagemode=none

[38] Ibid.

[39] In the Netherlands, SBIR has an annual budget of €2.5 million and takes the form of a competition: businesses with the best offers are awarded a feasibility study. Those companies with the most promising studies receive funding to further develop their products. In 2017, 89% of the petitioners were small businesses. Companies working on blockchain, mobility and renewable energy received early-stage funding from the programme.

[40] See Mazzucato report (2018), on FET Flagships: "the FET Flagships have not so far put the same emphasis on public engagement or on defining goals and milestones in terms of societal relevance, even though they do aim to turn scientific and technological developments into innovations that can be brought to market, and aim to support societal challenges. The experience from the current FET flagships should prove valuable for designing and implementing future missions, and applying the selection criteria, implementation requirements and public engagement criterion proposed here could increase the impact and visibility of FET flagships as future missions".

[41] Harberger speaks of two types of growth. One is characterised as "mushroom" growth, in which a limited number of sectors, industries or firms deliver much better productivity performance than others. "Yeasty" growth occurs when the productivity improvements spread more widely across the economy. Similarly, Carlota Perez (2002) speaks of an "installation phase" versus a "deployment phase" of a new technological paradigm.

[42] See the USPTO Congressional Justification for Fiscal year 2020, March 2019, at https://www.uspto.gov/sites/default/files/documents/fy20pbr.pdf

[43] Interestingly, the complaint alleges that AbbVie entered into unlawful market division agreements with the biosimilar manufacturers, which permit competition in Europe, but which delay biosimilars in the US market until at least January 2023 (*UFCW Local 1500 Welfare Fund v AbbVie Inc.*, March 18, 2019).

[44] The Economist, *Time to Fix Patents*, 8 August 2015. And see also the reply on Forbes by Marshall Phelps on Forbes, quoting extensive literature, https://www.forbes.com/sites/marshallphelps/2015/09/16/do-patents-really-promote-innovation-a-response-to-the-economist/#2b14cfa71921.

[45] http://www.wipo.int/edocs/pubdocs/en/wipo_pub_941_2017-chapter2.pdf

[46] In the conclusion of the European Council in Lisbon (March 2000), it was hoped that by 2001 a Community patent would be available for European applicants. As the Union replaced the Community, the "Community" patent became the "unitary" patent. Of course, the use of "European" was precluded to avoid confusion with the title granted by the European Patent Office under the EPC.

[47] The Commission focused only on the first two sources in their *ex ante* impact assessment (SEC 2011 482 final 13.4.2011)

[48] See Case AT.39612 - Perindopril (Servier). On 9 July 2014, the Commission imposed fines totalling EUR427.7 million on the French pharmaceutical company Servier and five generic companies for curbing entry of cheaper versions of cardiovascular medicine and thereby violating Article 101(1) of the TFEU. In 2006, Servier had launched an infringement proceedings against Apotex before the UK courts, claiming infringement of a patent and applying for an interim injunction. On 6 July 2007, almost a year after the EPO Opposition Division had confirmed its validity, the High Court found the English part of the patent invalid. See Judgment [2008] EWCA Civ 445, Case No A3/2007/1715, paragraphs 9 and 10 (ID5149).

[49] http://patentblog.kluweriplaw.com/2018/06/14/leading-german-patent-law-firms-criticize-epo-examination-proceedings/

[50] https://www.iptalks.eu/key-issues/sme-manifesto/

[51] See Prof. Ansgar Ohly. "The rejected complaint shows just how anti-competitive a law of unfair competition would or might be. What one man calls 'unfair' another calls 'fair'. (…) I think there are real difficulties in formulating a clear and rational line between that which is fair and that which is not, once one goes outside the requirement of no deception." (*L'Oréal v Bellure*, [2007] EWCA Civ 968 at paras 139, 140 per Jacob LJ).

[52] Regulation 1/2003 – while introducing a "convergence rule" (Article 3 para. 2) that seeks to create a level-playing field by providing for a single standard of assessment for agreements, concerted practices

and decisions by associations of undertakings (Article 101 TFEU) – does not prevent member states from enacting or maintaining rules that are stricter than Article 102 TFEU (formerly Article 82 EC). More specifically, Article 3(2) of Regulation 1/2003 allows Member States to enact or preserve legislation on unilateral conduct that is stricter than Article 102 TFEU; however, the same paragraph does not allow member states to apply rules that exactly mirror Article 102 TFEU in a stricter way than at EU level under the case law of the Court of Justice of the EU.

53 See Vestager's speech, "Fairness and competition", GCLC Annual Conference, Brussels, 25 January 2018.

54 Interestingly, the early jurisprudence of EU courts led to a significant emphasis on the need to preserve "workable competition". For example, see the Court of Justice decision in Case 26/76 *Metro v Commission* [1977] ECR 1875 (so-called *Metro I* decision).

55 https://www.law.cornell.edu/supct/pdf/02-682P.ZO

56 https://www.financialsecrecyindex.com/PDF/USA.pdf

57 As stated by Byrnes (2017), "the actual amount of tax collected by FATCA is statistically insignificant." Casi et al. (2018) find that since the enactment of the Automatic Exchange of Information in 2013, and more specifically for the period 2014-2017, the CRS induced a reduction of 14% in cross-border deposits parked in offshore locations for tax evasion purposes; however, such wealth and related income has not been repatriated but rather moved to new locations to avoid domestic tax obligations. In particular, the US has emerged as a "potentially attractive location for cross-border tax evasion". Zucman (2013) finds that around 8% of worldwide household wealth is located in tax havens. Alstadsæter et al. (2018) show that average values vary significantly across the world. 60% of the wealth in tax havens is held in the Gulf and certain Latin American countries, while only 15% in continental Europe and even less in Scandinavia. Moreover, Hanlon et al. (2015) estimate a tax gap of around $8 billion to $27 billion caused by US investors' round-tripping activities.

58 Amending Protocol to the Agreement between the European Community and the Swiss Confederation providing for measures equivalent to those laid down in Council Directive 2003/48/EC on taxation of savings income in the form of interest payments

59 Willem Pieter de Groen (2015), Corporate Taxation in Europe: Let's get it together! CEPS Commentary.

[60] A Fair and Efficient Corporate Tax System in the European Union: 5 Key Areas for Action, European Commission, Communication, 17 June 2015.

[61] The proposal builds on Action plan 13 of the OECD initiative against BEPS (OECD 2015e) but goes beyond the initial OECD proposal in that it requires MNEs to publicly disclose the information rather than confidentially reporting it to national tax authorities.

[62] https://www.cfr.org/backgrounder/inequality-and-tax-rates-global-comparison

[63] See European Parliament, Report on financial crimes, tax evasion and tax avoidance (2018/2121(INI)), Special Committee on financial crimes, tax evasion and tax avoidance. At http://www.europarl.europa.eu/doceo/document/A-8-2019-0170_EN.pdf

[64] OECD (2014), *The rationale for fighting corruption*, Background brief.

[65] RAND Corporation (2016), *The Cost of Non-Europe in the area of Organised Crime and Corruption*, European Union.

[66] Notices from European Union institutions, bodies, offices and agencies, European Council, *The Stockholm PROGRAMME – An open and secure Europe serving and protecting citizens* (2010/C 115/01).

[67] PwC, Ecorys (2013), *Identifying and Reducing Corruption in Public Procurement in the EU*, https://ec.europa.eu/anti-fraud/sites/antifraud/files/docs/body/identifying_reducing_corruption_in_public_procurement_en.pdf

[68] Global Integrity (2018), The Global Integrity Report, https://www.globalintegrity.org/.

[69] Transparency International (2017), *G20 Leaders or Laggards? Reviewing G20 Promises on Ending Anonymous Companies*, available online at: https://www.transparency.org/whatwedo/publication/g20_leaders_or_laggards

[70] Transparency International (2015), *Exporting Corruption. Progress Report 2015: Assessing Enforcement of the OECD Convention on Combatting Foreign Bribery*, https://www.transparency.org/whatwedo/publication/exporting_corruption_progress_report_2015_assessing_enforcement_of_the_oecd

[71] Higher indicator values reflect a better performance.

[72] The Global Competitiveness Index (GCI) assesses the competitiveness of over 130 countries based on 12 pillars, including aspects related to ethics and corruption in the public and the private

sector. Based on a survey of business (small, medium, and large enterprises), the GCI compiles individual scores for the level of ethics and corruption in the public sector, as well as for the level of corporate ethics. The former refers to the perceived level of public funds diversion, public trust in politicians, as well as the frequency of irregular payments to public institutions. The latter captures the perceived level of ethical behaviour of firms in their interactions with public officials, politicians or other firms. World Economic Forum (2018), *Global Competitiveness Report 2017-2018*, available online at https://www.weforum.org/reports/the-global-competitiveness-report-2017-2018.

[73] Conviction rates for corruption offences could serve as an additional indicator to measure anti-corruption efforts. To this end, the European Commission has developed an EU-wide data collection project in order to gain a comprehensive overview of the state of play in each member state. However, the classifications of corruption offences as well as the indicators available vary between the member states, thus rendering it difficult to create a fully formed picture of corruption convictions at the EU level. (European Commission (2016), *Collection of official data on corruption offences*, https://ec.europa.eu/home-affairs/sites/homeaffairs/files/what-we-do/policies/organized-crime-and-human-trafficking/corruption/docs/official_corruption_statistics_2011_2013_jan16_en.pdf).

[74] Center for Public Integrity *(2015) State Integrity Investigation*.

[75] Transparency International (2017), *Access all areas: when EU politicians become lobbyists*, available online at: http://transparency.eu/access-all-areas/

[76] EBRD and World Bank (2015), *Business Environment and Enterprise Performance Survey*, available online at https://ebrd-beeps.com/reports/beeps-v/beeps-v-report/

[77] UNODC, Corruption prevention to foster small and medium-sized enterprise development, Vol. II, available online at: https://www.unodc.org/documents/corruption/Publications/2012/Corruption_prevention_to_foster_small_and_medium_size_enterprise_development_Vol_2.pdf=

[78] Ibid.

[79] European Commission (2017), *Special Eurobarometer 470. Corruption*.

[80] European Commission (2017), *Flash Eurobarometer 457: Businesses' attitudes towards corruption in the EU*.

[81] European Commission (2014), *EU Anti-Corruption Report*, COM(2014) 38 final.
[82] RAND Corporation (2016), *The Cost of Non-Europe in the area of Organised Crime and Corruption*.
[83] Frans Timmermans (2017), *Letter to Claude Moraes, MEP, Chair of the Committee on Civil Liberties, Justice and Home Affairs (LIBE), European Parliament*, ARES(2017)455202, 25 Jan. 2017, Brussels.
[84] See the recent Proposal for a Directive of the European Parliament and of the Council on the protection of persons reporting on breaches of Union law, COM/2018/218 final - 2018/0106 (COD).
[85] Brookings Institution (2018), *Global Metro Monitor 2018*, available online at https://www.brookings.edu/research/global-metro-monitor-2018/
[86] 'Domestic' here means 'intra-EU'. In 2006 the Commission published a strategic trade policy document called 'Global Europe' [COM (2006) 567 of 4 Oct 2006], the main tenets of which are still followed in EU trade policy today. The quote is from the Commission Staff Document [background paper, as SWD (2006) 1230, p. 11].
[87] The term 'European business' comprises enterprises owned by Europeans (possibly also operating in other parts of the world) as well as non-EU companies doing business in Europe.
[88] The following is based on three surveys: European Commission (2015), OECD (2017) and IMF/World Bank & WTO (2017).
[89] EEA is the European Economic Area, i.e. the EU-28 plus Norway, Iceland and Liechtenstein (these three countries are fully in the single market, except for fisheries and agriculture).
[90] Such as Alcala & Ciccone (2004) with a ratio of 1.23%; Ahn et al. (2016) is slightly more specific: when cutting tariffs on inputs by 1%, the total factor productivity in that sector improves by no less than 2%.
[91] See Pelkmans, Hu, di Salvo, Francois et al. (2018), pp. 240/1 for data; the figure of up to €600 benefit for consumers is the result of an analogy with several empirical US studies (e.g. Hufbauer & Lu, 2017).
[92] See Autor, D. et al. (2014); Autor, D., D. Dorn & G. Hanson (2016).
[93] See Metivier, di Salvo & Pelkmans (2017) for a comparative analysis between the US and the EU of the cushioning and adjustment support of workers unemployed due to trade.
[94] See Cernat & Mustilli (2017) for a detailed and careful assessment.

[95] 'Plurilaterals' are agreements between a subset of WTO countries on a well-defined aspect of WTO rules (like public procurement or 'green goods'). Plurilaterals go further in liberalisation than other members of the WTO accept at a certain point in time. However, plurilaterals must be 'open' for all WTO countries.

[96] Thus, for example, the EU/Turkish customs union of 1995 includes a very long list of technical regulations (from the EU) for goods and reference to many thousands of related technical European standards for Turkey to be incorporated in their laws.

[97] TRIPs is about minimum regulatory levels of protection of IPRs as well as enforcement; TRIMs are about trade-related investment measures; TBTs are about the disciplines for technical barriers; SPS is about common rules, based on scientific risk assessment, for food and feed, including animal products.

[98] EU trade agreements which have to be signed by EU member states as well are called ' mixed agreements'.

[99] Remember the recent problems caused by the regional parliament of Wallonia for the ratification of CETA.

[100] 'Good [or, 'better'] regulation' is defined as regulation justified correctly by market failures, and proportional to the risk(s) involved, while considering various alternative regulatory options before choosing the one minimising the costs to market participants or the one with the highest benefit/cost ratio.

[101] The fifth freedom, not formally recognised in the Lisbon treaty – only in secondary legislation, consists of the free movement of codified technology (embodied technology moves freely anyway) in know-how agreements and IPRs, with the crucial European Unitary Patent waiting for ratification.

[102] See the annual World Bank indicators on Doing Business: www.doingbusiness.org; these are, for the most part, aspects of the national institutions and how (well) they operate (paying taxes, getting electricity, construction permits, resolving insolvency, getting credit, starting a business, registering property, etc.).

[103] Like the ones from IMD or the WEF. Economists tend to have problems with the arbitrariness and subjective nature of the measures, as well as the intrinsic incomparability between countries of what are subjective impressions of local managers and opinion leaders. Nevertheless, this does not mean that many of the numerous aspects listed in these Indices are irrelevant for the performance of enterprises and the benefits for consumers.

[104] Just to illustrate, in 2003 7 of the 10 top performers were EU member states or candidate members. By 2015 8 of the top 20 reformers still were EU member states and the differences between the higher scores became smaller.

[105] European Commission, SWD(2017) 439 of 10 Jan 2017, Proposal for a Regulation introducing e-card services, Impact Assessment, Annex 4, pp. 102 – 132, comprising an *ex post* evaluation of the working of the services directive. It shows that implementation is unsatisfactory. The difficulties in getting member states to improve on the implementation of the services directive are extensively documented in Pelkmans (2019, chapter 3).

[106] The only important result (after 12 years of negotiating) is the WTO Trade Facilitation Agreement concluded in Nairobi in 2015. It is of importance for developing countries as they have relatively high costs and time-loss in logistics connected to customs, port handling and some regulatory verification procedures. In fact, it results in pure cost-cutting (after some minor investments) and there are no losers. OECD countries gain too but less.

[107] It should not be forgotten that this applies to countries outside Europe. In Europe, the EU-12 had grown into EU-15 (1995) with the EU membership of Austria, Finland and Sweden, followed by the great eastern enlargement of 8 countries in 2004 and another 2 in 2007, plus Croatia in 2012. The pre-accession periods for all these new members are characterised by what amount to very 'deep and comprehensive' FTAs, mimicking the single market to a large extent. Again a strong manifestation of the twinning of the single market and EU trade policy.

[108] The complexity of four FTAs (CETA, EPA with Japan, Korea and TTIP [up to late 2016]) is explained in a more detailed analysis in Pelkmans (2017).

[109] Unlike the very recent 'me too' movement on the appropriate behaviour, especially vis-à-vis women, the term 'me too' comes from generic medicines, imitators with the identical active ingredient(s) as the originally patented one.

[110] TiSA, trade in services agreement.

[111] The 'environmental goods agreement'.

[112] Mutual Recognition Agreements, whereby accredited conformity assessment bodies in A can certify goods of A destined for a B market, given their recognised knowledge of B's regulations and standards.

113 International Maritime Organisation (of the UN).

114 See Pelkmans & Correia de Brito (2015) for details on such lingering conflicts between trade negotiators and regulators in the US, following the conclusions of MRAs in pharma and medical devices in 1998.

115 United Nations' Economic Commission for Europe, in Geneva.

116 For extensive analysis on the restrictions of investing in China and on the implications of China granting 'national treatment', see Pelkmans, Hu, di Salvo, Francois et al. (2018), chapter 15.

117 See Hu & Pelkmans (2017).

118 Late October 2018 in Ottawa, Canada brought these (13) WTO partners together on proposals for WTO reform but China was not invited.

119 https://www.euractiv.com/section/data-protection/news/supercomputers-eu-to-develop-high-performance-data-infrastructures/

120 The hosting sites will be located in Sofia (Bulgaria), Ostrava (Czechia), Kajaani (Finland), Bologna (Italy), Bissen (Luxembourg), Minho (Portugal), Maribor (Slovenia), and Barcelona (Spain).

121 https://ec.europa.eu/digital-single-market/en/news/final-report-high-level-expert-group-impact-digital-transformation-eu-labour-markets

122 Europe in May 2019. Preparing for a more united, stronger and more democratic Union in an increasingly uncertain world. The European Commission's contribution to the informal EU-27 leaders' meeting in Sibiu (Romania) on 9 May 2019. https://ec.europa.eu/commission/sites/beta-political/files/euco_sibiu_communication_en.pdf